# ADVFN'S
# BE RICH

How to make 25% a year investing sensibly in shares – a real time demonstration

Volume 1

Clem Chambers

Copyright © 2014 ADVFN
All rights reserved.
ISBN: 1908756551
ISBN-13: 978-1908756558 (ADVFN Books)

ADVFN BOOKS

ADVFN
the leading private investor website
Stock prices, charts and tools
Plus: financial news and forums
All FREE!
Register now: www.advfn.com

# CONTENTS

| | |
|---|---|
| Introduction | 1 |
| Welcome to Clem Chambers' Premium Blog | 7 |
| Promethean World | 10 |
| The Portfolio is Up and Running | 12 |
| Maths is My Friend | 13 |
| FCUK – Solid Pick in Dicey World of Retail | 15 |
| The Age of Aquarius Platinum | 16 |
| Aquarius – Up | 18 |
| Strong Santa Rally Boosts Portfolio | 19 |
| 2012: A Good Year For Mad Punting | 21 |
| How I Invest | 23 |
| The Fiscal Cliff and the Three Per Cent Lift | 25 |
| My Legacy Portfolio | 26 |
| Flybe Added to Portfolio | 28 |
| Banks Ballistic: Should I Buy More? | 29 |
| Premium Portfolio Progress Report | 30 |
| Watching the Portfolio: Part Two | 35 |
| Reviewing the Rest of the Premium Portfolio | 39 |
| The Difference Between Trading and Investing | 44 |
| Change is Due in the Market | 46 |
| A Waiting Game | 47 |
| Portfolio Update | 48 |
| Avocet Mining Has Cratered | 50 |
| Yen Shoots Up | 52 |
| A New Stock for the Portfolio: Volex | 53 |
| Market Due to Move – But Which Way? | 54 |
| Dow Hits All-Time High | 55 |
| Dow Breaks Its Record | 57 |
| A New Era in Equities | 58 |
| The Market is Patchy | 60 |
| Whoops! Trinity Mirror Takes a Tumble | 62 |
| Cyprus Madness, UK Sanity | 63 |
| Cupid Crashed But I Didn't Buy | 65 |
| Japan Will Cause Equity Markets to Rocket | 66 |
| Why Gold is Down | 68 |
| You Need an Investment Plan | 70 |

| | |
|---|---:|
| Will There be a May crash? | 72 |
| Timing the Market | 74 |
| Happy Days in Tokyo | 76 |
| Japan Crashes | 78 |
| Buying Small Cap Stocks | 81 |
| Buying in May | 83 |
| Is It Time To Sell? | 84 |
| First Group Share Price Makes No Sense | 86 |
| Sell in May... | 87 |
| Investing Hurts | 89 |
| Buying a Boring Share | 91 |
| Why You Should Diversify | 93 |
| The Portfolios Are Rallying | 95 |
| Boring is Good | 96 |
| Trying to See the Future | 98 |
| Barclays Rights Issue – Not Much Else Happening | 100 |
| Freudian Investing | 101 |
| Promethean Slumps – I Was Right Not to Buy | 102 |
| Degenerate Punting Account | 105 |
| Adding to the Portfolio | 107 |
| A Noble Investment | 111 |
| Specimen Portfolio Recovers Lost Ground | 113 |
| Portfolio Rally is Exhilarating | 115 |
| Investors Can't Be Fortune Tellers | 118 |
| Going Bananas | 120 |
| Momentary Profit | 122 |
| Nearly Out of the Summer Lull | 123 |
| Portfolio in Profit – Just! | 125 |
| Songbird Added to Portfolio | 128 |
| Songbird – Going for a Song | 129 |
| Buying Stock Brokers | 130 |
| Portfolio in Profit | 132 |
| Market Run Comes to an End | 135 |
| New Subscribers: Welcome | 136 |
| Preparing for a Drop | 139 |
| Outrageous Spread Stops Me Buying | 141 |
| The Mystic Art of Investing | 143 |
| The Market is Falling! | 145 |
| It's a Bear Market | 147 |
| Albemarle and Bond Bouncing at the Bottom | 150 |

| | |
|---|---:|
| US Default – Don't Panic! | 151 |
| My Buying Is On Hold | 153 |
| Default Crisis Averted – We Were Right Not to Panic | 155 |
| Specimen Portfolio Update | 157 |
| Newsflash: Northamber | 161 |
| The Frustration of Buying Northamber | 162 |
| Portfolio Update | 165 |
| Which Way is the Market Heading Now? | 168 |
| Investing is Easy – but Difficult | 170 |
| Flybe to the Moon | 174 |
| Flybe – The Missing Post | 175 |
| Flybe – It's Complicated | 177 |
| Portfolio Suddenly Shows a Loss Thanks to Volex | 178 |
| Don't Buy Mining Shares. No, Really, Don't! | 180 |
| Status Update | 181 |
| Bubbles are the Ultimate High Risk Trade | 184 |
| The Market Feels Unsteady | 186 |
| Not Much Action Right Now | 188 |
| Dead Quiet | 190 |
| Diversification is the Way to Go | 196 |
| Why Buy RSA? | 198 |
| May The Odds Ever Be In Your Favour | 201 |
| I've Got the Portfolio Blues | 204 |
| Why An Offline Broker Can Pay | 206 |
| How Will Tapering Affect Equities? | 208 |
| Our First Sale | 210 |
| Shares That Pay Dividends | 214 |
| We're In The Money | 216 |
| Why We Hold First Group | 218 |
| Portfolio Up Today | 221 |
| Investing Is Like Gardening | 223 |
| The Market is in a Correction | 226 |
| The Diversification Rule | 229 |
| Don't Panic! | 232 |
| The Art of Doing Nothing | 234 |
| Why I am Dabbling in Gold | 236 |
| Stop Press: Petropavlovsk | 239 |
| Buying Gold | 240 |
| The Portfolios are Strong | 241 |
| Small Cap Spreads are a Disgrace | 244 |

| | |
|---|---|
| Promethean and Flybe | 246 |
| Flybe Rights Issue Gives Us a Good Profit | 248 |
| Buying a Hedge Fund | 249 |
| Man Group Brings Profits | 251 |
| Reading the Charts | 252 |
| Going Bananas: Fyffes Takeover | 254 |
| Is That a Banana in Your Portfolio, or Are You Just Pleased to See Me? | 256 |
| Morrisons Takes a Fall So I've Bought It | 258 |
| The May Dip Is Coming | 259 |
| Betting on Ladbrokes | 262 |
| Essenden, Still Right to be Wrong | 265 |
| Tidying Up the Legacy Portfolio | 266 |
| A Good Day For The Portfolio | 272 |
| The Songbird Connection | 274 |
| Portfolio Spring Clean Continues | 275 |
| Not Buying Gold | 276 |
| Fasten Your Seatbelts... | 278 |
| Portfolio Profits | 280 |
| Aquarius Platinum Rights Issue Shenanigans | 282 |
| The Bear Necessities | 284 |
| Welcome, New Subscribers | 289 |
| AstraZeneca Share Price Up 15% | 291 |
| Serco Slump Shows the Importance of Diversification | 293 |
| The Dogs List of Shares to Watch | 295 |
| Winning with French Connection | 297 |
| Taking a Crazy Punt on Barclays | 298 |
| The Market is Flat | 301 |
| Going Bananas | 303 |
| Here Comes the Slump | 305 |
| AstraZeneca Takeover Off | 306 |
| The AstraZeneca Punt: Results Are In | 308 |
| Summer Lull is No Fun | 311 |
| One Way to Pick Stocks | 315 |
| Conclusion | 318 |
| About the Author | 321 |
| Also by Clem Chambers from ADVFN Books | 324 |

# Introduction

Investing is easy, or so it seems when you have been doing it all your life. As a child I would cycle after my friends who were coasting in a leisurely fashion on their way to the nearest sweetshop. They would be pulling away and disappearing over the next brow as I would be pedalling as hard as I could to try to keep up. For me on my small bike, it was hard; for them, older and on bigger bikes, it was easy.

Investing is the same; it's easy when you know how and hard when you don't.

For a new investor, "playing" the stock market can be a huge and often costly learning curve. How to climb it? There is no simple answer. You can read books, but that doesn't start to explain how the process works in practice.

This book sets out to take you up that mountain, at least the first year of the climb.

I have bought and sold shares since I was a little kid, mainly because trading was my father's "game." I bought £20 of a share called Metramar and my father docked half my pocket money for a full year. I recall at some point selling and receiving £100 in £1 notes and throwing them in the air in my bedroom to see them fall all around. I might have been eight or nine. My father had successfully imbued the idea that good things came from buying and selling shares, or at the very least toys and tuck bought autonomously from my own hard-won capital.

For me, things got serious when I started ADVFN, now one of the leading global destinations for private investors looking for the tools they need to play the Game of Markets. I decided to put a large percentage of my liquid assets into shares so that I would be on tiptoes when we built the site, as I would have a lot of "skin in the game."

Having started out in the early computer games industry then pivoted into massively multiplayer games, the stock market felt quite familiar. The stock market IS a multiplayer online game. I applied my understanding of games design and games playing to the market.

That sounds grand, but it isn't. Games are like machines: cogs rotate, dials turn, there are movements, controls, obstacles and goals. So I dug in.

These are a few key points I found.

- **The market pays people for the risk of funding a business.**
- **The market is very often efficient at setting the share price.**
- **In the short term the market moves randomly.**
- **To earn more than the average from shares you need to buy and sell when other people do not want to.**
- **To avoid bad luck you must diversify.**

The stock market is a fun game. It is especially fun because you can make lots of money from it. I found the process very enjoyable, if a little slow. I also discovered, like the kids disappearing over the hill, it is easy. Making solid returns from investing in shares IS easy.

Losing money, however, is also just as simple. It's called trading. Making money trading shares is nearly impossible. (Do not forget this.)

**Investing is not trading.**

Trading is buying and selling shares with <u>no</u> basis to know if the share is going to go up or down.
**Let's look at that more closely**. Here are some of the things that amount to, "**No** basis to know if the share is going to go up or down":

- Share tips.
- Charts analysis.
- Newspaper articles saying a company is good.
- What other people are doing.
- Advice, even from rich people, especially from your broker.
- How you feel.
- News headlines.

...The list is much longer but I won't bore you.

**Recall: In the short term the market moves randomly.**

If it didn't, money would be sucked from the market like blood from a virgin by traders and the market would dry up and die. So trading is a 50/50 bet and you lose the costs of the gamble, until you have no money left.

Investing is different. With investing you have a checklist of attributes you want your company to have and you buy a bunch of the best fits. This checklist is best closely connected with the financial status of the company which can be seen in its financial reports. Investors are financial gold-diggers and they need to check out the finances of their companies before they fall in love.

This, at least, is how I choose to do it.

The checklist is loosely based around "value investing." That is a method of investing created by Benjamin Graham in the 1950's. A student of his, Warren Buffett, took these ideas and made himself the richest man in the world. As such, it's a good place to begin one's investment education.

You can look at it this way:

- If a company can be bought for a few years' worth of its profits, it's probably cheap.
- Check it for cash; it should have enough to get by.
- Check to see if the directors are buying. They're not stupid.
- Look to see how much it is selling as a ratio to its share price. Sales are good.
- We like dividends.

There are a pile more things to think about, but low P/E, fat dividends, directors buying is probably almost enough to get a value investor taking a pinch into their portfolio.

Then there is a matter of being contrarian.

**Recall: To earn more than the average from shares you need to buy and sell when other people do not want to.**

This is the art of appearing foolish and making money.

People like to think themselves contrarian, but they aren't. Most people like the comfort of crowds. Manchester United supporters are legion, because they win and the hordes of red scarves make normal people want to buy into the movement. Whether people are herd creature or pack animals, few want to go wandering alone even if the grass is longer and the spoils of success theirs alone.

However, if you want to buy when everyone wants out and sell when everyone wants in, you have to be one of those cranky, asocial people that doesn't care what the group-think says.

You don't have to be contrarian to be a value investor, but it helps, because stocks get cheap when people don't want them and not cheap when people want to buy them.

I tend to be contrarian, in the same way as cats tend to like tuna. It works well. However, that just tells you about me, not how to make money in shares.

The key is, to build a portfolio. This in itself is quite contrarian. You will see lots of people say it is a silly idea. Those people are IDIOTS, or crooks, or both.

(The financial industry doesn't make much money from long term investors with portfolios. When the industry doesn't make money out of investors, you will hear cries of, "don't invest like that," and where the industry coins it from investors, you will hear all sorts of encouragement to continue to fill their coffers with such behaviour. Where there are resources there are always predators.)

**Recall: To avoid bad luck you must diversify.**

A portfolio is how you diversify.

Heads or tails. Luck cuts both ways. However, you can't have good luck without bad and bad luck can take you out of the game completely. Therefore, I am a contrarian value investor that has a diversified portfolio of UK value investments. This works well for me.

So I decided to start a premium newsletter on ADVFN.

Why?

Firstly I get paid for it. I like money, I like it no less the more of it I get. My book *101 Ways to Pick Stock Market Winners* has been in the top of the stocks and shares charts on Amazon for years now and it occurred to me I might get a few subscribers, if I documented my investments on ADVFN.

ADVFN has literally millions of users and many have heard of me. I write a lot of articles for the likes of Forbes, so it seemed like a good idea to turn my full time curating of ADVFN and my husbandry of my portfolio into a newsletter.

The goal quickly became to:

- Show a new investor how to build a portfolio of investments by practical example.
- Expose the realities of investing including mistakes, costs and failures while using only foresight.
- Invest like a very small private investor with all the nasty dis-economies that go with it.
- Be bluntly honest and try not to be boring.

So what follows is exactly what happened when a successful, highly informed, financial guru (so called) actually starts a new portfolio and builds it like a small private investor.

This is the first year (and a bit), from nothing to something with all the ups and downs a new investor won't expect but will come up against. It's a diary of my progress, as written in real-time as I bought and sold shares, from the start of the blog in December 2012 up to May 2014. The blog is still going and if you subscribe you'll be able to follow me in real-time as I continue to work on the portfolio:
(go to http://newsletters.advfn.com/clemchambers/) – or you can wait until next year to buy the next volume of Be Rich!

If I had made a "pigs ear" of it, this book would still be a solid and practically free education in investment, but happily I didn't.

So read on and see first-hand and in real time how you can build wealth in the stock market. You will see that, in the end, it is easy and that perhaps it doesn't take a guru to make a lot of money from the stock market, only a road map.

# Welcome to Clem Chambers' Premium Blog

### 6 December 2012

This is my first post on my premium blog.

Firstly, welcome. I am a value investor and I am a portfolio builder. I aim to get returns of between 15-25% and in the main hit 25%, though some years can be much better. This is a huge outperformance and strictly speaking should not be possible. Perhaps this is because we live in special times.

Occasionally I leave the market – it happened three times in the last ten years – and I might be out for six months. This could prove trying for any of my readers but we will deal with that if and when it happens.

Currently I am very bullish short and long term, though there is a medium term question mark as you might expect in a cyclical and volatile market.

I hold my positions on average for about a year, but it can be longer or shorter depending on performance, events and news. This means I don't churn my investments, which helps returns.

I do not operate stop losses as I have a portfolio and do not need to. I will let companies go bust rather than sell. It happens but it makes no difference to returns. I will avail you of some amusing stories later about why stop losses are not your friend.

I often average down, but never to the extent of becoming concentrated.

Many people would suggest I am a contrarian investor and they are probably right. Betting against the pack is where the great returns are. I am also contrarian because I believe in the efficient market hypothesis and I will go to great lengths to use the theory to highlight how to use it for profit. There are great profits to be had when the efficient market breaks down or gets bent, because efficiency is always pulling on prices to get them back to the right level.

From this blog I will start a new portfolio, which will be of my buys and sells from here on in. They will in effect be a continuation of my latest portfolio started last November which is now up a ridiculous 45%. Here is a chart of its performance which is very illuminating:

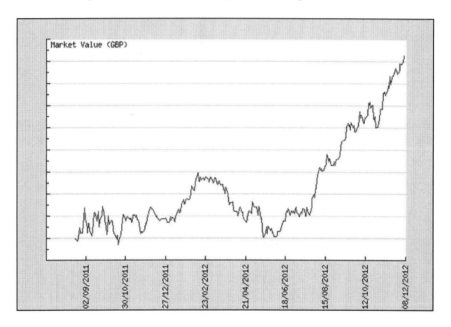

You can see how the volatility declines as the portfolio is built. It contains 32 stocks. You can also see it went nowhere for the first six months, which was incredibly frustrating. It is now off to the moon with plenty of upside. There are thirteen losers as of today in the portfolio. There have been ten sales, all winners, representing about 15% of the current profit. There has been about 2% worth of dividends in there too.

However, in effect we will be starting a new portfolio, all the while continuing the process I will be following for myself. I will tell you what and when I buy and sell and my reasoning.

It is the technique that you should focus on, rather than the stocks themselves. What I think and what stocks do are not strongly linked; it is the final profit that is the key and that is driven by investment principles.

Firstly I will be buying in "clips." We will call a clip £3,000. You could scale that up or down to suit your pocket. £1,000 is the smallest comfortable number; any less is not good as costs will eat into your returns.

I will track returns including trading costs and spreads.

Alongside buying and selling I will burble on about my opinions on the current markets and what is affecting them. As such you will see my ideas in advance of what I write for folks like Forbes, The Scotsman, Mac Format and Gulf News.

Please feel free to comment and throw in questions and ideas.

# Promethean World

### 11 December 2012

I have bought another clip of Promethean World (PRW) at 16.5p and it is now a significant part (4-5%) of my portfolio. I would buy more but the company has shown nothing but bad news since its floatation in early 2010 at around 200p.

It could go bust which is, of course, always a risk in a company that has fallen 90%. As part of a portfolio it makes perfect sense, but as a starting point for a portfolio it's a high risk candidate.

However, you have to start somewhere, so I am starting the specimen portfolio with this purchase. The portfolio will be seeded with £30,000 of cash and will be built out as I buy and sell in my own portfolio. A clip will be £1,000 and we will have 30 stocks.

Initially as it builds returns will be volatile and fragile. I will track it with real costs and spreads so the outcome is true to life.

Outside of my portfolios I have what I call "a stupid punt fund." This is a spread betting account I have used for R&D purposes for over ten years. Its purpose was originally to help me understand what ADVFN customers go through punting in a leveraged account on all sorts of wild bets. It is important for me and ADVFN to understand the experience and the original thousands have ebbed and flowed over the years and today the balance reached a high water mark of roughly 100% profit, after ten years of messing around. When Trinity Mirror was absolutely down on its luck I bought £150 a point at 26p, because I couldn't take any more on board within my rules in my proper account. My maximum level for an initial position is 10% of the total portfolio and is a rarity.

As luck would have it, it is now 95p. I sold £50 at 90p and another £50 at 95p. This is a kind of "scratching an itch" to sell, because I am not the sort to hold out for massive wins and fat profits. The main position in my portfolio is 100% up so it is my instinct to sell with a smile, even though I believe there is further significant upside. So I've uploaded a little in the "punt account" to scratch that itch and I will sell the last £50 piece at 105p.

Meanwhile I shall grit my teeth on the main position and try to run my profits to a logical exit point.

It is galling to see companies you sell run on, as has been the case with Enterprise Inns, but it must happen over and over again by the laws of probability. However, over the last few years I've been trying to force myself to run the winners further, yet greed is not my strong suit.

In any event, the bull market continues and the first entry into the trial portfolio is in place.

# The Portfolio is Up and Running

### 13 December 2012

Today I set up the model portfolio and entered the initial investment into it. It highlights several important investment issues but one is immediately apparent.

The cost of ownership of Promethean World is 11%. There is of course stamp duty at 0.5%. Then there are brokerage charges, which as I use an old fashioned voice broker come to about 1%, but of even more importance there is the bid offer spread.

The bid offer spread is the best part of 10%. This is a high hurdle to get over in any investment and we will meet fat spreads time and again.

You have to be very sure in buying a stock with such a spread and I will turn stocks away simply because the spread is too big. Ten per cent is about my limit and it still grieves me. However, when stocks are at rock bottom, they can be perversely hard to buy and so spreads are wide.

The key idea is to always remember the spread on a stock is a hidden cost and you mustn't forget that it can be an enormous impediment to your profits. You need to judge the size of the spread and check whether it's sensible to buy.

When stocks are in an illiquid phase, especially when their price is low, the spreads do get large and will shrink if the share recovers and trading picks up.

However, the main reason I have an old style voice broker is I can get him to call a market maker and haggle. This often pays for itself many times over because a decent spread price improvement can be hundreds of pounds on some stocks and easily cover a 0.75% commission. Online broking offers no such flexibility and can, when the markets go crazy, simply become unusable.

You can also call your broker from a bus in Kathmandu – something that can't be said for an online broker. So sometimes old is better.

# Maths is My Friend

### 17 December 2012

I like maths. Maths is a very important tool for me to look at the markets. Take "game theory" for example. This is the maths of games, how games work and ways to win and lose.

There are three basic games: "positive sum," "zero sum" and "negative sum." The only game you want to play is positive sum. This is a game where the pot grows with the playing. If the pot is shrinking, if you play long enough, even if you are good at the game you will lose.

Equities are a positive sum game because of economic growth, so it's a game worth playing.

The pot grows anywhere between 3-7% a year on average depending on whose numbers you want to use. This means you should get 3-7% profit on an average year if you bought a random balanced portfolio of equities. Its modern equivalent is an ETF, which mimics the market. Some say this is how to play shares, just buy the FTSE 100 ETF and let the positive sum game deliver.

However we want a bit more profit so we are going to stock pick.

The first thing to realise is, if we spend more than 7% investing in shares a year we are not going to make money. Hence we are careful of the spread some shares have. We are also shy of using leverage, because often leverage costs 7% a year in interest, in effect eating all our profit.

By trading slowly we help capture the full average profit offered by the market for playing the stock market game. The more we trade the more of this profit we spend. So slow and steady is the way to go.

This is one of the reasons we are not going to get hyperactive or for that matter start this premium blog with a completed specimen portfolio. We are just going to build it up over time and discuss the market as the days pass.

Friday I dumped all my leveraged bets in my "stupid punting account." I've made a fat profit this year there and with the fiscal cliff looming, leverage can strip you to the bone really quickly. I haven't sold anything in my portfolio because unlevered it can safely sail through all but the nastiest storms and come out of the other side unscathed.

That is the beauty of a proper portfolio: you can run it, it doesn't run you.

I have added Volex and Aggrekko to my watch list. Not buys yet but on the radar for the future.

# FCUK – Solid Pick in Dicey World of Retail

### 19 December 2012

I'm pretty bullish on French Connection, which I've built a position in. It isn't in the portfolio as I'm only putting my future position in that so people reading the blog who wish to emulate the process can see the results.

At 29p I see value beyond 40p, with upsides to the 60-80p level.

Retail is of course tricky, but a company with profits and as near enough no debt and a fat cash balance are in a different world from the HMVs and Game Groups. Especially if they have a brand, something the fashion industry has in spades. I seem to be the only one who thought French Connection's FCUK idea was brilliant. For the life of me I don't know why they pulled the plug on it all those years ago, and I notice it's back in evidence.

Fcuk has a 5 P/E, a 5% divvy, £34 million of cash, a market cap of £27m and net assets of £75m. I like the numbers so much I second sourced the data. Sales are roughly six times market cap. The only thing not to love is, I can't find directors buying. If they did I would buy a bit more, to add to a position which is approximately 2.5 times my normal position.

This is exactly the kind of stock I like to buy. It's what pays off time and again. Cheap, unfashionable companies with solid fundamentals.

In happier times I'd be looking to buy Aggrekko for the dead cat bounce, but not these days. Sometime between tonight and the weekend the company will jump 5%, but these are not the times to trade.

# The Age of Aquarius Platinum

### 19 December 2012

Japan is going to rock the world: in a good way. Abe will most likely strip the Bank of Japan of its independence and reflate. Japan's economy will go ballistic and this will trigger a global withdrawal of central bank independence in the first world. This will in turn set the printing press whirring.

This is great news for the employed and bad news for the retired. Good news for the young and bad news for the old. It is good news for the private sector and bad news for the public sector. Good news for equity holders and bad news for bond holders. Sovereign debt gets shredded.

So in a nutshell a boom is coming. However, it is still a way away. I'd like to think 2013 but it's probably 2014... even 2015 before it gets hot or even 2017/2018 before times are swinging. However the great recession is dead, or at least the worse is over. The only way is up.

Of course, that doesn't mean it isn't gritty and horrible now. It just means the trend is now bullish until further notice.

This will be the basic plank of my investing now for years unless something ruins the picture, which is always a possibility.

Today I bought a unit of Aquarius Platinum (LSE:AQP). I don't like miners, because I do not trust management or the countries they dig in; however, I can't resist a bargain and as part of a portfolio you can take silly risks to chase big returns. I love this chart:

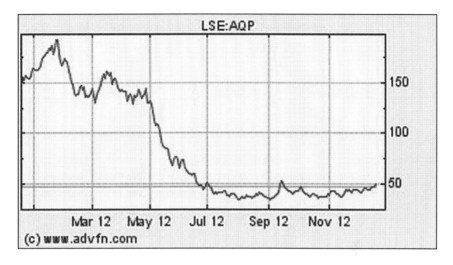

I will buy stocks making this pattern all day long if the fundamentals aren't shot to pieces.

A single stock pick like this would be very dicey, but as 3% now of my portfolio, it's not an issue. It's slightly non-optimal to be introducing these picks at the start of our journey but it will provide a rough initial ride, which will be instructive to many. Portfolio building is always rocky at the beginning but it smooths out as the portfolio spreads.

# Aquarius – Up

### 20 December 2012

Aquarius Platinum shot up to 55p after I bought it. Nice luck.

The buy price of any share in this portfolio consists of a commission, stamp duty and a brokerage "compliance charge." Calculated on a £1,000 block of stock the average price was 51.35p. The naked price was 49.9p but costs are real and any performance must include them to be "real."

Promethean was horribly expensive due to its terrible spread. However, we ate that on the basis that its upside is mighty, if it has one, and because bombed out stocks can be impossible to get into at a decent spread sometimes and as an investor you just have to jump on board or be damned. However, I often don't jump on board if I can't get significant improvement, so expect to read about that in due course.

I did a CNBC show this morning and suggested the fiscal cliff would be a good thing to fall off. But people are too scared of tomorrow to stop storing up catastrophe in a couple of years. To the active investor, however, it is an opportunity and we will see how this pans out in the week ahead.

I'm itching to buy more stocks but making haste slowly is the sensible approach.

# Strong Santa Rally Boosts Portfolio

### 24 December 2012

The proto-portfolio is apparently 5.17% up already. This is, of course, pure luck and a little silly. Aquarius Platinum is up 8.5% and Promethean is already over its 11% cost hurdle and 2% ahead. All this is at the bid and after buying costs.

This is not skill and is of course very nice but nonetheless not what a portfolio building process is all about.

We have been getting a very strong Santa rally created by several factors but the main one being funds balancing their books and some would say pumping them for a strong year finish. This is all fun when it's in your favour but it's just a nice sideshow in a long, often boring, journey.

Last year had six months of returns best considered lacklustre. OK, so the portfolio was up 15% by around February but by June it was back to square one, with hardly a happy or satisfactory moment from its birth in November to then. If it had been a premium service a subscriber would have very likely been extremely sceptical of what was going to happen next.

What's more, there was little to say except, IT'S A GRIM WORLD. Yet this portfolio is now up a ridiculous 50%, all coming from the last six months.

Patience is a virtue.

Don't be misled. 50% return in a year is too high. The target is 25% which is way too much in most people's books. However, I can usually hit that number on average, with 15% being a low floor. Of course, the past is no guide to the future.

This kind of massive alpha is theoretically impossible which is ironic as I'm an adherent to the theory. It is probably because following the ideas of efficient market hypothesis is so rare that the market has opportunities. If so many use the market to gamble then there will be inefficiencies to profit from. Long may that continue.

However, making 5% a week is not going to happen very often and things will go against us, get boring and take determination, positive mental attitude and grit.

Meanwhile, however, we can drink to the father of investment genius: luck.

# 2012: A Good Year For Mad Punting

### 31 December 2012

Subscribers will know I have what I call a 'mad punting account' which I use as an experimental account for wildly dangerous speculation. It has had a great 2012, effectively up 400% on the year. But don't get excited, it is up 100% in ten years, roughly twice the return in a decade that my safe boring portfolio has made since May.

You have to remember that spread betting can cost you 7% in interest charges. So when you lever it up ten times that's a 70% charge on your capital, if nothing happens. Obviously you hope to lever up your profits too, but beating 7% just to break even is tricky. Effectively in ten years you give up 100% worth of profit just to stand still, 1,000% if you are levered up. So if you use spread betting to punt indices, where the speculator is lucky to make more than zilch, your capital is doomed pretty quickly.

Anyway, Pace and TNI in particular and some fortunate speculations delivered a big year and I closed the lot the Friday before Christmas because I couldn't be bothered to care about it and a thumping big potential dump care of the fiscal cliff. Leverage means a small move against you can be a financial avalanche, so you should be a scared rabbit when you play with leverage. I missed out on a nice Nikkei profit but I missed out on a euro loss. More importantly, I could look at the fat profit lying safely in cash and relax.

Of course, you can't keep a gambler at bay for long, so yesterday I re-entered the Nikkei long and today took couple of small punts on Petrofac and RIM. I like the Petrofac Schlumberger takeover rumour and RIM is just plain cheap. Of course Research in Motion, the maker of the Blackberry, is having a bad time but its valuation is daft. $6 billion dollars wins you $10 billion in sales, a billion in EBITDA and over $2.5bn in cash and equivalents. Meanwhile, a dollar in Apple's sales is worth per dollar of market cap, ten times that of RIM. That looks bargain basement to me.

But all this punting is in my crash dummy account. It's not about making money, it's about playing around. This is why it is separated from the master portfolio, the one we are building here.

I'd urge any of you forced to "trade," to separate your trading account from your investment portfolio. Investing is not trading. While people like to think in terms of trading, investing is about value, while trading is about speculation. Investing is easy, trading is hard. Don't mix them up.

Why? Simply, it will confuse you. You may be a rubbish investor and a great trader, or vice versa. Keep the accounts separate and you will easily know where your strengths lie. Mix them up and it will be very time consuming to pull them apart again to know what you did right or wrong.

In my opinion you will clearly see that you should invest to become wealthy and you should trade for fun. It is like hunting for food and shooting clay pigeons. They have different purposes and what is more, clay pigeon pie tastes terrible.

As I write, the US seems highly likely to tip over the fiscal cliff. My portfolio will take a hit, but I can't time the exit or the entry so I will ride it out. I will load up on buys if it's a big drop.

So Obama and Boehner, bring it on! I'm ready for some action.

# How I Invest

## 2 January 2013

I think it is important for followers of this blog to understand my current investment thesis.

Firstly, I like shares because it is the only positive sum game there is. This means a game in which all can win because money is created by the game itself, making it easier to win. The stock market is likely the only market game you can win as a player, though the house wins in all markets. That's the basic platform: play a winning game.

The next layer of the thesis: efficient market hypothesis. From day to day, markets are pretty random and very efficient. If you do a little maths with the FTSE index you can prove this for yourself. There is a tiny non-random element equal to the long term profit. This is about 3-7% a year depending on how you want to calculate it. If you put a long term moving average on the FTSE you will see the randomness disappear and a long term "return" appear in the form of a gently rising curve.

Randomness means there is no right or wrong time to buy per se; it's all just a process of averages. You already know the tropes – win some lose some, swings and roundabouts, eggs in one basket etc.

The layer above this is: Value Investing. Buy cheap stocks and sell them when they aren't cheap. I do this by following unpopular stocks, which I try my best to get at rock bottom. By checking out their balance sheet and applying all sorts of rules of thumb I end up with a portfolio of candidates in the least "real trouble", which means that they are undervalued. History shows us that these shares give a pretty good return; for me somewhere in the mid 20% a year, often more.

The layer above this is: Macro. This layer starts getting into the realms of speculation. Speculation is fascinating but it is alchemy not science. It can be fluffy nonsense that may or may not add the cheese on the bread and butter of value investing.

At present the macro situation means that the first world is going to dig itself out of debt through inflation. For me, there is no other plausible position to imagine, except to believe the unsustainable levels of debt and deficit are sustainable.

Europe and the US need to cut their debt roughly in half. That means 7% inflation for ten years or 10% inflation for seven years or 25% for three years.

Shortly, (two to three years) we will see +10% inflation for a year or five. This might not show up in the official figures but you will see it in "hard asset" prices and "hard priced assets" like haircuts, hotel rooms and other service industries and, of course, energy and utilities.

To get complicated for a moment, QE has put a large proportion of a country's long term debt towards the short term end. The US will simply turn their short term debt into cash (monetisation) as it comes due and then boom! We get inflation.

At some point interest rates will shoot up to 5-10% and bonds will implode. I would guess this will be another slow motion crisis so there will be plenty of time to move when things start to go pear shaped but it will have a big effect on equities and other fixed assets.

The thing to remember is the passive are the ones that take the brunt, while the active will adapt and ride out such difficulties. As such, readers of this blog will probably be just fine, even though it will of course be quite stressful, or as I used to think, fun.

The key to the macro is not to be absolutely right, but instead to be on one's toes to take advantage of the opportunities and avoid the pitfalls.

Anyway, that is where I'm coming from and 2013 could be a huge year in equities. Just saying so won't make it happen, but 1 January is looking very nice indeed.

Meanwhile, my Nikkei punt paid off big and I closed it this morning for what looks like a 3-4% profit. I always take a really fat profit quickly because profit = square root of time. For those of you who are not mathematically minded you can take this as meaning "it does well to cash out quick if you hit it lucky".

I'll look at the Nikkei again in a day or two and probably rue my snap profit take. Trading really is silly but again, it is fun. My portfolio has made me six times my Nikkei punt today but the quick profit is first in my mind.

This is why people lose their shirt trading; it is not about profit, it is about adrenaline.

# The Fiscal Cliff and the Three Per Cent Lift

### 3 January 2013

We haven't built up much of a portfolio yet, which is a little frustrating but how it should be. Hyperactivity is a costly business in investing, slow and steady wins the race.

Yesterday was spectacular as the "fiscal cliff" downdraft lifted. My long term portfolio took a 3% lift. As a broker at TSC Trade remarked, it's good if you are long beta, which suggests my portfolio is full of rubbish. I replied it's full of "value" which is not the same at all.

Beta is defined as volatility around the norm; this means that in a rally high beta will zip up more and in a slump fall more. It's a technical value derived from looking at the chart of the past and deriving its jiggliness from the data. The more it jiggles the more beta it has. It's the size of the jiggle that defines whether it's high beta or not. The more it flails around, the higher the beta.

Beta has its uses, but my stocks are often low beta because they fell off a cliff and have been lying motionless for a long time. Dead equals low beta. So much of my portfolio has been low beta. However, I select stocks on their balance sheet not their volatility so beta isn't a big factor. In fact I like to buy a dead stock when it starts marching with low volatility upwards. But that's another story.

Meanwhile I bought a clip of Avocet Mining. It's a bit irritating that all the first three stocks I have bought in the portfolio are miners. I hate them! But you can't go against the flow of your system.

In my historic portfolio I only have three out of thirty-two.

# My Legacy Portfolio

### 7 January 2013

So this is my legacy portfolio. As I add to it I will post here and the buy will become part of the specimen portfolio. The below performance includes costs and stamp duty and the sell price is at the bid.

| Holding | | Avg.Price | Price Now @ bid | Profit/ Loss % | Opening weighting | Weighting Now |
|---|---|---|---|---|---|---|
| AGA | Aga Rangemaster | 0.7463 | 0.765 | 2.5 | 3.5 | 2.8 |
| AQP | Aquarius Plat. | 0.4589 | 0.6725 | 46.56 | 4.1 | 4.7 |
| AV. | Aviva | 3.274 | 3.865 | 18.05 | 4.1 | 3.8 |
| AVM | Avocet Mining | 0.8165 | 0.7175 | -12.12 | 3.3 | 2.3 |
| AVR | Avarae | 0.107 | 0.1025 | -4.17 | 1.6 | 1.2 |
| AZN | Astrazeneca | 29.0833 | 29.81 | 2.5 | 2.5 | 2 |
| BARC | Barclays | 1.7232 | 2.875 | 66.84 | 3 | 3.9 |
| BKIR | Bank Ireland | 0.0989 | 0.123 | 0.99 | 3.3 | 2.6 |
| CNKS | Cenkos Sec | 0.7581 | 0.7 | -7.66 | 1.5 | 1.1 |
| DRX | Drax | 5.196 | 5.595 | 7.68 | 1.5 | 1.3 |
| DXNS | Dixons Retail | 0.1623 | 0.2812 | 73.31 | 4.1 | 5.5 |
| FCCN | French Cnctn. | 0.2511 | 0.305 | 21.45 | 4.6 | 4.4 |
| FDL | Findel | 0.0405 | 0.0875 | 116.15 | 1.7 | 2.9 |
| FGP | Firstgroup | 2.0056 | 2.087 | 4.06 | 1.5 | 1.2 |
| FLYB | Flybe Grp | 0.7199 | 0.4925 | -31.59 | 1.7 | 0.9 |
| GDP | Goldplat | 0.1374 | 0.1275 | -7.21 | 1.5 | 1.1 |
| HOME | Home Retail | 0.9585 | 1.248 | 30.2 | 1.5 | 1.5 |
| HRN | Hornby | 0.6494 | 0.7225 | 11.27 | 1.3 | 1.1 |
| LAM | Lamprell | 1.0108 | 1.1375 | 12.53 | 1 | 0.9 |
| LGT | Lighthouse Grp. | 0.0646 | 0.035 | -45.79 | 2.6 | 1.1 |
| LLOY | Lloyds Grp. | 0.3179 | 0.5045 | 58.72 | 9.9 | 12.3 |
| LSE | Lon.Stk.Exch | 10.2433 | 11.44 | 11.68 | 2.5 | 2.2 |
| PDG | Pendragon | 0.1261 | 0.1775 | 40.74 | 1.2 | 1.4 |
| PRW | Promethean | 0.2489 | 0.19 | -23.67 | 6.3 | 3.8 |
| RBS | Royal Bank Scot | 2.7532 | 3.345 | 21.5 | 3 | 2.8 |
| RDSA | Rds A | 22.8234 | 21.295 | -6.7 | 1.5 | 1.1 |
| RM. | RM | 0.701 | 0.7425 | 5.92 | 9.9 | 8.2 |
| SIXH | 600 Grp. | 0.1113 | 0.14 | 25.79 | 1.1 | 1.1 |
| SSE | SSE | 13.72 | 14.64 | 6.71 | 2.5 | 2.1 |
| TNI | Trinity Mirror | 0.454 | 0.9725 | 114.2 | 10.1 | 16.9 |
| TNO | Rsm Tenon | 0.0653 | 0.0666 | 1.94 | 1 | 0.8 |
| TSCO | Tesco | 3.2875 | 3.4925 | 6.24 | 1.5 | 1.2 |

The first thing that is clear is I'm overweight on Trinity Mirror. This is caused by a mixture of going in heavy and being right. I should lighten up and this will be in the back of my mind now.

Since this portfolio was started at the end of 2011 through early 2012 there have been a few nice profits taken including Pace, Enterprise Inns, PV Crystalox, Cable and Wireless, Mothercare, Transense, Robert Wiseman and a Findel top slice. Many have zoomed on up. Profit taken is about equivalent to a 20% profit on the original capital and dividends so far about 3%. The gross profit is about 56%, which is a huge outperform even for me.

It will take a huge year for me to repeat this in 2013 and I'm not expecting it. I'm aiming for 25% and normally get it but I'm happy with anything over 15%. This would be shooting for the moon if I was a fund manager but being below the radar and not having to take giant positions is a big edge in investing.

So onwards and upwards!

# Flybe Added to Portfolio

## 11 January 2013

I topped up on Flybe in the legacy portfolio today, so that is a new entry into the "get rich slow" portfolio. Before it goes in, the portfolio is at 10.5% profit.

Flybe is a bet on the recovery. Aren't they all. Airlines do go bust on the stock market; in fact they go bust a lot, but they also do well as you can see from Ryanair and Easyjet.

The chart looks good. I like it when stocks form a sideways base at a low level. £36 million in market cap gets you £600m in sales. Let's call it as £1 of market cap gets you £20 in sales, with Easyjet it's £1 to £1, BAY £1 gets you £2 and in Ryanair £1 gets you 50p in sales.

Of course, they can always drop like a rock again, which is why I often top up at lower levels and build a conviction position if I feel the company is worthy of it.

Trinity Mirror had an RNS today that spiked the price to 112p. It is now below the open as I write at 98p. A cynic would say someone wanted an updraft to get out on at 100p. An optimist will say the chart has to fill the 112p gap now, so that's good! I don't really like this kind of weird behaviour but I'll sit it out. I had promised to sell some at £1 but that was just a target a long time ago. It's better to be patient.

I sold the last of my Findel yesterday from the legacy portfolio. It then went up. That's life. I bagged 110% or thereabouts.

The market is feeling a bit softer now and on the trading side I bought some Barrick Gold which also has a tight range. Tight ranges are good because they say, "this company is stably priced." After stability can come growth. It is hard to have growth without stability first. But Barrick is just crazy punting, so not part of the portfolio.

I am also keen to go long on Nikkei but I'll wait till I'm on the right time zone next week. Frankly I'm feeling a little risk adverse this minute and I couldn't really be more long.

# Banks Ballistic: Should I Buy More?

### 14 January 2013

On the way to the ADVFN US office. Banks are going ballistic and I would buy some more but I'm up to my ears in banks so I'm holding off. Instead I'm topping up on First Group, which is therefore a new entrant to the model portfolio. It's low P/E and high dividend. It's a bit like buying a bank really, in an odd, recovery play way.

Adding new stocks is killing the average return on the portfolio but that's the way it goes – portfolio building is like farming. Currently we are planting a crop.

In crazy punting land, RIM punt is doing well cancelling out the damage on the HMV Hollywood or bust punt. I really like RIM as its business is strong; it's just its future that crushes its valuation. Classic!

# Premium Portfolio Progress Report

### 22 January 2013

The premium portfolio is doing well even though it has had to jump the hurdle of buying new stocks that dilutes the fat profits of the early buys.

It's funny, but imagine you bought 2 stocks and they halved. You would be nursing a 50% loss. Now buy eight shares of say super blue cheap quality, hence your costs are low. Now you'd be showing a portfolio loss of 5% and overnight you wouldn't be looking so stupid.

Sadly this fact has worked in reverse. Our early luck has been diluted by our recent purchases. This will be the case for a fair amount of time as we will be building for at least a year, perhaps more.

However we are overall 3.68% up after costs since roughly a month ago. So that would be over 40% annualised. It's possible to keep this up but unlikely. 25% is the yearly target and there is no timing it. A rally or a crash can mess the numbers up horribly in the short term as the above simply shows, but as the weeks go by the trend will show itself.

So far it's:

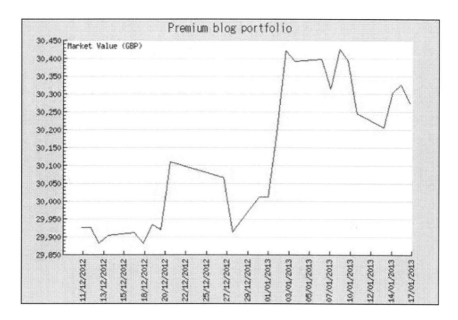

Meanwhile the legacy portfolio is looking like this:

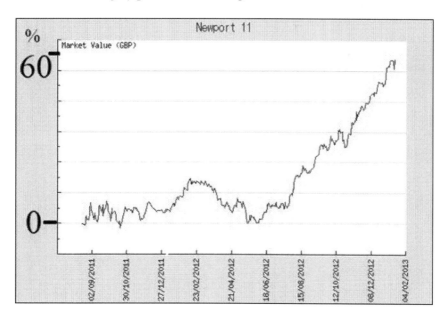

I think this underlines how important patience is and how difficult timing can be.

Anyway, back to evaluating the legacy portfolio. What follow is a one liner take on the status quo.

## Aga

People are addicted to these stupid things. Balance sheet strong, near historic lows. P/E minimal. Value 150-400p. 84p now.

## Aquarius Platinum

Easy 150p on the chart. Precious metal play. If you believe in inflation you have to have precious metal exposure. Political/mining risk a big downer, but most people love that. Could go to 400p in a perfect world. 71p now bought at 46p for the legacy portfolio and 51p for the specimen portfolio.

## Aviva

Credit crunch smashed insurers just like banks. Banks back up to their old highs, if not killed by the fall, eg: HSBC/Stan, likewise insurers will get there. That mean AV goes from 366p to 600p-800p one fine day. Insurer very unpopular, these sentiments will change especially if asset inflation gets underway, especially in equities. Meanwhile 7% dividend.

## Avocet Mining

Gold play of course. What a shaggy dog. 2 P/E. Is 65p, should be 150p. Of course the company has done itself over, but that makes it a punt on them putting that right. I will buy more if it tanks unless something awful causes it. The chart is looking a little wobbly though the Chairman has bought some recently. I don't like miners but I do like this kind of opportunity and I do like gold. Need to keep a beady eye on news flow.

## Avarac

I'm non-exec of this company. The drawback is I can buy but not sell without grovelling apologies to the board. This is therefore a long term hold. However, can't resist 14.2p of assets for 10.4p. I know the inventory and the assets are golden.

## Astrazenica

A 6.6 P/E with a 5.8% dividend. It's a no brainer. Then compare with GSK. AZN has more sales and more profit and is worth half.

Will hold until these ratios equalise and take the divvy while I'm at it. Will of course score on a general rally.

## Barclays

Barclays is an old friend. Sat on 72% profit. 20%-50% upside in it if conditions remain stable. 100% on recovery. Still loving banks. Scale back around 100% on recovery. Still loving banks. Scale back around 400p is an option if I'm feeling cautious.

## Bank of Ireland

Love this opportunity. In effect I have bought in around the price the US rescuers paid. Ireland is coming back quick and even after dilution the upside is 100%. After all you can imagine Wilbur Ross and co have done their due diligence. Are they going to punt this kind of huge money out for less than a 100% upside? Will crunch the numbers again at 0.2c.

## Cenkos

Hum.. not sure why I hold these. Probably because I think they are a great broker and will fight back. Not a good enough reason to hold really but they are rallying so they get the benefit of the doubt on a "run profits" kind of reasoning. Definitely on the potential cull list. A 2013 rally will of course be good for business. Looks like a 100-110p sell target.

**Drax**

I can't resist 4.5 P/E and 5% dividends. Should have topped up the day this summer it got kicked, but was too bearish in general at the time. Remains sleeping beauty. Good for around 700p.

....another ten thumbnails on Wednesday.

# Watching the Portfolio: Part Two

### 23 January 2013

It is good to remember that my opinions are not irrefutable, invincible, incontrovertible or even correct. Like a workman I have a set of tools and with them I get down to the job of selecting stocks. There is a fair amount of bodging to be done. Stock picking is like plumbing not cabinet making, there is a lot of brute force involved; it simply doesn't need to be any other way.

As a whole the market is very efficient, but in certain particular instances it is woeful. That's where I like to invest. That's where the money is. Like all fat picking grounds one can be laid back and even lazy, because the key call is, is this a part of the market that is badly served, ill understood or simply neglected for a good reason? If it is you can lazily pick the harvest.

Contrarian value investing has been fat city since it was discovered in the 1950s. Long may it remain so...

**Dixons**

Have done very well on this (+66%). The chart looks great. However, Dixons is a lamentable retailer. It looks like "the last man standing" but is there such a thing in its segment? I'll let the market tell me. It's got a strong trend. I'll follow that, if it breaks I'll drop it. It's probably good for 50p all being well and maybe just maybe 100p if something good happens like they find a format that isn't generic rubbishy retailing. It is there to be found. Shops will not go away, walk into an Apple store to see the future.

Just noticed Dixons have had fat directors buys. Good. However, a pet hate of mine is when good news comes out after close on Friday. This is bad IR and a sign of weak coordination from management. PLCs have a duty to spread good news with as much diligence as bad.

## French Connection

This is a company with great fundamentals hampered by what I consider "gauche" management. That's not to say they aren't good at fashion retail, just that they are weak in the city walk part of their job. A perfect example of that was Sly Baily. She was great at her job at the Mirror but a disaster in the city. FCUK seem to have that kind of thing going on.

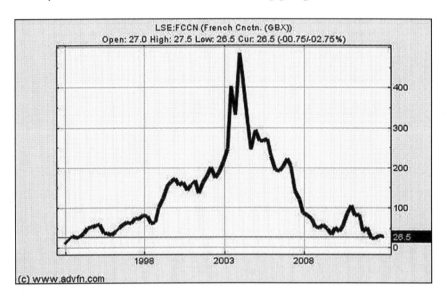

This is a 50p-100p-200p stock if they can sort themselves out. They just need to "chin up, chest out."

## First Group

It's hard to resist a sub 5 P/E for a company with £6 billion in sales and a semi-monopoly. Its dividend is fat even if it's frozen or even cut back. The stock fell like a stone when it didn't win the poisoned chalice of the Glasgow to London route. A proper P/E means this share is good for 300-400p from its current level.

## Flybe Group

I love this chart. So it might go down heavily again, but for now I like the look of this base. Two years ago this company floated at 300p, it's now 49p. So the question is, is this a dud or a comeback kid? Crudely, it's valued at about 33% of BA's sales (IAG as it is now). If I looked at EasyJet the number would be 1/20. Of course as it's priced for doom it could very well go bust like the other minor airlines but if it doesn't it has a large upside. Note to myself, keep an eye on IAG, twice the profit of EasyJet same market cap... and four times the sales.

## Goldplat

A gold miner that mines other gold mines' rubbish for gold and makes good money doing it. Crazy mining opportunities attached. All mining is a punt, but this is at the value end and well positioned to do well if gold takes the next leg up. A dark horse and a long term one at that. Chart says it's at the bottom of its expected channel so expect a bounce. But at £20m market cap and sales of £26m, could go far if a number of what-ifs panned out.

## Home Retail

Will see this back over 200p. Giant sales. OK balance sheet. Seems to be cracking the online retail problem. Performing well. Takeover target? Will get a kick up the pants from any recovery. Should buy more of this... hum...

## Hornby

Coming back from its poor numbers, looking for 100p. Solid balance sheet. Killed divvy to build up cash which is sensible. Nice double bottom chart pattern and a history of "zero to hero" share price moves. Not going to double but a nice potential winner in any event.

## Lamprell

Another mess. Worth 250p if there isn't something terminal in the cupboard. You'd think there was when the price collapsed early 2012, but it is still in business. This is not a small company with £700m plus in sales. This is a straight recovery play. On the cusp of a big jump or dump according to the chart. A stock that needs a fair amount of attention as it suffers from a future with poor visibility and could go bust unlike much in the portfolio. None of my stocks are safe but when they go up they fly – that's the trade, Hollywood or bust.

## Lighthouse

Big sales, great customers, lowly value. To annoy people I ask what is the difference between Hargreaves Lansdowne and Lighthouse. The answer appears to be a fund platform. There is of course the issue of skill and vision but if you were a bleary eyed alien the big difference you'd note is the valuation ratios. The IFA rule change is the big what-if of course but the idea is that a big group of commission driven salesmen will find a way. Long shot with big up side. Close call with going private though. Should be on the iffy list really. However this is not cheap because it's not a mess. (This is why a review is good practice, the world changes and good buys can look less good as time passes.)

## Lloyds

I love banks. Lloyds is worth 150p and will hit 100p if nothing kicks them down the stairs. The chart looks ballistic so makes a good guide. At 53p still a snip. End of PPI a bonus. Like Barclays I look to HSBC/Stan as the benchmark.

Part 3 to follow.

# Reviewing the Rest of the Premium Portfolio

### 25 January 2013

Firstly I bought some Xerox in my crazy punting fund. The RIM I took a little of a week or two back has exploded. More luck but it does mean the punting fund continues to swell. This is simply a function of a bull market I suspect.

However, meanwhile Apple imploded. This is strangely satisfying though I wish holders no harm, because I've been writing for months how Apple is a bubble. I even drew some charts at Christmas predicting exactly what has happened. You can see these on Forbes if you have a moment to gawp.

OK, this newsletter is not about US stocks so back at the legacy portfolio...

I don't seem to meet many people that have a practical grasp of portfolio building. You need to work towards getting 30 plus stocks into your investment portfolio to get the magic working. That seems like a mountain to climb but it isn't. It just takes time.

To build up a portfolio is easy, like getting rich. It's just the time it takes that is the issue. If you don't have a portfolio you will probably never make a six or seven figure share portfolio. You will be stuck with trading and never getting anywhere. One year you will be a genius and make a lot then the next you will get wiped out. That's why it's worse if you don't invest with a portfolio.

So I hear back from a lot of people, "Warren Buffett says you have to concentrate on a few stocks you know are good." My reply is "really?" Berkshire Hathaway is hugely diversified. If you count the companies that make up his net worth it's well over 30.

Portfolios are unpopular with investors and the industry because they are boring. Brokers don't like them because the owner will be a slow boring customer, that doesn't ring them once a day to thrash their stock around and make them commission. This is another reason to be contrarian.

Always be very cautious when the investment industry is welcoming you in. Always think of the banner outside the City Poker room off Queen Victoria Street: "Beginners always welcome."

If you go around the city and talk about building a portfolio of value investments you will find yourself not the centre of attention. Try the process again talking about crazy mining stocks almost bound to go belly up. Suddenly you will be popular, as popular as the man in the betting shop talking about the next potential 100-1 winner.

So how to build a portfolio.

Firstly don't make big positions until you have built to 30 stocks. If you have a great stock zooming or crashing down, don't play with it. Buy a different stock with new money. If a stock doubles and you sell it, buy two different stocks next. Get to 30 stocks before getting clever.

Then think about clips. Let's say it's £1,000. You have say £33,000 now in play.

Now you have £1,000 and £2,000 clips to play with, or one or two units. So if you wanted to buy more of a stock you had £1,000 in, you can now buy one more clip. Likewise if you love an opportunity you could dive in with two clips.

Now let's say you have £50,000, you could go one, two, three clips. One clip for normal stocks, two for terrific ones and a max of £3,000 in anything.

I'm sure you see how it pans out. I've got from 1 to 5:

1. Exciting but wildly risky.
2. Slight hesitation due to timing.
3. Normal.
4. I like this a lot or have topped up , 2+2 for example.
5. Probably topped up to get here or it's red hot.

Then 6 to 10 I've got here because this stock is a conviction play. I've probably topped up three times mainly on the drop. With this model you can still end up with 50% of your capital in ten of your stocks.

But then there are the running profits. Don't sell until you start to sweat. Then you can top slice back if you wish to an allocation you feel comfortable with or just sell. A share is a piece of paper not a puppy.

The point is that most and hopefully all the stocks you pick are a sideshow to the portfolio. They give you not only safety but comfort.

When a stock gets overweight then you need to watch it like a hawk, a position I have with two stocks: Lloyds and Trinity Mirror. I could top slice them but I'm going to hang on and keep a close watch. Meanwhile, when I find another stock I will buy two to three units of it.

## London Stock Exchange

This sector is M&A-ville. ICE's takeover of NYSE is the latest instalment of this saga. So when I saw the CEO of the LSE in a French magazine promoting his wine, I thought, WHY? Like Cincinnatus would he be retiring to his farm soon? Tenuous I know, but if equities come back into fashion the LSE/Italian Bourse will flourish, so the takeover idea is in for free.

## Pendragon

Cheap turnover, £3bn turnover for £300m. A 5 P/E. Meanwhile the company is in breakout mode. 30-100% upside.

## Promethean

Where to start on this one? A high tech company with a low P/E, market cap 20% of historic sales. Listed three years ago at 200p, it's now 20p. If it doesn't go bust, which shouldn't be on the cards, then it must double at least.

Downsides are it has a VC backer. VCs are toxic.

Sales have collapsed but they are still big, £123m or thereabout. This is a bit of a mystery company as the story doesn't really pan out in my head. However, if there isn't a dead elephant in the basement, and there may be, this has giant upside. But I would not be surprised if there wasn't a nasty surprise coming up. It's a straight bet on the odds and expected returns.

## RBS

Nice upside if the politicians don't bring the house crashing down. The likelihood of that is decreasing. Using the STAN/HSBC benchmark it is an easy doubler.

## RDSA

Shell. 7 P/E, a market cap of 25% of sales, a 4.8% dividend. No brainer. Unless I need the money for a much better bet, this is a perfect bit of stodge for my portfolio. I must own this stock, the numbers are perfect.

## RM

When I was a kid I used one of this company's computers. RM has been out of fashion for a decade on the market but 150p-200p feels right to me for it. It is now 76p. Public sector suppliers aren't in vogue and I suspect the education sector is further out of fashion. It has a 4% dividend. More importantly, it's been cleaning house.

## 600 Group

Bought this small industrial at 11p, it's nearly 13p now, looking for 20p. It has turned a corner and is now in profit after a CEO change. It's a small dabble. It seems to be turning out positive news suggesting renewed energy. £40 sales for £11 market cap. Non-exec bought stock. The company is worth a small position.

## SSE

I have a history of buying this company, wondering why I have and selling it again. A portfolio gives you leeway for this kind of silliness because against the big picture, a little inconsistency is of little consequence. OK, it has a 5.8% dividend. It's a stodgy big cap to give some gravitas to more risky portfolio members. It's a steady performer and I hope it's in the takeover frame as a bit of spice. The CEO just left in a hurry which cut my outstanding profit off. I should really sell, but then I'd remember why it's a good pick and buy again.

## Trinity Mirror

This has been a star. I'm up 118% on this as I write and I went fully committed by buying as it fell. I think this has 150p in it, but I have to be mindful I'm overweight in the stock. I'm holding for now. When it nears anything like the valuation metric to DMGT I'd sell, but it's still miles from that.

## RSM Tenon

This is a wild punt. Accountants should not go bust, but they do. If this doesn't it should be a lot higher that the current prices. A splash of shares is a punt on the obvious upside.

## Tesco

A blue chip on a 10 P/E with a 4% dividend? It should be 400p. Will sell it there.

This might all seem perfunctory and it is. My feeling is, the more complex argument you have to make to own a stock, the less chance your thinking is correct. If you think it's gold it isn't, when you know it's gold it is. It works for gold miners and it works for me.

# The Difference Between Trading and Investing

### 30 January 2013

The trouble with proper investing is it can be boring, which is one of the reasons I have a crazy punting account. If you punt you need to keep that money separate from your investments.

Trading and investing are not the same. Don't muddle them up. For one thing, you can benchmark your profits quickly if you keep trading and investing in different accounts.

The one thing about investing is you need to keep looking for opportunities and on the weekend I noticed Ford and GM were badly out of whack. Ford was much more expensive than GM, so the obvious idea is to buy GM and sell Ford for a lovely hedged position.

In my case I wasn't going for the hedge, I was going to jump into GM in my punting fund.

So here is golden rule no 874. Keep checking your data.

What do you know, the data was wrong. GM and Ford were valued roughly the same when you found good data. So I didn't buy GM.

If you can, always check your data. An aberration is only an aberration if the numbers are true.

Investing can be full of false starts which is why patience and diligence is needed. Investing is not hard in its own right, but being patient and diligent seems to many too much to bear.

Today a company called TOYE went mad, shooting up 70% at one stage. I used to own this stock and did well in it but it's another lesson waiting to be learned. I simply couldn't buy much of this share, it was and is pretty much completely illiquid and has a massively wide spread. The market will also refuse to sell you much or any stock.

For all intents and purposes you can't invest in a share like this, even if it's dirt cheap. On the surface TOYE still is dirt cheap. However, if you buy in it might be years until you can sell out. Buying a share like that is a snare.

To add insult to injury it is very hard to get much of a position even if you wanted it, which in a funny way was how I sold my holding, by "crossing it" to a private investor building up a stake.

Save yourself the hassle, don't buy very illiquid stocks with wide spreads and no trading volume. It's too much effort.

Meanwhile, if you want to consider a trade like Ford short, GM long, look at GSK and AZN. The correct answer is long AstraZenica and short GSK, look at the fundamentals and see if you agree.

# Change is Due in the Market

## 5 February 2013

The market feels toppy and there are changes in the works. After rocketing, the euro suddenly looks wobbly again, with Italy, Spain and Greece looking fragile. I'm pretty sure all this is not being caused by the various rationalisations by the so called MSM (mainstream media.)

Firstly it must be understood that the level of insider trading is titanic. It is not people in the know, it's institutions in the know. For example if the UK AAA rating got downgraded in the near future, you would know that someone knew the UK was lined up for this and was re-hedging themselves.

Politicians are as leaky as hell, so those near to them will get the nod days, even weeks, before the outsiders. This is why we as outsiders need a model to navigate by; we have to work out the big picture and position ourselves ahead of the action. This is not as hard as it seems because those hands that have taken much control of the market, move slowly and only when necessity absolutely demands action.

It's a fine balance between a correction and a historic break out. A correction is most likely, I feel. The pound action is to me a bit ominous. It says something is coming but to be honest I do not know what.

As investors, nine times out of ten we should sit tight. This makes for boring stock picking but we are investing not trading.

People seem to have forgotten about the fiscal cliff and the US debt ceiling coming up soon. If this was fixed it could create that rally, if it blows up we will get that correction.

I'm groping for the bottom of sterling. Sounds like a rude joke but it is true. 1.15 could be it, but that's a guess.

# A Waiting Game

### 7 February 2013

Sometimes you just have to sit and wait. I would love to buy but I've bought enough and I will wait for the breakout which will mean a historic new era dawns. Nice thought, so probably we are in for a correction. So with only four stocks in the portfolio nothing too bad can really happen.

Meanwhile we are sat on a 7.4% profit or £380 of £5,137 of stock after costs. This is, of course, great. However, if you tipped £30,000 into your account when we got going, then you are only 1% up, about what you will get in the bank in a year if you didn't lock it up for ages. Hence if we can do that all year we will be very happy.

But that's not how things work. Volatility ahead.

The euro is a mess as is the pound. The yen's weakness is ballooning the euro as the euro is the anti-yen. It's a case of the yen being the least weak currency. This is not really a position to invest in as not only is it highly volatile and based on lots of hidden variables, it is a semi-fixed game. It is however hard to sit and watch the situation unfold, so I am long some Nikkei 225. If Japan takes off the equity boom of the decade will begin. If we correct from here it will just be delayed.

The main problem is that the absolutely obvious is taking so long to unfold. Governments are so slow and huge that it's easy to think the story will be told in months when it in fact will take years. This is another reason to take it easy.

Get rich slow is the way to go.

# Portfolio Update

## 13 February 2013

The legacy portfolio had a giant day yesterday with the banks rallying and Trinity Mirror up 7.5%. The market is struggling to break up into new levels.

Combined, the five shares in the portfolio are doing fine. Promethean and Aquarius are the stars, up 31% and 37%. Avocet is the dog down 31% and Flybe and First Group are treading water. Yesterday Barclays released its figures and future plans and the banks rallied hard. This stuck about 1.5% onto the value of the portfolio and as much again coming from Trinity Mirror with its 7% pop.

This portfolio seems to be breaking up ahead of a market rally.

It is always easy to take on further risk after a good day, but the thing to do is to be dismissive of good fortunes and keep plodding on. I really want to buy Bank of Ireland but will wait a little because I have enough/too much bank exposure already. However it might fit in the new portfolio but before I decide I'm going to wait. The profit to be made won't go anywhere as it's not the stock that makes investor money, it's the method.

Of course this is all very boring and you might think you didn't subscribe to be bored. As the portfolio is in profit more than a yearly subscription after only a few weeks I hope readers can stomach the calm.

I am in Tokyo right now and have been looking at a stock called "Chiome" Bioscience which is a sketchy biotech. A Japanese professor has just won a Nobel Prize for Medicine and biotechs are rocking! Pity the private investors piling in.

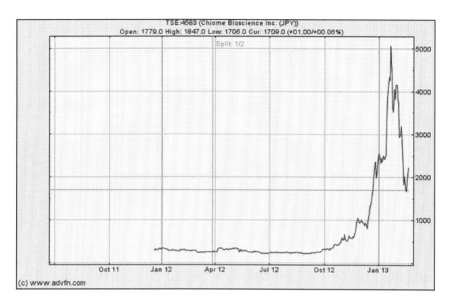

We've all seen this wealth death trap before!!! Up like a rocket and down like a stick.

Slow and steady wins the race.

**Update:**

After consideration I bought a unit of Bank of Ireland. It will be good for the portfolio to have some banking exposure and the recovery potential of Ireland is starting to show through.

I looked at Bumi again but I see nothing but trouble there even if the chart looks great. Meanwhile, I've been looking at African Barrick. Words fail me on this company; what the blazes is going on there? Sometimes the goings on at companies like African Barrick and Bumi just beggar belief. Still it's worth keeping tabs on them even if only to see performances that show that no matter how much regulation there is in the world nothing will stop investors being lead a merry dance.

# Avocet Mining Has Cratered

### 14 February 2013

Avocet (LSE:AVM) has cratered today. This is why we have a portfolio. If you don't have a portfolio it is these kinds of events that kill you. Instead, if you do have a portfolio, you merely scowl. An investor who had all his money in this company would now be down 50%. Meanwhile we are still a mighty £7 in profit overall, which probably still outperforms a gilt security on an annual basis.

Normally I would top up on this company in the legacy portfolio but this story is too shaggy to go big on.

The charts say this was all known in July, perhaps even obvious to some in January 2012. This is the trouble with miners. They are not transparent. This is a kind way to say something rude.

It seems possible that there will now be a rights issue, so if we top up we will do it then.

The question that needs to be asked is how these gold mines lose money with gold at record highs. The Occam's razor answer is of course unprintable for legal reasons. However, it's hard to know how these things will pan out. I buy and hold and let the dogs go bust and take profits when they seem good and the company is no longer cheap. In a year this company could be a pound or it could be 10p. It seems odd to therefore hold but risk does equal reward and for everyone that fails more succeed and choosing the winner ahead of time appears impossible.

Of course, it's always easier to predict the past.

What did the announcement say? They've got 1.2m ounces rather than 1.8m in the ground at their Inata reserve. They claim they should dig 100-135,000 a year at $1,100 cost. Blah, blah, blah. The bomb is their statement that the hedging position with their bank is crippling them and they might have to dilute through an issue of shares. As they used to say, "What a shower."

But it's just one company in the portfolio, so life goes on. The more companies we have the less this thing affects us. It remains, however, highly annoying.

# Yen Shoots Up

### 18 February 2013

Yen shot up overnight on the basis that the G20 weren't going to spank Japan for devaluing its currency. Japan looks likely to lead the first rally of the new era – if another asteroid doesn't spoil the picture.

It is, of course, nerve-racking sitting on a resistance line on the charts. If the market goes higher, especially in a hurry, it will be the starting gun of a new long-term era. Unsurprisingly, people find this unlikely.

In a way I do too, but I am simply looking at the indexes and their charts tell the story that if we rally from here and don't slump, something big is underway.

I'm in no hurry to jump in more because a break out will be the beginning of a long term trend which I can sit on for years. I don't mind missing a few per cent to establish it clearly in my mind. If there is a pullback I will buy. It is that simple. Heads buy, tails buy. It is just a matter of trying to time it.

Meanwhile it is fascinating to watch the pound. 115 to the euro seems like the level for a rally but we will see.

Trading currency is just backing random politico-economists. How random is that!!!

# A New Stock for the Portfolio: Volex

### 19 February 2013

A new stock for the portfolio. As the market hesitates and oscillates at the top of its long term channel we continue to build the portfolio. We've added Volex.

When you look at the chart you will see it has taken a pounding. This is a theme we will be following over the long term. Watch angels fall from the sky and buy them when they look like they are making a comeback.

It can be tough as we have quickly found with Avocet. Some of these dogs will die. Some will look like they are dying and come roaring back. Sometimes we will get the bottom, sometimes we won't even be close. Overall we will do well. It will often feel pretty grim, especially when the market has a correction/crash. We simply plough on.

Volex was an old favourite a long time ago and it rocketed. It has now fallen back to earth. However, the directors have been piling in and that is always a sign to buy a cheap share, because directors don't throw big chunks of their cash down the drain. In fact they do the opposite, they are cautious buyers of their own stock because not only do they know where all the bad news is and are constantly dealing with it, they are also locked into the stock they buy because they have to send out a negative RNS release when they come to take profits and that's a most uncomfortable thing.

In September they were 250p a share and today they opened at 120p.

We now have seven shares in the portfolio and we are still a country mile from diversification. As such the P/L will shoot all over the place, sometimes making us look clever, sometimes stupid. To have taken a 71% hit on a stock and still only be 5% down is a good example of why diversification is so important.

Promethean's results are due on 27 February, which is sure to bring champagne or chagrin.

Investing is so much nicer when you have 30 shares in the portfolio.

# Market Due to Move – But Which Way?

### 25 February 2013

The market is waiting for a signal to rally hard or slump. The jury is out as to which way.

Japan had a massive Monday jump. The idea is that Abe the Japanese PM is serious in getting inflation in the system. The many-headed deflation hydra that is the BOJ is acquiescing. That means a huge shot of QE in the arm of the world economy.

At some point bonds are going to buckle and in advance equities are rallying. 13,000 is on the cards. Weak yen = market rally in Japan and the world.

Meanwhile back in London the day got off to a nice start. The downgrade should trigger a sterling rally as the insider traders tipped off at the turn of the year cover their shorts. I will go long the pound in a few days once the idea is established. I entered at 1.15 to the euro weeks back and I am happy to buy in on further falls if they come.

With the market deciding whether to rocket or correct, the only thing to do is sit and wait. This will prove boring and I will be forced to witter about secondary matters while we wait, hoping for opportunities to come our way.

This is far better than trading one's stomach lining away and much cheaper.

# Dow Hits All-Time High

### 5 March 2013

It only goes to show you shouldn't listen to the doom and gloom merchants in the media. After unending bad news since the crash of 2008 here we are at an all-time high on the Dow. More to come no doubt.

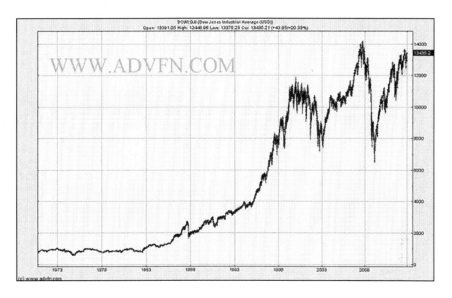

Meanwhile as the main indices rally, the small caps and recovery plays have been struggling. We are still in the idiot corner with the portfolio even if it is up a couple of per cent today. When the main indices are booming it is often the case that the minor stocks take a breather.

The markets have been in hibernation since the new year as far as value investing goes, even while the Dow has been heading upward to break records.

Some young investors I'm helping in Japan are well ahead on their investing in UK stocks, bringing in huge profits. However, this is purely the result of the collapse of the yen. Currency can totally mess up your portfolio strategy if you are not careful, a key thing to bear in mind in US stocks. Of course a bunch of US stocks would have done well because of the falling pound, but I feel the pound has had its slump and is well set to rally.

Sell in May is starting to loom ahead, of course, but again I'm not too sure it will precipitate an exit for me this year – unlike 2010 and for that matter 2008. But we shall see.

Meanwhile, I can't get too excited about new stocks. That can change quickly, of course, but for now I'm holding back.

# Dow Breaks Its Record

### 6 March 2013

The Dow is now in new territory. The FTSE is still 500 points away.

Under normal circumstances I would increase the Avocet position but in this case I'm not going to do that. This may turn out wrong as holding off buying Thomas Cook was wrong last year. However, there is method to my decision.

Firstly, when a company says "...may need at some point and are therefore thinking of considering xxxxx" it means "we will do xxxx." Therefore as far as I'm concerned Avocet will do a money raise and it will be at a big discount with significant dilution. As such it is not a good idea to buy before this is announced even if you were going to buy more.

The second thing is, I've lost trust in the management and therefore will not grow my position in any event. If there are any nasty surprises like restatements of accounts, I will consider exiting.

I really should steer clear of mines altogether but it's hard to do a blanket. The prevalence of crooks in mining is pestilential.

# A New Era in Equities

### 7 March 2013

As the youngsters would say: WTF. Indices go wild. The Dow now has no technical resistance, only support. All-time highs are a wild event. I think this is very bullish.

I've been saying for weeks, if the market breaks up from here we have entered a new era for equities. Well, I think we have entered a new era in equities. This is inherently a silly statement to make but I feel I need to make the big calls, because this blog is about investment thinking, not about always being right. It's about profits in the long run, not being right today.

What I notice is, the value end is not rocketing while the big cap index is.

What does this mean? It means the big money is moving into stocks oblivious of stock picking. It is an event driven by money flow. It's money into stocks, probably from bonds. This is great because money flow is the key driver of markets. Once the flock of money has flapped into the game it then allocates itself at a finer resolution so that good shares rise more than poor value propositions. Think of it as buying a FTSE ETF now, then picking stocks over the next three months while selling down the ETF as you go.

So what we may be seeing is money moving from bonds into equities in advance of interest rate rises a year out from now. In effect, we are seeing a financial beachhead being formed. This will trickle down later to the sort of value stocks I invest in. Rising tides raise all boats and we are seeing that rising tide begin in earnest.

These rallies are always a bit hair-raising if you trade the indices directly and while index trading is better avoided I can't resist. I've done pretty well on the Nikkei but I keep taking profits and hiding, so I have definitely not optimised my profits. I have got perhaps 60% of the rise from 9,500. But a profit is a profit. Right now UK, Japan and US look like they are going to explode upwards. However, that is exactly how it feels at the top of the market but sometimes you just need to go with it.

Meanwhile, back at the specimen portfolio we remain in the dumps while the legacy portfolio is effectively stuck going nowhere.

Aviva just took a kick to the head because its fat dividend has been slashed. However, Trinity Mirror has helped performance, but as a whole the portfolio is stuck in a day to day range.

If I'm right, in a few weeks this FTSE 100 rally will feed into the portfolio and it will take off.

# The Market is Patchy

### 13 March 2013

The market grinds up against headwinds. It's actually a good sign when the market sneaks up bit by bit, but it doesn't feel that great. The market looks on its way to 7,000 but while the technical looks great, the ride is laborious.

I topped up on First Group yesterday in the legacy portfolio. I didn't put any more into the specimen portfolio because we are building it out in depth rather than size. I say we are building it out, but in fact we haven't bought anything recently, just sat back and watched a bear run in its few constituents knock it down. It's bounced a little but nothing to write home about.

The market is at best patchy.

Avocet is still flat on its back and we wait for what is almost certain to be a cash call rights issue. Bank of Ireland is rallying hard and Aquarius Platinum is coming back a little.

I've mentioned before that I am almost allergic to mining stocks, all the while we have two out of seven members in our nascent portfolio. You can't blanket ban anything, but I'm tempted to do it for mining.

A couple of days ago the un-spell-able Finnish miner Talvivaara announced a rights issue, effectively asking the shareholders to pony up the whole value of their current stake in the business and at the same time nuked the current value. How could that happen? Only a miner could get away with it. It is like returning home to find your house burnt down, leaving you just your old garage behind, only to be presented with the bill to build a new one by the arsonist.

Granted, a few non-mining companies pulled this trick in the depth of the credit crunch; 3i and Inchcape come to mind. However, that was in the pit of financial collapse.

If I was a shareholder I'd be frothing at the mouth.

So this is why we won't be seeing too many mines in the portfolio. However, I like gold and I love value so it may be hard to resist. The key to mining stocks is to recall the Mark Twain saying, which I named my thriller

*The Twain Maxim* for: "A mine is a hole in the ground with a fool at the bottom and a crook at the top."

Happily we don't hold Talvivaara.

# Whoops! Trinity Mirror Takes a Tumble

### 14 March 2013

Trinity Mirror fell out of bed. The year end report was strong but it appeared that the initial fall was a "buy on rumour sell on fact" but then... four of their ex-reporters got arrested in the ongoing phone hacking investigation. So from 120p last night the price is now 100p.

I bought some in my crazy punting fund at 103.5. This is probably two days too early but I simply feel like having more.

The crazy punting account is long Blackberry, Xerox, pound v euro and long Nikkei, Bank of Ireland and Petrofac. These are all trading lunacy but performing well. So now there is some phone hacking in there.

Meanwhile I would buy some more Volex in the specimen portfolio were it not for the fact we are in diversification mode. That is frustrating.

I bought a clip of First Group in the legacy portfolio which could be said to be doing well were it not for today's Trinity Mirror dump.

As I write, the 100p stop losses just fired and the price slumped to 96... oh to be a trader. Now the stops are gone, up she goes to 102. I so want to jump in and play, but that is not where the real money is. However much it seems like it is in trading, the millions are in investing. I say this with gritted teeth as TNI hits 102.75. That's 8% in minutes.

You have to look away.

# Cyprus Madness, UK Sanity

### 20 March 2013

As Cyprus totters on the brink of meltdown there are glimmers of governmental sanity in the UK. This is turning into an interesting week. The market still has its motor on.

I have bought a clip of Cobham. It's a nice solid piece of FTSE 100 stodge. This isn't a stock that has done much in the rally but I feel it has a chunk of upside potential. Currently the specimen portfolio has nothing but explosive candidates and there needs to be some solid ballast.

I often buy Shell for this, but I'm starting to feel Shell is just too big to be beautiful even with its thumping dividend. However I might buy as I'm tempted to add some ballast at the moment in general.

The Cyprus mess has had me messing around in the punting fund. I took profits off my swooning Nikkei and bought gold for a few hours to clip a little profit. I turned completely around on the Nikkei and bought back in for a bigger position than I'd left. Silly but profitable. The market says Cyprus is no big deal now. Why, I can't imagine. I remain short euro/pound even if euro strength or rather lack of weakness says Cyprus is of little matter. In any event, the lunatics are in charge of the asylum which makes it hard on us all.

Meanwhile back in the legacy portfolio, Trinity Mirror's slump hurt badly. A 160% profit is now 100%. I've grown the position in my punting account as I believe in TNI at 150p. The trouble with being overweight is clearly shown in this whole affair. However, to be frank I'm trying to modify my normal "scaredy rabbit" style with increased aggression on positions I feel strongly on. I used to sell at a 30% profit but while this is great discipline and sensible and safe it very often leaves big profits behind.

My thought is that we are at the beginning of a huge bull so I must force myself to be greedy. It's hard and unpleasant but I must increase my aggression with the circumstances. Offense in a bull, defence in a bear.

Meanwhile I must remind myself not to buy a slumping stock for three days. It's overly intricate but still the way to play slumping stocks like

Trinity Mirror. However, that's just fiddling on the margins. The key is to buy cheap stocks and hold them until they are no longer cheap. I keep reminding myself of this and doing so over and over does no harm.

Meanwhile stamp duty goes on AIM stocks. Hurrah, another 0.5% profit per position for us.

# Cupid Crashed But I Didn't Buy

### 28 March 2013

My natural instinct is to buy big share crashes and Cupid could not have been more spectacular. My phone was out to buy but I stopped myself.

A company like Cupid is a very intangible business, unlike say De La Rue which I bought into or for that matter Trinity Mirror. Buying crashes should be limited to companies with material businesses, or at least that should be a big weighting.

Then there is a matter of bull or bear markets. If the market is looking bearish, the top is not a time to take on risky trades, it's the time to go silent. Risk on/risk off is a good model. I am risk off right now. This was the second strike against it.

Then of course it bounced high on Monday. However, you make your calls and you stick to them. Being right for the wrong reason is no use at all, even though it can be galling when you think you are wrong for the right reasons.

The game of speculation is not about being right all the time, it's about your profits at the end of the day. Much better still to not even play and instead invest. This is the most solid reason to resist the temptations of the likes of Cupid.

The May correction is around the corner and whether that is caused by developed world rebalancing or US pension rebalancing I still think caution is called for. While so many markets are trapped in this sideways channel and small caps are suffering, this is not a time to be brave. Tomorrow will always serve up another opportunity.

# Japan Will Cause Equity Markets to Rocket

### 5 April 2013

Japan has kicked off the new global economic era, for real. Equity markets will rocket, especially in the developed world – but first the May correction???

Caught between Scylla and Charybdis. The May correction is close and the bear market we are in is real. However, we are on the rim of a massive bull run. This is horrible. Who wants to buy before a 5-10% dip due for the first week in May? But equities are on the edge of exploding upwards. QE is about to morph into QQE and it will drive vast pools of capital into equities. (QQE is what the BOJ has named their program. What is the extra Q? It is quality. They are going to lower the quality of the yen.)

So I'm sat waiting for mid-May to get in.

Today's BOE news spiked the Nikkei from 12,200 to 13,000. The BOJ's $1.5 trillion reflation is a massive news. The yen fell from 140 to the pound to 146. The Nikkei is headed to 16,000.

The rally in the index we've been seeing has not been popping in the lower levels of the market. This means the rally is a technical money flow rally. This means money from other places is being parked in index stocks for safe keeping. There is no stock picking going on, no linkage to things like earnings and P/E, just a parking of capital. This is not necessarily bad because if this money sticks around, arbitrage will kick in and drag the non-index stuff up and money will flow around and rebalance the index stocks based on stock picking fundamentals. But this takes time.

Right now market fundamentals are secondary. The market is controlled at a political level and if the economy improves that will fall into the economic level and finally, sometime in the long term, stocks will be back trading at the market level. However, for now the big picture revolves around moves like the BOJ's this week and the EU's moves on Cyprus last week. Japan is signalling a new economic reality and it is monetisation.

Sterilisation of new money was what QE does... QQE is good old fashioned Zimbabwean money printing.

However, May is coming. Will we dodge the 1 May bullet? It seems unlikely but possible. We are long, after all, but it seems silly to go yet longer now, not unless something amazing crops up worth buying.

Meanwhile it's a matter of sitting out this bear market and waiting for the money to seep into the real market. When it does there will be a fat rally, but for now we are going to have to sit and suffer.

This is very frustrating.

# Why Gold is Down

## 16 April 2013

Gold crashes because...

The market is up a lot one day because QE is failing so there is more to come. The next day the market is up because QE is succeeding so the economy is better.

I remember a company I ran whose share price had rocketed and we knew exactly why it had suddenly jumped. Of all the stories and rumours that consequently flew about not one was even close to true. What was more interesting was that no one would believe the real reason when told.

Of course maths says that things like gold's crash can be simply random. It probably isn't and this is what I think it is. It's...

...The yearly portfolio rebalancing of the BRICs. BRICs countries get 1,000 billion in trade surplus every year and a lot of it goes to governments, especially non-BRIC Arab states. You can't leave this money lying around, you have to manage it. Managing hundreds of millions is not easy and you can imagine the politics that go with that kind of progress.

As such I believe the big portfolio changes of at least one of these players goes into effect about now every year. You can imagine the rebalancing process taking three-four months. Imagine how long it will take to have all the meetings to set such a process up, all the recommendations from the bankers to consider, all the spreadsheets to pore over, the coding of trading engines to execute the new allocations and trade them as efficiently as possible. Then someone hits 'return' on a computer and off the multi-billion (trillion???) dollar process goes.

Take a look at the still properly unexplained 'flash crash' of 2010. I've always thought that was the fattest of fat fingers of all time. It was apparently just an S&P 500 trade, but funnily enough it showed up in all the commodities and currencies too. Of course, all financial instruments are tied together so you would expect this, but tellingly the yearly slump hit the same limits in the end as the ephemeral flash crash. This a classic sign of algo trading malfunction and long term trajectory limits are reached in m = minutes = 1, rather than M = Month = 1.

That's mainly conjecture... but here we are and gold just went off a cliff. As such we need to be wary of the summer slump being nigh. Normally it kicks off 1 May. It should come early as people pre-empt it. If it happens we are going to buy the fall heavily. If it doesn't we are going to start buying on the third week of May.

This process will kick off, but it depends on the portfolio shift as to what happens. If it's portfolio money to come out of bonds into equities, stocks might explode; but that's a long shot. The key process will be how much shifting of resources will there be because the slump is caused by one-way sucking out market liquidity. Prices slump because the move hurts market efficiency because the size of the action is too large to easily swallow. That is why when it ends the market snaps back.

It could, of course, just be folks going on holiday, the old 'sell in May' reason, but let's face it, Americans don't do that, nor do the Asian nations. As such the outcome of holiday fever in Europe shouldn't be so dramatic.

Anyway, it's here. Get your money ready to buy the dip.

# You Need an Investment Plan

### 23 April 2013

You need a plan when you invest and you need to use it to navigate the markets. This can be very frustrating if, for example, you decide not to buy stock until the third week in May, as I have.

The last couple of years have been very difficult markets to navigate because they have been what's best called 'stop/start.' The first half of last year was dead. The second half of the year glorious. It's not surprising because the markets are carrying a heavy load of government manipulation. This time it is a conspiracy, and the G20 won't say it isn't one. Governments are firmly in direct control of the markets through fixing the mother of all instruments, interest rates.

The governments of the developed world are trying hard to save their 'welfare states.' You could imagine the welfare they are defending is that of their bureaucrats but ultimately who cares; this blog isn't about politics, it is about investing.

The setup is, governments are going to try and stretch out readjustment in the hope growth will catch up with their deficit spending. They will keep interest rates artificially low to fund themselves and confiscate through osmosis the money of savers through 'financial repression.'

It is going to be horribly drawn out. With the markets dammed in, things move slowly. Recovery is slow, readjustment is slow and yawningly obvious outcomes are delayed and delayed until the dam bursts. Dams don't have to burst, but they generally do in economics.

I must say that I no longer trust official figures on GDP, inflation etc, so we are left having to estimate what is really going on. Food is a good benchmark. In the end this is all about inflation and money supply.

We are looking to ride opportunities where there is fundamental disagreement over outcomes, so the price is debateable until one side wins. We try to be on the right side and get the prize.

The debate is: inflation or no.

In my opinion there is strong inflation where China isn't making the stuff involved: food, education, transport... you can create your own list. This is where we should consider buying assets. Taking sides in these debates is where there is plenty of money to be made. Divided opinion is the fundamental dynamic behind value investing. The argument goes:

"This stock is way too cheap."

"Oh no it isn't."

"I'll buy some then."

It's that simple.

However, governments and other such bubbles can fix prices for a long time. Only when the gravity of reality strikes does the bubble burst.

Meanwhile the markets are in hiatus. I believe we will breakout upwards later in the year, strongly, but now is not the time to load up.

Waiting is a pain!

# Will There be a May crash?

### 30 April 2013

May is soon upon us and then we will see if the markets will crash as they have for the last few years. If they do we will then buy, if they don't we will start buying. It's a simple strategy... try and miss a likely correction.

After the first two weeks is over we will be moving into buying mode. This will be slow at first because there is no rush and because markets work to their own time schedule and if there is no crash I'll still be nervous. We haven't covered ourselves in glory so far, but that's not surprising or even unexpected.

This chart of the small cap index is the background to the market we are in:

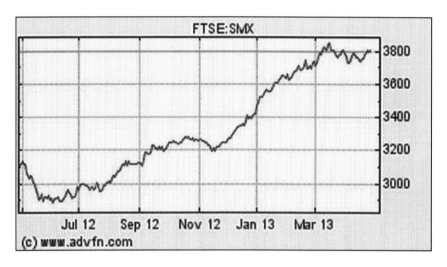

So from March we've been in a static market and we've been fishing in the high risk end a bit too much.

The effect of Avocet's collapse will wash out over time in the same way as if we had a big winner, but it doesn't help nonetheless. Tricks with numbers are a curse but half the point of having a broad portfolio is that it smooths lumps and bumps.

So let's perform a trick. Tomorrow I'll buy 30 FTSE stocks at random. Now our portfolio will show a 3.5% loss overall. That will feel and look better but it will not be so.

Normally I would buy a big chunk of Avocet, but I cannot bring myself to. Even without the latest sagas of ENRC and Bumi you don't have to be too paranoid to see that the mining sector is rife with, well I can't use a pertinent word without risking defamation...

Volex is intriguing. Again I'm tempted to buy more but the long term chart is so very eccentric I'm going to stay pat.

Frankly this waiting game is most frustrating.

Meanwhile in crazy punting, I'm very long Nikkei and short euro against the pound. Don't take any notice of this because index trading might as well be random. I think Nikkei is going to 16,000 and the pound will rally hard but this is just pie in the sky.

Until the next few weeks pass the right thing to do is simply sit back and watch.

# Timing the Market

### 8 May 2013

Market timing is difficult. Actually it is not difficult, it is impossible. Here is why. If you could "market time" people would make such huge profits everyone would get massively rich.

Market timing is the holy grail of investing. There are armies of people employed on the vague hope of being able to market time. This is the second reason you can't market time. With everyone attempting to do it, if there is any way to do it, the timing would be pre-empted to death. Which is exactly what happens.

People in banks who try to do this, from the biggest investment banks to the smallest hedge funds, are called quants. They trawl through the data to try and find a pattern to trade. To pay their wages they measure how the banks are doing meanwhile and what their risks are, but they dream of finding a way to market time. However, if they find such a scheme they trade it and when enough people know the scheme, it is destroyed by everyone queue jumping it to death.

You can get the time series of any stock for yourself and try to see if any series of moves predicts another. But an army of math PhDs is doing the same, so funnily enough there is none to be had.

The key trouble for those like us always tempted to time the market is that it involves getting out right and getting in right too. You don't need to time the market once but twice. That's a 4 to 1 manoeuvre. Therefore even the "sell in May" idea is very tricky.

So here we are wallowing in misery with a 15% loss, waiting for the May crash and BANG!!!, suddenly the market changes and our proto-portfolio levitates and it's a 9% loss. In the bat of an eye a third of the loss is gone.

When markets turn they turn fast. A huge rally can be over and done in three or four days. If you miss that, you've missed much of the benefit of getting out in the first place. So in a few days we have gone from idiots to simply fools. It's a nice demonstration of why buying and holding and forgetting the noise is the best way to go.

So this is the week the market is meant to keel over and flop. Right now there is no sign of it. I shall start buying in a week or so. Slowly at first.

Meanwhile G4S slumped today on a disappointing update. This is the sort of company I do not understand. It is one of those service companies which are government stooges, that make barely any money yet have vast sales and have an effectively broke balance sheet once you remove the intangibles. Bar the fact that intangibles are generally worthless in any event, how can a company of brain dead security guards have intangible assets of 2.5 billion pounds? Their auditors will tell you of course, but my point is rhetorical. If I had 1.2 billion in net assets of which 2.4 billion were intangible, I'd be in a cold hard place... But G4S doesn't seem to mind being in such a tricky spot.

So I doubt I'll be buying any of that.

# Happy Days in Tokyo

### 15 May 2013

It's all kicking off in Tokyo. The Nikkei is now over 15,000 from under 10,000 at Christmas. The mother's market – Japan's equivalent to AIM – has gone from 400 to over 1,000. Happy days!! But what next?

Meanwhile the JGB, the Government bond, is going mental. Interest rates are exploding... at least by Japanese standards. From zip to nearly 1%. I bailed out last Friday at 14,750 on the basis that 5,000 points of profits were enough even for me.

Trading indexes on margin is madness even when it's going your way and I do that in my crazy punting account which is now uncomfortably fat for an account that is meant as a test bed for trading rather than a place to accumulate wealth. It's a nice problem.

I closed my euro short today as currencies are just too hard to call because they are driven by political whim not markets. I have decided the euro is strong to keep high yield bond countries like Spain afloat. 5% on a bond backed by the ECB is just what the guys hunting for yield want. Hence Spain's highly successful recent bond placement. It hurts France and the Club Med countries but floats their public sector deficits. At least for now.

Back to our portfolio: we've gone from 15% down to 6.7% in the bat of an eye. This is why you have to grin and bear a portfolio. You just can't time the market.

I'm still nervous about the market but we are today adding French Connection. I bought some more for my old portfolio on Monday and wondered whether that qualifies for the blog portfolio and the answer is yes. So in it goes today at 31p.

I'm still cautious about the markets in general because May is when it implodes every year. It hasn't and I said if it didn't it would go madly up and it is. But but but...

You can't time the market... Argh!

Anyway, at this rate the FTSE will hit an all-time high and then soon the money entering the market at the top FTSE 100 level will trickle down into stock picking and our value end will move.

That's the theory.

# Japan Crashes

### 23 May 2013

Boom crash goes Japan. It crashed today 9% from peak to close. This has set off chaos in the European open. Is this the May crash?? Well it could be, the market certainly is high. However, I believe we are in a completely different market from the last few years; in effect a new era.

This market will correct but who knows by how much. This is volatility re-entering the market and the future is full of rallies and slumps. You can't let them bother you.

Meanwhile back at the portfolio, which has been waiting for a slump to buy more, First Group pulled a rights issue. We are taking up these rights.

Before today we were back to only 5% down, coming back 10% in a few days.

The rights actually underpin the First Group story. Now look at the following. First Group's Balance sheet:

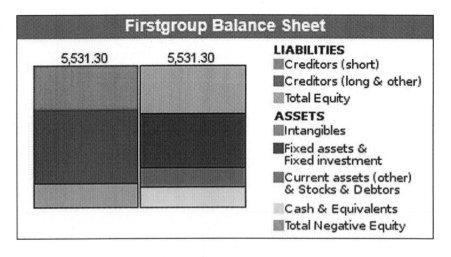

Now at Stagecoach's:

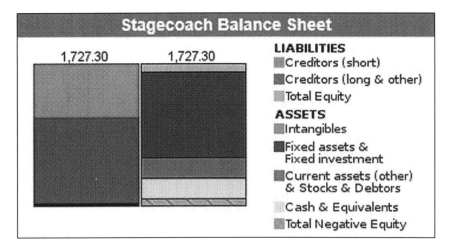

Stagecoach's balance sheet is much weaker, yet its share price has been zooming for years. Actually Stagecoach's balance sheet is a shocker. Negative equity is a hugely weak sign. A rights issue soon for them?

Here's First Group's in comparison.

So with a new slug of capital and a new chairman, this could be a turning point for the company.

Meanwhile the market may have a bad time in the near term.

# Buying Small Cap Stocks

### 29 May 2013

It's a nasty fact but buying small caps is a very costly business.

We bought Total Produce near the close yesterday. It's non-UK so stamp duty alone is 1%. That just catches in my throat. It's basically robbery.

The UK moans about a potential Tobin Tax and it already has one: it's 1% on Irish stocks. So if you buy £1,000, as we are, bang goes 3.5% on costs then another 4% on the bid offer spread. Talk about making everyone else rich.

It is outrageous that a £200m stock should have a 5% bid offer spread, but there it is. Calling the market makers direct for a deal it was discovered they wanted about another 3% on top, so the brokers had to go via RSP, the robot market maker, to get inside the offer price. This in effect saved most of their commission but it remains daylight robbery that a stock should have a 55p-58p spread.

This highlights that the London small cap market is still dysfunctional and that this rotten state of affairs gives the investor a high hurdle to vault. There are pluses to this but that's a long convoluted discussion. In essence this nonsense is what causes a share like Total Produce to be mispriced. It takes time to correct itself but there is a fat return to be had by the patient.

That is as maybe, but it is still a flaming outrage. There is simply no excuse for shares to have a spread much over 1%. Meanwhile, this stock has a 10 P/E, sells ten times its market cap and pays a 3% dividend.

Now with First Group corrected, we sit at an 8% loss. Only Cobham and Bank of Ireland are not in the dog house, though roughly speaking Avocet is the sum total of our losses.

Off this stream I'm building a very long term boring portfolio. It's half US and half UK. Initially it's doing great. So far in there is:

- AstraZeneca
- Cobham

- Imperial Tobacco
- Ladbrokes
- RDSA
- Vodafone
- AMD
- Citigroup
- Goldman Sachs
- Xerox

The idea is to buy interesting blue chips and leave indefinitely. It's not trying for anything sensational. I'll update you when I add to it. Being blue chip it's getting a fat updraft from the current bond equity stock rally but the idea is to have a pound/dollar hedged portfolio of big caps for a change.

It's getting tricky to get in and out of small caps in scale, so I need to get some practice on the whales and see if I can beat the index from within.

# Buying in May

## 29 May 2013

So the market didn't crash in May, and therefore we are buying again. You can't time the market so it would be poetic justice if the market crashed in June. However, you can't go on thinking like that, you have to buy. So we bought Land.

I'm a strong believer in this recovery. I think we have entered a new economic era. That's brave and it's good to be brave early on with a caveat to change tack if circumstances prove you wrong. In this model property will do well, as it is doing well at the residential level now. So long market and long economy means long property.

And there is a kicker. Land and British Land are the two main players in this arena and for the life of me I can't see why Land Securities isn't roughly at half price to British Land as far as fundamentals are concerned. OK, so maybe not exactly half price but significantly cheaper.

Opinions differ on the two companies close up, but from arm's length I can't see why they should be so disparately valued. Land is cheap in comparison with British Land.

You could do a pairs trade, long LAND and short BLND but to be honest I can never be bothered.

So to recap here are the reasons:

- Long market.
- Long economy.
- Cheap in peer comparison.
- Fat dividend.
- I should think this is good for 1,400p so a nice 40% upside.
- All this and a blue chip to boot.

# Is It Time To Sell?

## 5 June 2013

Sell in June and go to the moon? The market is feeling bearish. Is it time to pull the plug?

The answer has to be, never sell your portfolio outright unless you think the world is ending. You simply can't time it. It costs you a fortune in fees. It is hard to psychologically re-enter and it is impossible to get right on average. You can only sell shares when they aren't cheap and buy shares when they are; through thick and thin.

So here is some advice and it is likely wrong. It will sound good, but it isn't likely true: If you think the market is going to crash, stop buying, save your money till the crash comes then buy. This is 'buy the dips' in effect.

Theory says, you can't anticipate a crash. So this won't work. It is as simple as that. So as far as theory is concerned this advice is null.

Do I do this? Yes.

As the youngsters say: WTF???

Random walk, efficient market hypothesis needs to be the bedrock of your thinking. It doesn't have to be a cause for religious zealotry, but as an investor it should be an anchor point.

*A Random Walk down Wall Street* by Burton Malkiel is the key book to read. The market is not totally random, but it is highly random. The market is not perfect, but it's amazingly efficient. In the same way a mirror is not perfectly smooth, but from our standpoint it may as well be. As such, we should attach ourselves to the doghouse of the random walk with a leash of a certain length, because to stray too far can court disaster.

I say this as I am getting pummelled by the Nikkei which has showered me with gold and seems intent on recovering it. This is the point of my punting account, to feel the joy and pain of my speculator customer base. It's nigh on a kind of S&M experience. It's horrible even when you are on top.

Back to the portfolios.

This market really is very different from the post 2008 crash market. There is a lot of noise in the market. It looks like volatility but I don't think it is what traditionally you'd think of as "Vol."

The legacy portfolio is doing well, but I'm not happy, because a large part of the performance is coming from one stock: Trinity Mirror. This is of course how a portfolio can work, but the performance is narrow even if the profits are quite fat. That is not reassuring.

The specimen portfolio just can't get arrested, which is frustrating to say the least. Contrarian investing and value investing can be like this but it can be a test of resolve.

So from idiot to genius to idiot again, this is the outcome of volatility. At least that's what I'd like you to believe.

# First Group Share Price Makes No Sense

### 13 June 2013

Sometimes you have to scratch your head and wonder if someone changed the rules when you weren't looking, or wonder whether the world is wrong and you are right. First Group should not be below £1 but it is...

As I write it is 98p. It should be 135p. Or rather if you take the rough level of where it was before the rights issue and put all the number in and swirl them around, the current share price should be 135p. In fact when the rights were announced that is the level it fell to. Since then it has tumbled much lower. Why?

If you were bearish, you'd say the company was a basket case. You could say it is no longer going to pay 22p a year in dividend.

However, the likelihood is, many holders will sell their holding of old stock to buy their lower priced rights as they can't afford to hold and buy more, which is what we have done.

This tempts me to buy more. However, this market is just not encouraging me. It's bearish right now, but even when it was rallying, I still had my reservations. We are still taking a pounding, while in general the market is, so we continue to hold back. Until I feel the dunce cap lifted, we are going to be cautious.

Equities are being driven by bonds and currencies so index moves at the big cap end are technical and not about value.

We grin and bear it.

# Sell in May...

## 17 June 2013

Come back on St Ledger day. Perhaps the best thing about "Sell in May" is that you can rest easy in the glorious summer and forget the markets. This might just be a big enough dividend to make it worthwhile, come boom or bust.

The numbers look good if you study them in a certain way, but it has to be said, buying in the summer after a big correction is also an excellent way to make money, so leaving it till the St Ledger is far from the optimal strategy.

I can't remember being so lethargic in the market. The small caps index (SMX) is down 5% but we may as well be down 20%.

Outside of the specimen portfolio I have loaded up on First Group. It's one of those opportunities where I'm tempted to go in heavy, but I'm simply just going to my natural limit of 7-8% because it seems crazy for the share to be priced near its rights issue price of 85p. 135p is about the right price. 120p would be fine. So I'm left hanging onto the idea of staying diversified rather than risking having a nasty surprise.

What nasty surprise could one suffer? The reality in the stock market is that a small proportion of shares will always suffer scandalously from all sorts of misdemeanours and felonies and you just can't tell when they might strike. As such you should never truly pile in on any stock because bad things can happen. This is the point of diversification. Having said that, our current fledging portfolio – while not exactly diversified yet – is getting killed.

The legacy portfolio is doing much better but that is because Trinity Mirror is holding up well and its runaway success is offsetting a lot of pain. This was kind of the situation last year where it was the tail end of the year that provided for bumper profits. 2012 was six months grief and six months exultation. It may or may not happen again in 2013.

The thing is, you simply have to take the rough with the smooth. This can be spread over stocks or over time, it can be either or both, it's the only way. So now we are wearing an increasingly big dunce's hat and we must sit in the corner and wait in the hope that time will make us a genius again. It is not only a test of patience but it is also a test of confidence.

Meanwhile back in stupid punting land, I've been taking a pounding from the Nikkei, which having showered me with treasure is now proceeding to pulverise me. The Nikkei's dramatic crash has gone a lot further than I was expecting and is demonstrating the sort of volatility I recall in the 90s. This is meant to be experimental trading but the sums have become fat enough to make it rather real.

The entertainment value of juggling hundreds of thousands in a market that is swinging around in percentage points a minute has a distinct shelf life. This is another reason that trading is for the birds; to make the big money you have to have the kind of engagement level that would suggest you'd had a lobotomy.

Investing is far more sustainable.

# Investing Hurts

## 25 June 2013

We are all used to getting paid to work and many of us are used to getting paid even when we aren't working, be that through statutory measures like paid holidays or sickness, or through downtime or sloth or unemployment. So working and losing money is not something we are used to. People just don't like it.

Sadly, investing is not a one way street, you win and you lose and in the end you win overall. A bad start is about a 50/50 chance. It's not pretty when it happens.

Here is a 2008 portfolio which was epic and you will see what I mean. The initial loss is similar to where we are right now.

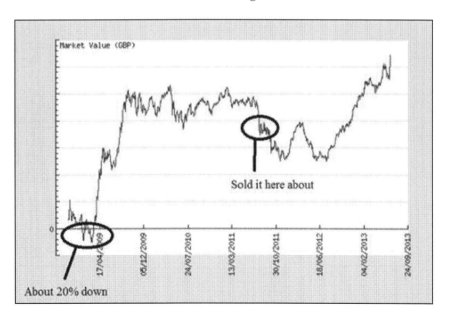

You will notice long periods of boredom and churn and also that the profits come in strong nearly vertical rallies. This is why an investor has to show a huge amount of stoicism and hence why investing is not a very popular game.

The FTSE is down 12% from its recent high and we are down 21%. If you account for the 3-4% of costs factored into our loss, we are still down 6% more than the market. This negative alpha should be a factor of buying out of fashion stocks. It would be easy to blame Avocet which is down 90% but in a portfolio you expect to have big winners and large losers which cancel out so you can't pass off losses or profits by taking individual shares into account.

We only have two winners right now, Bank of Ireland and Cobham, and everything else is in the dumps. So am I, but that's how this game works. When we bought the first stocks and they shot up and we were 20% ahead it felt great and now it feels awful.

This is where people give up. They can't take the pain.

What we have to do is soldier on. If there is a crash this summer we will get yet more pain and we will buy into it. For now it's just wait and see.

Meanwhile, First Group is a complete mystery to me. There is either something catastrophically wrong with this company which is about to strike or the share is utterly the wrong price. I think it's the latter and that is what this game is all about, separating the muck from the brass. It seems impossible that a massive rights could be achieved if the company was broken, but it remains to be seen for sure. We should buy another lot but that would be breaking the rules of continuing to spread the portfolio, so I will reluctantly hold back.

I have bought more in my legacy portfolio which is also taking a pounding. Even my new experimental blue chip UK/US portfolio which shot up 8% on initiation has been hacked down to -5%. For the record that has: AZN, Cobham, Imperial Tobacco, Ladbrokes, Land, Shell, Vodafone, AMD, Citigroup, Goldman Sachs and Xerox in it. I'm just playing in this portfolio, trying to get alpha in stocks with no real liquidity limitation.

Rising bond yields, aka rising interest rates, should push money into equities but it's going to be a rough ride and for now the market is just shivering with fright. It will settle and we will find out what this new era really has in store.

Maybe I should come back on St Leger day. However, soon bargains are going to start to appear, so it pays to keep paying attention.

# Buying a Boring Share

## 4 July 2013

We have a new stock selection. In the current market it's hard to get excited about shares. That is not a bad thing, because excitement costs money in investing in the same way as it costs money in entertainment.

Entertainment value of shares is low because the cost is high and the entertainment is generally restricted to the emotions of the rollercoaster or at best a good thriller, but more like a horror movie.

Boring is good.

So we have bought a 6 P/E stock which is a long-standing media agency cum consultancy cum marketing agency cum PR outfit. It is called Creston. I could wax lyrical about it but frankly it's simply a nice piece of diversification. The company is on the cheapish side. It has been going for a long time and it has solid customers. Its cash pile has jumped.

I'm bullish on all things internet marketing and it's simply not going to be a shrinking market, with or without a recovery. Internet marketing is tricky stuff and Creston seems to be on its game. Are you yawning? I hope so. It has a 3.4% dividend and for the record a P/E of 6.7 and strong cash generation – what is not to like?

It was a very long time ago when I would buy £1,000 of a share and it is slightly shocking to see the impact of trading costs buying at that level.

We have bought £1,000 of Creston in line with the rest of the model portfolio and the net cost including spread and stamp duty etc is a wretched 3.97%. You have to work hard to get that under 2.5% in any event no matter how much you bought. The share has a 2% spread, so even if there was no stamp duty or commission you'd still be down 2% from the get go. In theory this comes out in the wash, but it is galling. It really shouldn't cost that much to invest.

Meanwhile, we have had a little portfolio bounce and we are only down a rotten 16%. I will have to adjust for dividends which will make this poor performance a little less lame, but again, it will come out in the wash even if it looks depressing at this moment.

This is the important part of understanding the random walk and knowing/believing that over time you will earn 10-30% per annum investing properly. The reason so few people do invest is that it takes grit to put up with the setbacks. However, talk is cheap, we will see how theory transfers into reality by year end.

Meanwhile my new book is out: *Letters to my Broker*. Buy it from Amazon in paperback or for the Kindle. It's a cracker.

# Why You Should Diversify

### 8 July 2013

We've been buying approximately two shares a month, which is likely too fast for many of you who are starting out. This means if you are buying shares to mirror my buys you may have only bought three or six shares by now.

So how might you be doing?

Here is the result of buying three or six of the twelve shares in the portfolio and getting – by luck or judgement – the best or worse or the middling performers:

|        | 3 shares % | 6 shares % |
|--------|------------|------------|
| Best   | 5.52%      | -6.81%     |
| Middle | -18.80%    | -14.93%    |
| Worse  | -29.88%    | -20.30%    |

First off you can see the effect of diversification. The best is less good and the worse is less bad if you have six rather than three. The spread, ie the range of outcomes, is also tighter between the best and worst performance. So you can see how variable a small portfolio can be even if you pick from a simple group of shares selected with at least some kind of plan.

Meanwhile, the markets are continuing to go mad. A few days ago we were 21% down and now we are 14%. Yesterday was a huge day for the markets but it's not the beginning of a new era, rather the delay of one that caused the jump. This kind of volatility is a function of market confusion so it's not really good news. However, you can't complain about a random win.

Flybe has got itself a new boss, flown in from the stellar EasyJet. If Flybe turns itself around it will go to the moon and we will see the flipside of buying out of fashion companies which is the fantastic return companies produce when they come back from the brink. Maybe it will be Flybe, maybe it won't. It's the general idea not the specific company we back because you cannot be sure of any one operation but the odds are high in aggregate.

Meanwhile, I simply find it hard to resist buying gold miners because they are so down on their luck, but I must recall they are mainly a bunch of shady operators and I must resist their siren song. Some companies are not high risk at all, because there is no chance in making money from them. There is no risk in the certainty of a bad outcome and miners fit this bill very closely. However the bait is there and I'm sniffing it... nooooooo!

# The Portfolios Are Rallying

## 9 July 2013

We have had a massive rally on the legacy portfolio and a nice spike on the specimen portfolio. The specimen portfolio is up about 10% in a few days, that is to say, it has clawed back a long way. It is still down a long way.

Flybe is being a star. This is how companies go from zero to hero. EasyJet and Ryanair's valuations are insane and even if Flybe came within a country mile we would make a massive profit. To give you an idea, Flybe's market cap to sales is 15/1 or around 6%, Ryanair's is 200%. So if Flybe was valued like Ryanair as far as sales goes its share price would be 1,800p not 57p. Of course it won't get there, there are a million reasons why it won't – but it gives an idea of why it could go to £1. If it recovered to its float price it would be £3.

We can, after all, wait ten years for that and still claim a fat rate of return. But we can't think it will, we just think one or two of the shaggy dogs we bought most likely will do something similar at some point. Every year a company or two does it.

You can't be right in the market, only profitable.

So today the market is rocketing and I say, "this is mad." That's shorthand for, "I don't understand." I think I do but I'm still not happy, so it's still mad. But do I sell? No.

I know why I bought my stocks and the rest is just noise. Forget the noise. Trading noise is pure cost. Follow it, marvel at it, laugh at it, rail at it, but don't trade it.

Meanwhile Dow has hit the ceiling of its trend – if it breaks it could go to the moon. That would be bonkers, but I'm long... so bring it on, rally or correction, because I'm not long because of the index, I'm long because I've bought cheap stock and am waiting for them to correct, whether that's three days or three years.

Meanwhile the insanity brought on by rising interest rates has only just begun.

# Boring is Good

## 18 July 2013

Boring investment is good. However, it is rather, well, boring. Risking money is fun, so when things go quiet the entertainment value drops to zero. However, money and fun don't go together. Silence is in fact golden. This is how it works.

If something is fun, it has value. A fun stock pays you in fun and as such doesn't have to pay you so much in money. So fun stocks cost you cash. Boring stocks have to pay you in cash. Therefore, in the long run, exciting times in the markets are expensive.

You may of course find making money enjoyable but strangely people get more into losing games than winning ones. This is why gamblers gamble. It is not the winning that drives them, it's the losing. It doesn't seem right, but I learnt this lesson as a child with my own pub fruit machine.

The moment you can open a fruit machine and reimburse yourself your losses, the reason to play is gone. The moment you can set up a jackpot every time the joy is over.

Meanwhile, back in the markets we are still scraping our knuckles around on the ground. It's not quite as miserable as it was but we are still 14.6% down on the invested amount or 6.3% if we imagine we put £30,000 into the broker to get going. There are probably some dividends to take into account but that's just small change. Bank of Ireland, Cobham and Flybe are up, but the other nine are down. First Group is a stand out, in as much as in my book it's far below its correct price. It should at least be 130p. It should be 200p. If it was Stagecoach it would be 400p. But it isn't and might never be 130p again. However, you make your call and wait.

Lots of nasty things could happen and you lose the lot. Think Marconi, First Star, Gartmore and a constellation of shockers that flutter past every year. However, you hope for a Trinity Mirror, one year at 25p and next at 120p. One TNI pays for a few busts.

So I'm left looking at lots of gold miners thinking BUY! However they are such a mess I'm not going to. I might change my mind because they have cratered but even my contrarian tendencies can't be kicked into action by companies that, at best, squandered the opportunities of one of the biggest, longest commodity bull markets ever.

A few more weeks and St Ledger day will be on us. Then the fun will start, hopefully not of the costly type.

# Trying to See the Future

## 26 July 2013

Way back when Thomas Cook was under 20p I wrote that in normal circumstances I'd buy some. However, I didn't because the market was in a very fragile way and I didn't need to buy into a company likely to go bust. It didn't go down and rallied 1,000%. Still, I do not think it was the wrong decision at the time, even though months later you can see a ten bagger you missed staring you in the face.

You cannot clearly see the future – even if you could see the next five minutes you would become the richest man in the world. So we are forced to see the world as a function of risk. You can only take on the right level of risk for the circumstances and if the risk is too high for you, you should never play no matter how tasty the bait.

This leads me on to gold miners. I so really want to buy gold stocks. Petropavlosk is a perfect example. It is down over 90% from its high. Gold mines across the board have cratered, as has our Avocet, which I would love to load up on. But I won't and they may fly and make me feel like a fool.

However, you cannot invest in companies where the management has no credibility. It is simple mad these companies are all effectively zombies. It is mad that Petropavlosk can be said to have a cash cost of extraction over $2,000 an ounce.

How did that happen? It's a mine. You blow rock up, put it in big buckets, swirl it around and take out gold. How does this ever get so out of control it would be cheaper to buy gold chains at retail and grind them up, than run your mine? How could the stock market even let this happen? So how can you buy into such nonsense, even if it looks so tantalisingly cheap?

Meanwhile, Avocet jumped 35% today. This looks good but it isn't. 100 − 90% = 10%, 10% +3% = +35% or 13% of what you started with. Of course if you bought the bottom it feels good, but that is a level of risk we can't entertain and frankly a mug's game in general. The big movers up and down are always in such zombie stocks. Punters love them, but they don't get rich playing them. So like Ulysses, I'm tying myself to the mast and stuffing wax in my ears.

The portfolio is recovering, it is now only a rotten 11% down. However you can see how fast a portfolio can snap back especially one full of such "smart beta."

"Smart beta" is the new buzz word for hedge funds, meaning crazy stocks you bought because they are going up because you are a smart guy who knows the difference between crazy bad and crazy good. Hedge funds really are the pits. The fact that many have ten times more salesmen than traders should tell you all you need to know.

Here is a chart of our progress so far. The chart is drawn as if we put £30,000 in a broker's account to get going:

If we were just buying as we went along, we would have spent £ 12,991 including costs and it's worth £11,533 at the price we can sell it for (the bid), which is 11.2% in the hole. If I was a scumbag fund manager I'd say we were down £1,458 on £30,000 which is 4.9%, but of course that's not how it feels and no one is doing it this way.

The whole point of this blog is to take you through the process of investing and the swings and roundabouts that are unavoidable.

# Barclays Rights Issue – Not Much Else Happening

### 30 July 2013

It's a rat race at a snail pace. The end of the month approaches but not much is going on as the world is on holiday.

Barclays is having a rights issue and looks to hit the new diluted price as of today, 30 July. With our FGP the price then skidded massively lower effectively hitting the rights price. If Barclays repeats the FGP outcome it would plummet to around 200p. Barclays was in the legacy portfolio and I have sold it at about 292p. FGP was high in my mind but so is the fact that every regulator on the block is suing/investigating Barclays for one thing or another. It feels like a bit of a witch hunt, but of course there might be witches in there too.

So I decided to bail on Barclays for now. The profit was a fat 75%, so I'm not going to grumble and there is too much bank in the portfolio in general, so it achieves my need to un-concentrate in the legacy portfolio.

Back at the specimen portfolio we are still improving a little with the loss now down to 10.7%. Still miserable but less so. Twelve shares is only diversified a little and I should be picking new entrants soon. However I'm being very sluggish in my investment this year, it is like living in slow motion. This is meant to be good, but it doesn't feel like it. Everything feels very tentative.

In the background the Nikkei 225 in Japan is all over the place, which is for me a kind of leading indicator for what is going to happen in the US/UK. In a nutshell Japan today portends rallies and chaos in the future. Currencies are being nailed in tight ranges agreed by the various G8/G20 countries, which is kind of weird to watch, while commodities are thrashing around in a long term bear market set to run and run.

The broken markets spoiled by fixed low interest rates and QE make for a disjointed picture but one in which equities look to rally and rally.

Roll on the autumn!

# Freudian Investing

## 31 July 2013

I can't remember a market that felt so dull and yet so uncomfortable. However, I realise that a key to investing is to forget your feelings without trying to suppress them.

The specimen portfolio jumped to only 9.6% down today as Promethean took another nice jump. My emotions are, unavoidably, "I wish I'd bought a ton of this stock when it was languishing," but when I was thinking about doing just that before it began to rally, I couldn't face the prospect. Tomorrow if the share slumps I'll be sighing in relief I didn't load up to the gunnels. This is the emotional rollercoaster that traps so many people into bad investing habits.

However, feeling these emotions is inescapable; it is how you react to them that determines the outcome. Some gurus say you should invest and trade without emotion, but that's as impossible as eating without noticing the flavour. Instead it occurred to me that investing is best undertaken in a Freudian way.

That's not to say your father needs to look out for javelins etc. In the Freudian model there is the id, which is the wild emotional child in all of us, there is the ego, the big adult-ish "me" and the super-ego, the parent personality that tries to keep the id and ego in check and out of trouble. It is the super-ego that is the good investor or rather the voice a good investor will listen to most.

As my id laments not buying more Promethean, my super-ego is smiling happily that I haven't taken on too much risk. There is emotion but there is also control. Making sensible decisions in investing is about control. The funny thing is a lack of control simply makes you thrash your investing between fast buys and sells which of course drains your capital in costs.

High emotions don't make someone pick good or bad stocks, they just make them blow their money in buying and selling too much.

So in the end you have to let your phlegmatic super-ego lead the way.

# Promethean Slumps – I Was Right Not to Buy

### 1 August 2013

Well, well, Promethean World down 10%, now my id can be relieved I didn't buy more and my investing super-ego can be smug.

Promethean is a strange stock, which is why it is so "cheap." It released interims today which show a slowing of the decline of their business. This is the summary:

Trading in line with market expectations

Financial results

-- Revenue GBP70.0m, down 15.8% (H1 2012: GBP83.2m, down 22.9% versus H1 2011)
-- Adjusted EBITDA(1) GBP2.5m (H1 2012: loss GBP0.3m)
-- Adjusted operating loss(1) GBP2.6m (H1 2012: loss GBP5.7m)

– Operating loss GBP3.4m (H1 2012: loss GBP148.5m post exceptional items, including goodwill impairment)

-- Pro forma net loss(1,2) GBP3.4m (H1 2012: net loss GBP4.1m)
-- Cash balance GBP9.1m as at 30 June 2013 (30 June 2012: GBP8.5m; 31 Dec 2012 GBP8.0m)

Operational highlights

– Continued progress with software strategy and large-group interactive display new product launches

-- Operating cost base reduced 31.5% below H1 2012

-- 22% growth in Promethean Planet community in the last year to c.1.7m members

-- Signed new GBP25m bank facility – which matures in September 2017

(1) Excluding exceptional items, share-based payments and amortisation of acquired intangible assets.

(2) Stated on a pro forma basis using a tax rate of 24.0% (H1 2012: 26.0%).

-----

This time last year their numbers chopped them down from 35p to 20p. This is the company's long term chart:

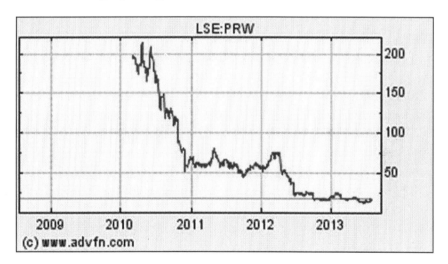

So you are getting 200p of 2010 value for 15p today and roughly £140m of sales for £30m in what is a high tech growth industry. Education is a massive global market and growing. But that is just jawboning, Promethean is a loathed stock which is why its value is so low. If it turns around it will rocket, if it doesn't it will go bust. The downside is 100%, the upside 200-500%, that's why we are in this game.

However, whatever the story of this company is, it feels to me more complicated than what is on show, it shouldn't be 15p. It should be at least 50p. But it isn't and the market is always right.

Then again as First Group clears 100p having traded at 90p on an ex-rights diluted valuation of 135p, it can be seen that the market isn't always perfect when situations are unusual. The market therefore pays us to invest in the inefficient margin where the market needs risk takers to play to make the price eventually right. This is where we are playing, which is seen as high risk but over the years, at least to me, if played with diversification, no risk at all.

Of course, as we sit on a 9.5% loss or about 4% if we put in a starting pot of £30,000, it looks pretty risky indeed. However, the effect of entry timing needs time to wear off. When you start investing you will make short to medium term effects on your results. Our timing hasn't been lucky overall but imagine if you had subscribed on the 23 June and bought all the existing stocks, you would be over 10% up!!! That subscriber would think me a genius, while someone who joined early on might still consider me a dunce.

Meanwhile, I went long pound versus euro in my "stupid punting account." This account has swung massively this year due to me punting the Nikkei 225 – it has rocketed 600% and fallen by 60% to rally 80% over that period. I need to rename the account the "degenerate gambling account."

Even though it is making interesting money, more than is fun to punt with, it is basically a waste of time when it comes to the prospects of long term profits, because no gains are safe, so no money in that account has any long term reality.

The only way to win, as anyone who has won a stack of chips at the roulette table finds out, is not to play any longer and take the money off the table. However, that account is there to remind me of the game ADVFN users are generally playing and what our site needs to do to help them.

Perhaps I should take some of the profits off that table then. Hum....

# Degenerate Punting Account

### 2 August 2013

Well I did it, I took money out of my spread betting account. I've had a "degenerate punting account" for ten years. The purpose of it was to trade recklessly like many ADVFN users and understand how it works and feels.

Surprisingly, it never went broke and I didn't have to charge it up much, except in 2008. Even then it never had more than a few thousand pounds put in. I know because when it was recently flush with success I went back to day one to check how much I had tossed into it. I was surprised how little.

The account, however, had flapped around from 100% up to 40% off in a cycle over that decade, but it must be said it wasn't over used. The whole point of the account was to mess around. Every time it hit a certain level the market would crash and I'd be back to square one or less. Strangely, I seemed to win on indexes, which shouldn't be possible, indexes being the most random of equity devices.

The key element of a spread betting account is leverage and the high cost of positions. This is hidden but the interest on your ten times leveraged position is titanic, often around 70% a year. However, I can forget all the technical about spread betting because like a test pilot flying a prototype, it's not about flying, it's about nearly crashing.

Anyway, yesterday I took out every penny ever put in and left the remaining (three times as much) there to play with. Apparently I've made 12% per annum compounded over the ten years though all the profit has come in the last two years.

What a mess. Well, it was meant to be. It was meant to be an exercise and it has turned out to be so. It clearly shows that leverage is not good for profits as I compound my capital without it at a much higher rate, although you'd be forgiven in questioning that from the performance of the specimen portfolio... which as of now is 8% down, which is 14% up from the low of a few weeks ago. The legacy portfolio is meanwhile storming away.

What did I do with my withdrawal? I paid it into my stock brokerage account.

# Adding to the Portfolio

### 5 August 2013

Today we have added Darty to the portfolio. Darty has 3.2 billion euros of business and is worth £400 million. It's a recovery plan pure and simple. It pays a dividend but that might go away because it is in negative equity, a parlous state to be in as HMV found out. However, it is very light on intangibles, the way most companies manage to look in positive equity. It has a new management team operating in what I believe to be a general recovery.

Even still the company needs to continue its come back which the chart shows as underway.

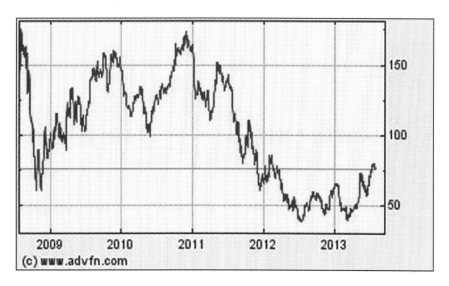

What I like is that the new management is loading up on shares. This is a classic positive sign. The non-execs buying £10-20K is a nice small positive, but it still can only be thought of as a gesture, but when the Chairman picks up a couple of hundred thousand and the CEO the same, this is proper money going in and must take a lot of confidence in the future of the business.

With a recovery underway and property hot again, things should go better for the company in any event. New management after all shouldn't be there to bury the company, meanwhile a resurrection of the company would resurrect the share price.

I topped up on Flybe in the legacy portfolio because the reorg is well underway, with more EasyJet management being parachuted in, whilst directors are being pushed off the board and back to operational duties, no doubt under the gun to deliver or leave. Ryanair and EasyJet valuations spin my head, pound per pound of turnover Flybe would be £10 a share!!!! It won't happen but it's a stark comparison, one that helped the company to IPO over £3 around 2011.

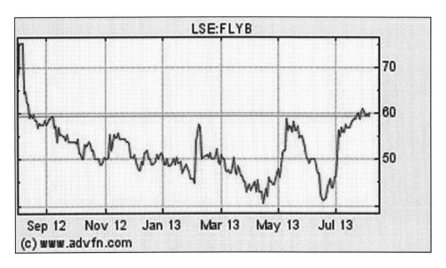

The chart pattern is most odd... looks like a fight between two forces is underway. Who knows...

Meanwhile the portfolio is down 8%.

As the legacy portfolio roars away, it is interesting to note that the same methodology to pick both is the same. There is an element of maturing that is going on which is not that surprising. We are in general picking out-of-fashion stocks and awaiting their rehabilitation. The legacy portfolio was started, if you average the various entry points, around December 2011 and it took months to take off.

The legacy portfolio:

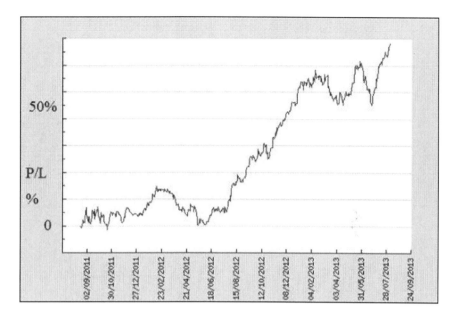

This is the performance of the specimen portfolio. Tracked as if it was started with £30,000 in cash. (No adjustment for dividends.):

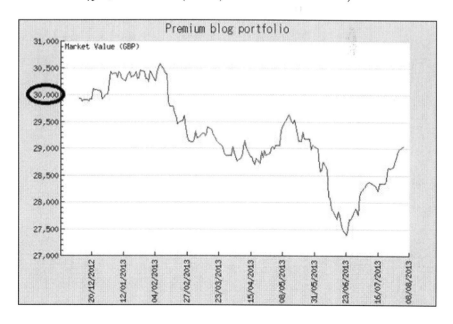

They are interesting to compare and contrast.
　　Investing is a patient game.

# A Noble Investment

### 9 August 2013

Yesterday we bought Noble and today it is up 2.5%. I've owned this stock on and off for a long time. The management are very smart and they are buying up auction houses in what is a muster market.

I am a long-standing coin investor. I perhaps should say collector because my pernickety investment style is not very present when I buy coins. I buy ultra-rare stuff and am too price insensitive for my own good. However, they are to be held for the ultra-long term, so I say "phooey!"

The thing is Noble's is one of my suppliers and what is more the CEO used to be ADVFN's broker before he went AWOL and into the numismatic business. So such detailed knowledge means I know a lot about the quality of this firm and it is high.

They have recently acquired Dreweatts and Bloomsbury Auctions. I have followed Dreweatts for some time as they have lovely stuff for auction. Their acquisition alone is a solid step up in terms of scale and Bloomsbury's is yet more growth. Acquisitions are tough to manage but the Noble's management are smart and respected. I feel they are on their way to the big league.

With a 12 P/E and a dividend of a couple of per cent, plus a growth story, I couldn't resist. Noble's has a 50-100% upside, as a wild guess, with an increase of sales to £20m and an improvement of P/E to say 15.

I don't normally do growth, I like recovery, but Noble's is the kind of story I like.

Meanwhile Avocet Mining went ape this morning, up 33% at one point. Apparently they say things are better now, blah, blah, blah. I fancied buying some, but then, why buy shares in a company when the management has no credibility to you? So I didn't.

On the other hand First Group is on its way up. The price should be 135p and as the effects of the liquidity shock of the rights wear off it seems to be heading there. I want to buy more, but we have enough, so we can't. I find myself generally full up on FGP so I can't even buy for my crazy punting account.

Oh well, such are the demands of discipline in investing.

# Specimen Portfolio Recovers Lost Ground

### 12 August 2013

So right now it looks like I might be able to start holding my head up in public. The specimen portfolio is now only down 5.8%. This is still very poor but this recovery is a perfect example of the swings and roundabouts of investing. As such I'm glad it has worked out this way because this kind of gut wrenching performance is something you have to experience to understand that this is the kind of path can happen on your way to fat profits.

At the end of June we were down well over 20%. I must say this kind of performance has never happened to me before like this. When I picked the bottom in 2008 I went down about this much, but those were massively volatile times. Buying a new portfolio and getting stomped is a first. I suppose this is a function of not having a choice of entry point as the portfolio had to be started when the blog was started, but even so it takes nothing more than the random walk to clobber you like this.

The legacy portfolio was doing roughly OK during this period. However, there is no difference in selection criteria between the two, only timing and scale. So in due course the specimen portfolio should perform the same as the legacy portfolio. This seems farfetched but it is inevitable because they will over time become approximately the same group of stocks.

Meanwhile the mad punting account has exploded. The pound euro long is doing well, the "way too much" FGP is helping and the Blackberry mess has recovered a little. It all adds up to a nice slug of money. I'm waiting for the Nikkei to fall back to re-enter that market, but I'm happy to not be pummelled by ridiculously risky positions. The account balance is pure profit now, which is nice, and I've decided to pull chunks of cash out as/when/if I hit further milestones.

Back in the land of sensible investing FGP continues to do what it's supposed to, head for 135p. The Chairman sold what looks like the rights he bought, which is somewhat of a worry. I suppose roughly £250,000 of extra FGP shares might have left him financially stretched but it seems a little odd to me in the circumstances. For me this is a little black mark that will nag.

Bank of Ireland is the star of the show right now, up 46%. Flybe is up 23% and I have high hopes for it. Even so of thirteen shares, only four are up.

Since I have been writing, the portfolio has recovered another per cent to lay at -4.8% which is approaching our transaction costs and spread.

So on we go.

# Portfolio Rally is Exhilarating

## 13 August 2013

In the last few weeks we have gone from Dunce to Genius. Here is the chart:

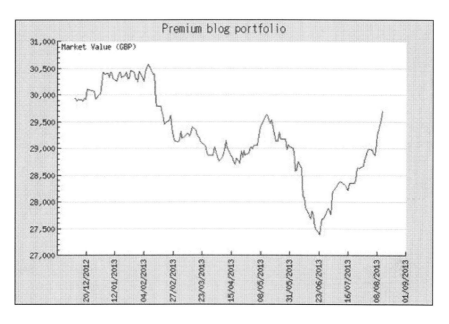

What magic potion did we take? What sacrifices to the gods? What powers of positive thinking did we use? The questions are rhetorical but it underlines the fact that a bear market makes everyone a fool and a bull market everyone a genius.

It is our performance in about a year that will give a true indication of how well we are doing.

Having said that, this rally is exhilarating and the legacy portfolio has gone vertical. It is carrying about 32% in profit with roughly as much again banked since its inception about eighteen months ago. This is a stellar return, but not one I expect to maintain.

The specimen portfolio is now only 3.3% down and as I add a new share to the legacy portfolio, so it is added to the specimen one.

Below is a reminder of the constituents of the legacy portfolio:

| Ticker | Share | Buy price £ | Bid price | P/L | Units invested | Units now |
|---|---|---|---|---|---|---|
| LSE:TNI | Trinity Mirror | 0.45 | 1.18 | 159.35 | 2.9 | 7.6 |
| LSE:LLOY | Lloyds | 0.32 | 0.76 | 138.00 | 2.9 | 6.9 |
| LSE:RM. | RM | 0.70 | 0.81 | 15.91 | 2.9 | 3.4 |
| LSE:FGP | Firstgroup | 1.19 | 1.17 | -2.13 | 2.8 | 2.8 |
| LSE:BKIR | Bank Ireland | 0.11 | €0.2120 | 72.81 | 1.5 | 2.6 |
| LSE:FCCN | French Cnctn. | 0.26 | 0.30 | 12.72 | 1.8 | 2.0 |
| LSE:PRW | Promethean | 0.21 | 0.17 | -20.93 | 2.3 | 1.8 |
| LSE:AV. | Aviva | 3.27 | 3.99 | 21.84 | 1.2 | 1.4 |
| LSE:AGA | Aga Rangemaster | 0.75 | 1.00 | 33.99 | 1.0 | 1.4 |
| LSE:FLYB | Flybe Grp | 0.62 | 0.64 | 3.48 | 1.3 | 1.4 |
| LSE:AQP | Aquarius Plat. | 0.46 | 0.47 | 2.43 | 1.2 | 1.2 |
| LSE:PDG | Pendragon | 0.13 | 0.30 | 135.88 | 0.4 | 0.9 |
| LSE:AZN | Astrazeneca | 29.08 | 33.19 | 14.10 | 0.7 | 0.8 |
| LSE:SSE | SSE | 13.72 | 15.73 | 14.65 | 0.7 | 0.8 |
| LSE:HOMI | Home Retail | 0.96 | 1.53 | 59.83 | 0.4 | 0.7 |
| LSE:LAND | Land Secs. | 9.65 | 9.20 | -4.69 | 0.7 | 0.7 |
| LSE:NBL | Noble Inv | 2.24 | 2.24 | -0.01 | 0.6 | 0.6 |
| LSE:DRX | Drax | 5.20 | 6.84 | 31.54 | 0.4 | 0.6 |
| LSE:DRTY | Darty | 0.79 | 0.77 | -3.40 | 0.6 | 0.6 |
| LSE:CNKS | Cenkos Sec | 0.76 | 0.88 | 16.08 | 0.4 | 0.5 |
| LSE:VLX | Volex | 1.19 | 1.14 | -4.08 | 0.5 | 0.5 |
| LSE:TSCO | Tesco | 3.29 | 3.72 | 13.16 | 0.4 | 0.5 |
| LSE:LGT | Lighthouse Grp. | 0.06 | 0.04 | -38.04 | 0.8 | 0.5 |
| LSE:TOT | Total Produce | 0.58 | 0.61 | 4.56 | 0.4 | 0.5 |
| LSE:HRN | Hornby | 0.65 | 0.78 | 20.51 | 0.4 | 0.4 |
| LSE:AVR | Avarae | 0.11 | 0.10 | -6.51 | 0.5 | 0.4 |
| LSE:CRE | Creston | 1.09 | 1.03 | -5.50 | 0.4 | 0.4 |
| LSE:RDSA | Rds A | 22.82 | 20.90 | -8.43 | 0.4 | 0.4 |
| LSE:LAM | Lamprell | 1.01 | 1.38 | 36.52 | 0.3 | 0.4 |
| LSE:SIXH | 600 Grp. | 0.11 | 0.12 | 7.82 | 0.3 | 0.3 |
| LSE:GDP | Goldplat | 0.14 | 0.09 | -38.14 | 0.4 | 0.3 |
| LSE:AVM | Avocet Mining | 0.82 | 0.13 | -84.69 | 1.0 | 0.1 |
| LSE:TNO | Rsm Tenon | 0.07 | 0.02 | -73.98 | 0.3 | 0.1 |

In terms of winners and losers:

| Ticker | Share | Buy price £ | Bid price | P/L | Units invested | Units now |
|---|---|---|---|---|---|---|
| LSE:TNI | Trinity Mirror | 0.45 | 1.18 | 159.35 | 2.9 | 7.6 |
| LSE:LLOY | Lloyds | 0.32 | 0.76 | 138.00 | 2.9 | 6.9 |
| LSE:PDG | Pendragon | 0.13 | 0.30 | 135.88 | 0.4 | 0.9 |
| LSE:BKIR | Bank Ireland | 0.11 | €0.2120 | 72.81 | 1.5 | 2.6 |
| LSE:HOMI | Home Retail | 0.96 | 1.53 | 59.83 | 0.4 | 0.7 |
| LSE:LAM | Lamprell | 1.01 | 1.38 | 36.52 | 0.3 | 0.4 |
| LSE:AGA | Aga Rangemaster | 0.75 | 1.00 | 33.99 | 1.0 | 1.4 |
| LSE:DRX | Drax | 5.20 | 6.84 | 31.54 | 0.4 | 0.6 |
| LSE:AV. | Aviva | 3.27 | 3.99 | 21.84 | 1.2 | 1.4 |
| LSE:HRN | Hornby | 0.65 | 0.78 | 20.51 | 0.4 | 0.4 |
| LSE:CNKS | Cenkos Sec | 0.76 | 0.88 | 16.08 | 0.4 | 0.5 |
| LSE:RM. | RM | 0.70 | 0.81 | 15.91 | 2.9 | 3.4 |
| LSE:SSE | SSE | 13.72 | 15.73 | 14.65 | 0.7 | 0.8 |
| LSE:AZN | Astrazeneca | 29.08 | 33.19 | 14.10 | 0.7 | 0.8 |
| LSE:TSCO | Tesco | 3.29 | 3.72 | 13.16 | 0.4 | 0.5 |
| LSE:FCCN | French Cnctn. | 0.26 | 0.30 | 12.72 | 1.8 | 2.0 |
| LSE:SIXH | 600 Grp. | 0.11 | 0.12 | 7.82 | 0.3 | 0.3 |
| LSE:TOT | Total Produce | 0.58 | 0.61 | 4.56 | 0.4 | 0.5 |
| LSE:FLYB | Flybe Grp | 0.62 | 0.64 | 3.48 | 1.3 | 1.4 |
| LSE:AQP | Aquarius Plat. | 0.46 | 0.47 | 2.43 | 1.2 | 1.2 |
| LSE:NBL | Noble Inv | 2.24 | 2.24 | -0.01 | 0.6 | 0.6 |
| LSE:FGP | Firstgroup | 1.19 | 1.17 | -2.13 | 2.8 | 2.8 |
| LSE:DRTY | Darty | 0.79 | 0.77 | -3.40 | 0.6 | 0.6 |
| LSE:VLX | Volex | 1.19 | 1.14 | -4.08 | 0.5 | 0.5 |
| LSE:LAND | Land Secs. | 9.65 | 9.20 | -4.69 | 0.7 | 0.7 |
| LSE:CRE | Creston | 1.09 | 1.03 | -5.50 | 0.4 | 0.4 |
| LSE:AVR | Avarae | 0.11 | 0.10 | -6.51 | 0.5 | 0.4 |
| LSE:RDSA | Rds A | 22.82 | 20.90 | -8.43 | 0.4 | 0.4 |
| LSE:PRW | Promethean | 0.21 | 0.17 | -20.93 | 2.3 | 1.8 |
| LSE:LGT | Lighthouse Grp. | 0.06 | 0.04 | -38.04 | 0.8 | 0.5 |
| LSE:GDP | Goldplat | 0.14 | 0.09 | -38.14 | 0.4 | 0.3 |
| LSE:TNO | Rsm Tenon | 0.07 | 0.02 | -73.98 | 0.3 | 0.1 |
| LSE:AVM | Avocet Mining | 0.82 | 0.13 | -84.69 | 1.0 | 0.1 |

Long may this rally continue.

# Investors Can't Be Fortune Tellers

### 19 August 2013

"If only, if only, if only..." The specimen portfolio is now toying with breaking even. As I write we are less than 1% down (0.78%). The winner helping us aloft is Flybe, now up 66%, because the new management flown in from EasyJet makes the comeback story sound very tasty.

Am I excited? No. This is how investing goes. In a portfolio you get big winners, good recoveries and abject failures. Today's investing horror story can be tomorrow's heroic profit and vice versa.

This brings me on to Avocet, our worse dog which is now rocketing. If we had loaded up at the bottom with more shares, which I was tempted to do, we would have made a packet.

Am I dejected? No. Missing big wins happens a lot. Remember Thomas Cook? We didn't buy that because the situation was too horrible and the market so wobbly I considered it the sort of crazy gamble that HMV was. It was and still is a bad bet in my mind, but it paid off massively in any event. Avocet is in the same basket.

However, we don't sell these mistakes or chase them. We just do our thing and hope to get a fat profit, year in and out, over the portfolio of recovery candidates. We can't be fortune tellers. We are playing the odds.

Who'd have thought six weeks ago when we were down nearly 25%, we would be back to around flat today? (Remember this loss includes fat costs and the negative effects of selling at wide spreads at current prices.) The sort of rally which has brought us close to par is rare and impossible to predict. And it can't go on.

Actually, yes it can. But we don't know. We have to let go worrying about all the missed opportunities and speculative guessing. We buy cheap shares and sell them when they aren't cheap. We try to be as safe as possible in this high risk endeavour. That's all we try to do.

As an aside I realise I'm buying these stocks too early. Actually this is not really true. There is no right time to buy, only the right price. However, in this current market, the shares that fit our criteria seem to continue to fall.

Can we delay buying and make more money? No, because tomorrow that dynamic will change and suddenly waiting won't work to our advantage and only hindsight proves us right or wrong. We have to forget timing. Timing the market should be considered impossible, even when it isn't.

It is all too easy to view the past with perfect hindsight and regret one's decisions. It is an emotional trap to avoid. We have to work with only small amounts of foresight.

# Going Bananas

### 22 August 2013

We have bought Fyffes, the banana folk. I've owned this share several times over the years. P/E is 8.5 and it's on my filters with sales over four times market cap and a dividend of 2.7%. It's not screaming to me, but nothing is. The chart looks very strong:

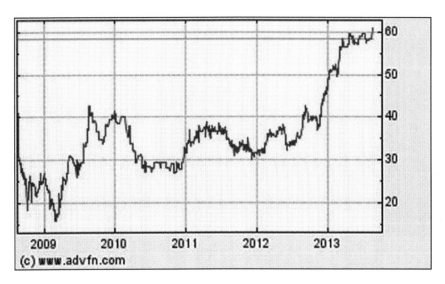

This looks like a break out to me. I always take this with a pinch of salt, but I'm sure you see what I mean. This is not a multibagger but it might give us 50%. 50% is fat but I've grown greedy and remind myself 50% would be very nice indeed with a dividend dropping in the letter box to pay us to wait for it.

At this second we are less than 1% down overall, even including the selling spread percentage which is a couple of per cent no doubt.

Darty came storming back, after the price fainted on us the instant we bought it. We are up 56% on Bank of Ireland and 38% on Flybe. Avocet remains the dog, down 75% and the rest are mildly bobbing about.

Here is a chart of the rollercoaster: it's plotted as if we put £30,000 in an account to get started:

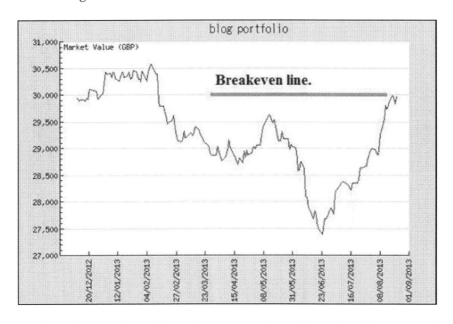

So after nine months we have fourteen stocks and have just about covered our costs. It's thankless but on we go.

For those who couldn't buy fourteen in nine months, this won't be a problem, because if you buy as we go along you should end up in the long run with the same result, you will in effect catch up over time. All the shares are picked using the same methodology, so one is not better than the other on average. That's not intuitive but that's probability for you.

# Momentary Profit

### 23 August 2013

For a moment there we were in profit. It might have been only £5 for half an hour but considering the portfolio was down well over 20% less than two months ago, it is surprising.

What happened in the market to create this turnaround? Nothing much. Certainly nothing outstandingly bullish has apparently happened in the market. (That's not to say something hasn't happened though.)

I keep writing about the highly random nature of the market and how you can't time things and you can't trade. While efficient market hypothesis is still the state of the art market theory, no one believes it. This is a kind of proof. Who would have predicted it? Who would have hoped for such a quick turnaround? It fits the theory perfectly.

My interpretation of the theory is, to be successful in the market you have to buy a basket of stocks you consider good value, for a good reason in niches and wait out all the random messing around. The market that people try to trade will make you look a fool or a genius but only time will reveal the real story.

Who knows what happens next, but we are building a portfolio of cheap stocks and over time they won't be cheap and we will bag a nice profit. Which stock will do what and when, we can't know.

The market is very random and highly efficient and we buy shares the market mis-values because it is not perfect. However, this randomness and high efficiency means this process takes time and patience and discipline and the market will pay us for that and the fact we are making it more efficient by doing so.

As I finish up we are back down 0.21%... 0.14% down... 0.17%... 0.18%... 0.17%...

# Nearly Out of the Summer Lull

### 29 August 2013

Not much to write about this week. There is nothing much moving.

Obama looks like he plans to try and drop a bomb on Assad's head. It occurs to me it's the only fun an American President gets to have. The "bombs away" button is the only one they get to press. However, they should do the math. Total national debt $15 trillion, cost of Middle East War $5 trillion. This shouldn't affect us much, whatever happens.

Meanwhile, nothing much has happened to the portfolio. We were up a few coppers and now we are down 1.26%, but after the huge fall and rise we have had, this is just noise. It has been very quiet even as the market has been pretty bearish and choppy. The legacy portfolio remains effectively becalmed.

Here is a list of our portfolio with its winners and losers. The sell price is at the bid and the cost includes all tax and charges.

| Ticker | Name | % P/L |
|---|---|---|
| LSE:BKIR | Bank Ireland | 53.9 |
| LSE:FLYB | Flybe Grp | 43.9 |
| LSE:COB | Cobham | 12.6 |
| LSE:DRTY | Darty | 8.4 |
| LSE:TOT | Total Produce | 6.3 |
| LSE:PRW | Promethean | -1.2 |
| LSE:FFY | Fyffes | -2.1 |
| LSE:FCCN | French Connection | -6.3 |
| LSE:CRE | Creston | -7.5 |
| LSE:LAND | Land Secs. | -9.5 |
| LSE:AQP | Aquarius Plat. | -11.8 |
| LSE:VLX | Volex | -12.6 |
| LSE:FGP | Firstgroup | -13.4 |
| LSE:AVM | Avocet Mining | -70.8 |

Five wins v nine loses, hardly stellar, but less abysmal than all but a few weeks ago. Let's see if the random walk can make us look like genius up to Christmas.

# Portfolio in Profit – Just!

### 3 September 2013

The specimen portfolio is bobbling around in profit. While 0.65% isn't exactly mind blowing for all this trouble it is a huge turnaround from over 20% down in less than ten weeks. If only we could know which ten weeks in a year to pick.

Selling in May and going away to 15 September as the saying goes would not have done us any good at all, we would be well over 10% down. It's hard to focus on the unknowable randomness of the market but it is good to keep bringing it to mind. Investing is not a game of tag, it's a game of wait and wait and wait and see.

Of course, if Mr Obama bombs Syria we will lose a packet for a bit and if he doesn't we will likely earn a few pounds. But who knows? If the market dives we may buy a few things.

While we are in profit over all, after costs and taking the need to sell at the bid into account, only four out of fourteen stocks are in profit. So that is an interesting lesson, only four of our selection of fourteen need be in the money for us to be in profit over all. The chances of being able to just pick those four from the selection of fourteen is one in a thousand and if you did the profit would have been just 34%. If you had picked the worse four you'd have the same odds and you would have lost 24%.

Instead of trying to win the 1/1000 lottery, we have a small portfolio and are flat for all our trouble and risk. This is the point that unsuccessful investors sell and grab back their money. They have lost, then waited a long time to get even before running away. This is, of course, no way to make money. You can't get even with the market because it doesn't care. Likewise you can't beat it, there is nothing to beat. It's like shouting at your cheque book: it is not listening.

In the stock market you either make money or lose money; you are either right or wrong; it's a place not a person. Waiting to get even is as pointless as selling if you actually do get even, waiting does not affect the outcome in any way. Trying to get even is not an investment or trading strategy.

Imagine, now we are back at even, I stopped this blog here! ...

...Don't worry, I won't!

# Songbird Added to Portfolio

**3 September 2013**

Bought Songbird, more info tomorrow.

# Songbird – Going for a Song

### 4 September 2013

I rather like property at the moment because if we are going to get inflation, a recovery or both, property will do well. Everywhere I go in the world the stupid money loves property. That's not to say anyone is stupid to like property, but the love of property in many parts of the world is blind. People buy smallish houses in the Riviera for a major fraction of the value of the whole of Canary Wharf. This is the kind of property lust that globally knows no bounds and it drives the idea that the best property cannot fail but to appreciate. It's a bubble mindset and we like bubbles before they inflate too much.

So I've bought Songbird, the holding company of much of Canary Wharf. The price today is 155p and the net assets per share is 240p a share. So as far as I'm concerned the company is for sale at an 85p a share discount, which means if it rose to 240p it would go up 54%. Of course, the value of the property would rise with more economic recovery, so the upside is tasty and will get tastier still.

There is a downside. The company structure is rather opaque and the management wiped out the shareholders in the midst of the credit crunch with a giant rights issue.

I did well out of that but it did show that the management was ruthless, to say the least. Ruthless management is not necessarily a good thing as shareholders can wake up and find themselves on the menu if the management are too predatory. This is a lesson I've learnt in many a people-based business in listed, fund management, recruitment and accountant PLCs.

Anyway we've taken the jump because Songbird is like Land or British Land but with a much higher risk reward ratio. The Canary Wharf and recovery story should play out well but there is never a free ride when the market values a stock at a fat discount.

# Buying Stock Brokers

### 9 September 2013

As I write we are 2% up on the specimen portfolio. However, I have just bought another share so this will push us back. It is Walker Crips. The idea is, its market cap now equals its cash and it has a business with sales about the same. So in effect, the business – which is stock broking, wealth management etc – is in for free. That is my hand-wavy analysis and if I can't keep it simple in my investments I don't want the share.

The trigger was today's announcement that they have sold some loan stock they received from selling their asset management business last year for considerable more than initially expected: http://uk.advfn.com/news/UKREG/2013/article/59119497.

I don't follow this company, so I took a look at the chart. Result: way down on five years ago. Other factors include: normal dividend 4-5%. The fat cash balance. A focus on reorganisation back to a solid core business. Pulling trading statements. All for free if you take out the cash.

I like stock brokers because they are down on their luck to say the least, but I'm expecting this to change. A new age of equities in the west is opening and brokers will flourish. That is blue sky thinking but it is one of those long term themes that nudge me one way or the other.

The trouble is the bloody stock has a 10% spread!!!! That is a killer. So to buy in we immediately lose 10-12% of our position because of the dysfunctional markets that market makers create. Even with a nice price improvement from my broker at TSC Trade we still ended up 9.75% all told in the hole for our trouble. Sometimes, though, you just have to, as the Americans say, suck it up, and we have. It has also pushed down our overall profit to 1.38%.

This is a very important point to always hold in your mind. If we buy shares which cost us say 5% to buy including stamp, commission and spread, that's a nasty bump. Over an average two year hold, however, that falls to 2.5% per annum. Still nasty but not drastic if we are looking to capture say 15%. The longer we hold the further the cost falls.

Now imagine we trade our portfolio four times a year. That's a 20% cost and that's simply unsustainable. This is why trading doesn't tend to work and why investing is easier.

# Portfolio in Profit

### 10 September 2013

Another fine day. The market is very strong and I'm left wondering if we are peaking. But we aren't trading so it doesn't really matter. We are 2.9% up as I write. Blowing past short term bond yields... OK, so I'm being ironic, but we are in profit.

There are two things to bear in mind. First, this recovery in our fortunes is not because of trading. We have sold nothing yet. This 20% fall and 20% rise is in the same portfolio of stocks. We have, as I hoped only a handful of weeks back, ridden out a market cycle.

This fall was a function of the cost of building a portfolio and random market factors. The passage of time is dealing with this as now we are enjoying an equally random but nonetheless welcome rally. This volatility should drop as we grow the portfolio but it underlines the uncertainty inherent in investing in shares. It is easy to be left asking: What changed? Who knows? But that is pointless, you have to make your choices and stick with them.

Secondly, costs significantly diminish our profits. The average spread on our portfolio is 2.1%. So valued at the current offer price, we would be up 5%. Pop on the .5% stamp duty and say 2% for commission (£20 a trade) and we see our un-truncated profit on our stock picking is 7.5%. This is a harsh reality often missed, costs can be swingeing.

But nonetheless even after all these costs we are up 2.9% and likely to be holding these stocks for a long time so time will heal these gouges.

Here is the list of spreads:

| ticker | bid | offer | spread |
|---|---|---|---|
| AQP | 50.25 | 51 | 1.470588 |
| AVM | 18.75 | 19 | 1.315789 |
| BKIR | 0.237 | 0.238 | 0.420168 |
| COB | 302.2 | 302.4 | 0.066138 |
| CRE | 102 | 104 | 1.923077 |
| DRTY | 79.75 | 80.5 | 0.931677 |
| FCCN | 32.75 | 34 | 3.676471 |
| FFY | 63 | 65 | 3.076923 |
| FGP | 119.3 | 119.6 | 0.250836 |
| FLYB | 87 | 88.25 | 1.416431 |
| LAND | 911 | 912 | 0.109649 |
| PRW | 16.75 | 17.75 | 5.633803 |
| SBD | 150 | 152.75 | 1.800327 |
| TOT | 65 | 67 | 2.985075 |
| VLX | 118.5 | 122 | 2.868852 |
| WCW | 38 | 40 | 5 |
|  |  |  | 2.059113 |

Meanwhile back in stupid punting land, I took another tranche out of my spread betting account. It is equivalent to what I put in all those years ago. I have decided that if I make one times my original capital from the previous withdrawal level, I will take one times my original capital out. It hasn't taken long to do that.

How? By being 15 times (1,500%) leveraged. This is, of course, madness but the whole point of that account is to trade like a beast.

One thing is clear, you can't trade and make a living, the scale is just too big. To make say £100,000, even if you were as lucky as I'm being, you would have to be throwing around multi-million pound index positions.

Let's keep it simple and say you can catch two pound euro moves from 115 to 120 a year. That's 10 euro cents. You would have to hold a 1,000,000 euro position to pull in a £100,000 profit. This isn't including funding costs but let's say you were holding for just two months of hell and you scraped a couple more points to cover that cost. Are you really going to be doing that year in and out, long after the thought of a ride on a motorbike stopped being fun or feasible?

Sitting on a carefully nurtured portfolio of stocks, however, is highly manageable. The difference is between bull fighting and bringing up chickens.

Anyway, for now at least the dunce cap is off.

...As I finish writing, (30 minutes) we are now up 3.1%. I've been a genius for 30 straight minutes. Life is good.

(0.4% returns per hour... Imagine compounding at that rate!)

# Market Run Comes to an End

### 12 September 2013

The market has suddenly gone bearish. This is not surprising after such a great run.

In the legacy portfolio we have two takeovers in two days – yikes: 600 Group and Noble's. I have sold them both. If the offers are firm and have a hostile tinge I would hold but when they are vague as in 600 Group and from an opaque source I will sell. The Noble offer has payment in shares as a big element. So I prefer to take the cash now. 600 was a 50% profit and Noble's 6-7%.

If Stanley Gibbons does this deal, which is effectively recommended, it will have done a brilliant takeover and will get a fat uplift. It is a growth share not a value share so I'm not really interested in it, as it doesn't fit neatly in my investment theme. I would have been very happy indeed to sit on Noble's stock for a year or two and watch it double, but that possibility appears to be receding fast.

In the specimen portfolio things are taking a breather too. Not much to report except Walker Crips is actually in profit which is a nice performance for a few days.

This weekend is the St Ledger of "Sell in May and go away" fame, so it will be interesting to see what "back to work" in the city brings. My flags are yen v dollar, weak yen equals strong equities.

Meanwhile the pound looks on its way up against the euro and dollar and if this is a final reversion to its correct rate, then we can expect a much stronger pound. Good or bad for equities? Too soon to tell, but probably good if the hot money decides to perch in UK equities to catch the FX updraft.

# New Subscribers: Welcome

### 16 September 2013

A welcome to all my new subscribers. You have missed much pain and pleasure.

I am building a contrarian value investing portfolio as if I was a new investor. I am buying only £1,000 of each stock, using a broker who is not the cheapest and taking into account the spread as we go. That means there are big real costs to climb over to get into profit. Results would look much better if I bought £5,000 of shares at a discount broker and did a valuation at the current price not the bid. But I'm trying to keep the record absolutely real.

This new portfolio is going into my legacy portfolio – my long term portfolio, so over time, perhaps another three years, the "specimen" portfolio and the "legacy portfolio" will be the same.

The legacy portfolio has had massive returns; the specimen portfolio has had a huge rollercoaster ride (see below). I like to think this rollercoaster is part of a maturing process. I buy when shares get cheap, but they can get cheaper. As such, building a new portfolio of value stocks is initially a costly business. In this model the profits come through later. This could be right, this might be just a convenient narrative for something else that's at work.

Investing is just about building a thesis and backing it with money. Sometimes you look like a genius, other times an idiot. We've certainly looked foolish, but now we seem just not particularly clever. Another year and we will know because we should be up 15-30% with a properly diversified portfolio by then if we are on the right track.

So here is the history of the specimen portfolio. The chart is calculated as if £30,000 went into a brokerage account from day one. Of course it is unlikely to happen like that as most people will drip funds in.

Here is the transaction log:

| ID | REF | Symbol | Type | Quantity | Price | Value | Charges | Total | M | Date | Time | Left | |
|---|---|---|---|---|---|---|---|---|---|---|---|---|---|
| 21 | | LSE:WCW | BUY | 2600 | £ 0.3991 | £ 1,037.54 | £ 0.0000 | £ -1,037.54 | | 09/09/2013 | 11:23 | 2600 | ×  |
| 20 | | LSE:SBD | BUY | 665 | £ 1.5577 | £ 1,035.84 | £ 0.0000 | £ -1,035.84 | | 03/09/2013 | 18:44 | 665 | ×  |
| 19 | | LSE:FFY | BUY | 1625 | £ 0.6335 | £ 1,029.37 | £ 0.0000 | £ -1,029.37 | | 22/08/2013 | 14:13 | 1625 | ×  |
| 18 | [17] | LSE:DIVI | SELL | 1 | £ 7.0000 | £ 7.00 | £ 0.0000 | £ 7.00 | | 12/08/2013 | 11:27 | | ×  |
| 17 | | LSE:DIVI | BUY | 1 | £ 1.0000 | £ 1.00 | £ 0.0000 | £ -1.00 | | 12/08/2013 | 11:25 | | ×  |
| 16 | | LSE:DRTY | BUY | 1276 | £ 0.8072 | £ 1,030.00 | £ 0.0000 | £ -1,030.00 | | 05/08/2013 | 14:51 | 1276 | ×  |
| 15 | | LSE:CRE | BUY | 950 | £ 1.1038 | £ 1,048.62 | £ 0.0000 | £ -1,048.62 | | 03/07/2013 | 13:25 | 950 | ×  |
| 14 | | LSE:LAND | BUY | 105 | £ 9.7621 | £ 1,025.02 | £ 0.0000 | £ -1,025.02 | | 29/05/2013 | 11:43 | 105 | ×  |
| 13 | | LSE:TOT | BUY | 1760 | £ 0.5923 | £ 1,042.51 | £ 0.0000 | £ -1,042.51 | | 28/05/2013 | 17:07 | 1760 | ×  |
| 12 | | LSE:FGP | BUY | 778 | £ 0.8500 | £ 661.30 | £ 0.0000 | £ -661.30 | | 23/05/2013 | 08:20 | 778 | ×  |
| 11 | | LSE:FCCN | BUY | 3200 | £ 0.3178 | £ 1,017.00 | £ 0.0000 | £ -1,017.00 | | 15/05/2013 | 09:42 | 3200 | ×  |
| 10 | | LSE:COB | BUY | 398 | £ 2.5126 | £ 1,000.00 | £ 0.0000 | £ -1,000.00 | | 20/03/2013 | 16:11 | 398 | ×  |
| 9 | | LSE:VLX | BUY | 851 | £ 1.2071 | £ 1,027.21 | £ 0.0000 | £ -1,027.21 | | 19/02/2013 | 10:10 | 851 | ×  |
| 8 | | LSE:BKIR | BUY | 8529 | € 0.1405 | € 1,198.73 | £ 0.0000 | £ -1,032.50 | | 13/02/2013 | 09:02 | 8529 | ×  |
| 7 | | LSE:FGP | BUY | 519 | £ 1.9861 | £ 1,030.77 | £ 0.0000 | £ -1,030.77 | | 15/01/2013 | 16:51 | 519 | ×  |
| 6 | | LSE:FLYB | BUY | 2000 | £ 0.5175 | £ 1,035.03 | £ 0.0000 | £ -1,035.03 | | 11/01/2013 | 16:46 | 2000 | ×  |
| 5 | | LSE:AVM | BUY | 1377 | £ 0.7462 | £ 1,027.50 | £ 0.0000 | £ -1,027.50 | | 03/01/2013 | 10:19 | 1377 | ×  |
| 4 | | LSE:AQP | BUY | 2000 | £ 0.5135 | £ 1,026.90 | £ 0.0000 | £ -1,026.90 | | 19/12/2012 | 15:50 | 2000 | ×  |
| 3 | | LSE:PRW | BUY | 6000 | £ 0.1696 | £ 1,017.45 | £ 0.0000 | £ -1,017.45 | | 11/12/2012 | 10:12 | 6000 | ×  |
| 2 | | - | CASH | | | | | £ 30,000.00 | | 11/12/2012 | 10:08 | | ×  |

Transactions 17 and 18 is how I keep track of dividends.

Interestingly, on average we've had this portfolio for 148 days. So at the average rate of performance, if we held this portfolio for 365 days and factored in the cost of the spread we will be up 6.5%. Of course if we projected out the performance since July we will be a ridiculous amount up. This is another reason why past performance is not connected to future performance and why randomness has the key role to play in the short term, but not the long term. In any event it's best not to count your chickens.

And here is the portfolio:

| Holding | | Quantity | Total Cost | Avg Price | Price | Basis | Cur Value | Profit/Loss | % | Daily Port |
|---|---|---|---|---|---|---|---|---|---|---|
| LSE:AQP | Aquarius Plat. | 2000 | £1,026.90 | £0.5135 | £0.5000 | BID | £1,000.00 | £-26.90 | -2.62% | £-15.00↓ |
| LSE:AVM | Avocet Mining | 1377 | £1,027.50 | £0.7462 | £0.1550 | BID | £213.44 | £-814.07 | -79.23% | £3.44↑ |
| LSE:BKIR | Bank Ireland | 8529 | £1,032.50 | £0.1211 | £0.2200 | BID | £1,573.09 | £540.59 | 52.36% | £42.90↑ |
| LSE:COB | Cobham | 398 | £1,000.00 | £2.5126 | £2.9450 | BID | £1,172.11 | £172.11 | 17.21% | £-26.27↓ |
| LSE:CRE | Creston | 950 | £1,048.62 | £1.1038 | £1.0350 | BID | £983.25 | £-65.37 | -6.23% | £0.00• |
| LSE:DRTY | Darty | 1276 | £1,030.00 | £0.8072 | £0.7325 | BID | £934.67 | £-95.33 | -9.26% | £-6.38↓ |
| LSE:FCCN | French Cnctn. | 3200 | £1,017.00 | £0.3178 | £0.3150 | BID | £1,008.00 | £-9.00 | -0.88% | £-32.00↓ |
| LSE:FFY | Fyffes | 1625 | £1,029.37 | £0.6335 | £0.6200 | BID | £1,007.50 | £-21.87 | -2.12% | £0.00• |
| LSE:FGP | Firstgroup | 1297 | £1,692.07 | £1.3046 | £1.2400 | BID | £1,608.28 | £-83.79 | -4.95% | £9.08↑ |
| LSE:FLYB | Flybe Grp | 2000 | £1,035.03 | £0.5175 | £0.8625 | BID | £1,725.00 | £689.97 | 66.66% | £-25.00↓ |
| LSE:LAND | Land Secs. | 105 | £1,025.02 | £9.7621 | £9.2450 | BID | £970.73 | £-54.29 | -5.30% | £5.25↑ |
| LSE:PRW | Promethean | 6000 | £1,017.45 | £0.1696 | £0.1650 | BID | £990.00 | £-27.45 | -2.70% | £-45.00↓ |
| LSE:SBD | Songbird | 665 | £1,035.84 | £1.5577 | £1.5775 | BID | £1,049.04 | £13.20 | 1.27% | £18.29↑ |
| LSE:TOT | Total Produce | 1760 | £1,042.51 | £0.5923 | £0.6500 | BID | £1,144.00 | £101.49 | 9.74% | £0.00• |
| LSE:VLX | Volex | 851 | £1,027.21 | £1.2071 | £1.1300 | BID | £961.63 | £-65.58 | -6.38% | £0.00• |
| LSE:WCW | Walker Crips | 2600 | £1,037.54 | £0.3991 | £0.4000 | BID | £1,040.00 | £2.46 | 0.24% | £0.00• |
| Total | | | £17,124.56 | | | | £17,380.73 | £256.17 | 1.50% | £-77.57↓ |

Now the investment industry is back from holiday it will be interesting to see what happens next.

FYI, Leading Light won the St Leger, so the stock market is meant to rally now. What did I say about past performance? Hopefully this particular 50/50 will come up in our favour.

# Preparing for a Drop

### 17 September 2013

It's a sure sign that a correction is ahead when things go too well. Before a crash you can generally feel it coming when the rubbish companies on the margin of the market, the tiddlers at the bottom of AIM, suddenly start exploding upwards. This is the firework display that says trouble is ahead.

A nice extra strong rally, however, isn't a portent of doom, just an indicator that a top is coming into view, at least for a bit. This is where I think we are now. We are at least at a plateaux. So I'm waiting, prepared for a bit of a drop now.

The market is bound to go a bit wild if the Federal Reserve does or doesn't cut back in pumping a trillion dollars a year into the US and world economy via QE3. However, who knows the short term outcome let alone the long term one? The end of zero interest rates will be choppy, but in the long run good news for equities.

When the market is bullish the big caps don't tend to fall much when there is bad news, conversely in a bear market they fall out of bed at the slight hiccup.

This morning finds Invesco and Asos in the sin bin, an indicator that the market is indeed feeling bearish. (As I write Invesco has bounced 2.5% back so this suggest we haven't necessarily entered serious bear territory.) So the days ahead will be likely glum.

The big action is in Forex at the moment, where in a sense not much is happening. You can practically see the agreed lines in the sand for the G8 currencies parity. While this control is successfully in place, then the lesser markets should be in good form. Currencies are the senior markets, followed by bonds, then equities. Stability comes from the top.

We will not sell the portfolio unless I believe the world is about to end. That happened in 2008. I sold again in 2010 but it turned out that I needn't have bothered, even though it seemed for about a year like a good idea. I think selling out is a very rare occasion and then only after a bubble and at the point before or around a bust. It can't be on a whim. You have to know why you are bailing and it has to be a massive reason.

I do not think such a future is ahead of us, for the foreseeable future, but that day will come and we will most likely miss it. I caught the last two early (2001, 2008) but getting three out of three is too much to ask.

# Outrageous Spread Stops Me Buying

### 25 September 2013

We nearly bought another share today but I put my foot down. It had a 10% spread. That's just an outrage. I had my broker ring up the market maker and try to do a deal, but no luck. It is just a scandal that the UK market can have such spreads. It isn't a new story of course. In this instance I refused to make the market maker rich. We can wait.

Meanwhile, the specimen portfolio is wibbling around at 1.38% up. I don't like the market right now, it feels toppy. However, I try to forget these thoughts because gut feeling is no guide.

Meanwhile I'm experimenting in the US market and I am building a multi-currency big cap portfolio. It's a very interesting task and not one I claim any skill in. The US end of it is most interesting. America really does have the most amazingly bent markets.

I have been following Blackberry closely because it is a classic value play. Today it delivered me an expensive lesson in US shenanigans and it is sure to be a cheap lesson in due course. I can't really express my analysis of the situation without risking defamation. However, it illuminates the jungle that is the US market and I think I'm going to enjoy my live fire exercises in it.

Meanwhile, as the market is in hiatus I am left feeling confused. How can Shell be so cheap? It is and threatens to remain cheap forever. I say this because I have bought it on many occasions on the obvious observation that the company is massively profitable, pays a huge dividend and is on a low P/E. Yet I always lose a few per cent and end up selling it for one housekeeping reason or another.

The only thing I can think is, the company is just too big. It's an elephant that can't jump because market liquidity is not big enough to lift it. It's the same with Exxon in the US. Yet compare Shell and Exxon balance sheets and fundamentals. They suggest that if Shell was Exxon it would be twice the market cap it is today. That doesn't smack of the efficient market.

But at the extremes the efficient market breaks down and perhaps too big is such an extreme.

I scratch my head sagely as if I know that's the reason, but looking at US stocks throws open a whole world of confusion that can easily leave you doubting your eyes.

Tesla, for example, makes cars, $400 million of them and the company is worth $20bln, 50 times its sales. It's worth about 30% of Ford's market cap, who sell $134,252 million of cars. Ford is worth roughly half times sales. So a $1 of Tesla cars is worth to the stock market $100 dollars of Ford cars. It is as if a Tesla car sold for $40,000 and a Ford for $400.

Clunk, my brain crashes.

But you can't sit on your laurels and make money from what you know you know, you have to keep pushing your investing as far as you can.

Multicurrency portfolio investment is fascinating – frustrating, but worth mastering. The trouble with it is it's extremely influenced by currency; and currency is technically impossible to predict. Make 20% on your dollar stocks and have the dollar move 20% down and you haven't made a dime or in this case a penny.

So, for example, rather than build just a dollar/sterling portfolio I should add a euro leg. However, I just know the euro must fall. (That's a fallacy but I can't fight it.) I simply can't bear to buy all those lovely French, German and Italian value stocks when I can see they are going to be held in cratering euros.

However this is all just gibbering, because there is little else to do but wait.

# The Mystic Art of Investing

### 27 September 2013

A lot of people think investing is occult knowledge and there can be an element of that. Knowledge is power, so if you know more you will make more money. So here is a bit of occult knowledge for my readers.

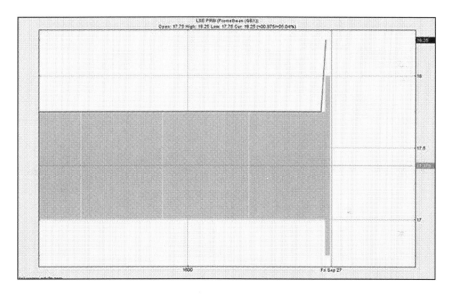

This is Promethean World, one of our more contrarian positions. Let's forget the narrative and look at the price action today. This stock is 5% but our portfolio shows a loss today. That could sting if you sold.

So this is what happened. The spread exploded on the last minute of trading so the BID price, which you sell at, fell by 0.25p. Then the share went into auction and "uncrossed", the moment the auction price is settled at 18.25. If you were buying on a RSP, the automated system, or perhaps via a spread betting platform, this price action would set the pace. If that was done on purpose to affect RSP or spread betting trading it would be an illegal market manipulation. However, that's another story.

What you can see is that your buying and selling price is heavily influenced in this and many other stocks by events like this. As such, as an investor you should avoid the open and close in illiquid stocks.

This particular case is more interesting still. These are the trades:

| Num | Exch | Price | Size | Type | C | T | Bid | Offer | Time | Buy | Sell | ? | Buy Ind. | Buy Vol. | Sell Vol. | ? Vol. |
|---|---|---|---|---|---|---|---|---|---|---|---|---|---|---|---|---|
| 2 | LSE | 18.25 | 16,033 | UT | | | 16.75 | 18 | 16:35:14 | 0 | 0 | 16,033 | | 16,033 | 1,714 | 16,033 |
| 1 | LSE | 17.15 | 1,714 | O | | | 17 | 17.75 | 15:04:25 | 0 | 1,714 | 0 | | 16,033 | 1,714 | 0 |
| 0 | LSE | 17.75 | 16,033 | AT | | | 16.75 | 17.75 | 10:37:05 | 16,033 | 0 | 0 | | 16,033 | 0 | 0 |

Someone made £40 on this trading £2,000 of stock and made us 5% on £1,000 (£50) if only the bid hadn't fallen one minute from the end of play. This is an inefficient market at work and a risky one too, at least in the short term. That might sound bad, but actually inefficiency and risk is where profit in the market lives. The market will pay us to make it more efficient. It turns out in my experience it will pay us quite a lot.

Here is hoping.

# The Market is Falling!

### 2 October 2013

For now at least, we are in a bear market. What we hope to see is our portfolio falling less than the market. Then when it rallies we hope it will rise more. This is the ratchet that makes us money.

As predicted in an earlier piece, the final moments of the rally were indeed aligned with when the market was pretending I was a genius. We are now in a period when I will be a dunce. When I feel particularly clever and the genius quotient is running high, that is always a sign of a market top. Hubris and Nemesis have been at it for millennia.

Being a dunce is not so much fun but we need to embrace the cycle.

How long this bear will last I don't know but it should be nearing a potential turn around point. You can see this on the Dow clearly:

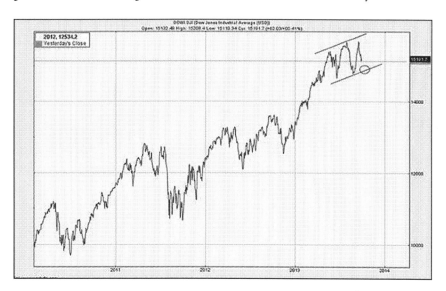

I use the Dow because it's clearer on its chart and the FTSE will follow. But always remember chart lines are not destiny. They are just frames of reference.

Meanwhile, the strong pound is interesting. Clearly, something important has changed and the pound looks set to rise and rise. This won't necessarily be bad for the FTSE because if you own sterling equities they appreciate in dollars and euros automatically. As such hot foreign money comes knocking.

Bear phases are of course less exciting than bull markets so I apologise in advance if I go a little quiet if things stay like this. I'll try to entertain but no promises or warranties given. Of course as soon as the rally starts I'll be crowing like any self-respecting pundit!

Good job we didn't sell in May and buy 15 September. As a side issue, Octobers used to be awful in the old days, so we should bear that in mind.

If you are wondering what I think about the US government shut down, my opinion is it's a joke. The US doesn't need to raise its ceiling at all.

Why? Well this isn't in the press, but it's simple. The Federal Reserve has $1.5 trillion in government debt on its balance sheet bought during QE. If it retired these bonds, the debt would fall by as much instantly, freeing up the ceiling.

There are plenty of reasons not to do this but none worse than default. As such the whole thing is nonsense and the market knows it.

At this level QE is very frightening if you think about it, which is why this option is never brought up. However, if you don't believe it is true then read how George Osbourne got billions back in interest the treasury paid the Bank of England on the gilts it bought during QE and you will see this option is real. Fascinating.

# It's a Bear Market

### 4 October 2013

Well here we are in a bear market. In the last couple of years the idiots of the media have redefined "bear market" as one that has fallen 20%. This is like defining a funeral as an accident.

A bear market is one where the market is falling. This is a useful definition as it says the trend is down. The new definition is useless as it says the trend *was* down. The market could be down 30% having turned and now be rallying hard and the new definition says, "we are in a bear market." It's enough to make you weep.

Bear market means the tendency is down. This can be for all kinds of reasons and there are a few right now, including the market being high and the American government being clueless.

Meanwhile the portfolio is back in the red again by a smidgen. We are losing £36 overall including expenses. Here is the chart:

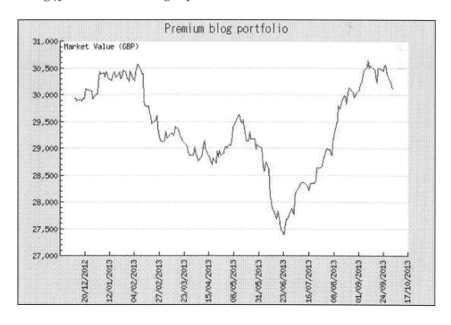

This is likely to get worse and I would be surprised if we didn't end up in the dumps again. However, we simply can't know. This is investing. You take the rough with the smooth. The thing to remember is markets turn fast on the upside. So in two to three days you can miss half of a bounce back.

If the market corrects we would expect our shares not to do as badly as the market as they are already crunched. This is what normally happens. We will see.

You only have to see our performance this year to see the impossibility of timing or at least how fast things can turn around.

The main risk currently is political and US-centric and there is really nothing to be done. Politicians are a prime class of fools capable of doing unbelievable damage if they get excited enough, leaving nothing certain.

Meanwhile I was on CNBC yesterday in America. Before me on the show was zillionaire bond king Bill Gross, later that afternoon CNBC interviewed President Obama. Not bad company but who was the odd man out? President Obama, of course, as he was the only one whose enterprise is closed for business.

Talking of the shutdown in the US, no one is considering the Fed and QE. The Fed has $1.5 trillion dollars of US debt. If the US government – of which the Fed is in effect part – was to cancel that, there would be no debt ceiling issue. I believe this is what will happen if the US actually gets near default. As such, this is just a political war between two sides of a dysfunctional and now malfunctioning democracy. It is just a distraction. The market panics easily and the hot money is running for cover in the euro.

However, times like this require a long holiday on a nice beach with a cocktail. There is little to be done except look for value.

Value investors right now might be tempted by Albemarle and Bond, the pawn brokers who have crashed in the last days by 80%.

Here is the chart:

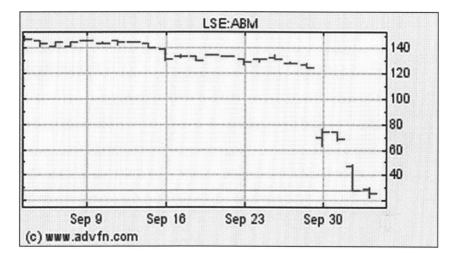

In the old days I would have been all over this, but in the days of pre-pack administrations for skimpy reasons I wouldn't touch this with a ten foot barge pole.

I took a punt on HMV. It went down. What do you know, they just reopened their flagship store on Oxford Street. Clinton Cards was another recent instance where shareholders were, as they say on the BBs, "shafted."

Remember New Star and Gartmore? Businesses still intact, management handed out fat slices of the new equity, shareholders obliterated. If you go back far enough Marconi was the template for this kind of financial slash and burn, and it will continue. As such, a value investment must withstand being able to be stolen. We therefore need to do a smell test on deep value investment opportunities. Albemarle doesn't pass it.

Sadly, when there is a US player or private equity in the frame, it is not a good sign that there will be a turnaround for the benefit of the shareholders.

# Albemarle and Bond Bouncing at the Bottom

### 4 October 2013

Funny how we mentioned Albemarle and Bond earlier today. Well, it bounced 50%. Hold on – in the three minutes since I typed that it's fallen back to 35% up. You can trade this stuff but it's not investing.

Why do these companies collapse and rally like this at the end? Well, first off if you are short this stock from high up, you don't want to be short when the company is suspended. If you are, you're locked into that position for maybe a year waiting for your money. Meanwhile a spread betting company might lock up your profits too or pick some weird price for settlement etc. As such, shorters don't want to be there to the bitter end, they want out before the death.

This short covering often causes these big spikes but blink and you've missed them. Sometimes they never happen and when the company goes under you lose the whole value of the stake you tried to catch the bounce with. It's ultra high risk.

Meanwhile, the share has an 8% spread so even buying in costs you 8% of your stake and you've hours to catch a profit. I'm too old for that kind of madness and hopefully you are too sensible.

# US Default – Don't Panic!

## 11 October 2013

I'm telling myself I should have perhaps written lots of blog posts about the potential US default. However, I haven't because we are investing and the last thing I want to do is build a level of panic. My position was that Monday 14 October was the day to decide to hold or fold as that was a few days from next Thursday when the balloon in theory could go up. The only reason for the US to default is because they want to kill the beast of government. As most politicians of all hues love the government which they run, this was unlikely to happen.

Secondly, Obama can simply say, "to hell with you" and print money.

So rather than write lots of "will they, won't they" stuff the correct response is lethargy.

The thing is, the market knows. Or put another way, Obama's bodyguards, brother's aunty's mother knows as does the equivalent up and down Washington. As such, the market is making a good estimation of the outcome. The market says don't sweat it.

So today the Republicans blinked and the market shot up.

However, complacency is not always the answer. What are the signs of terrible events ahead?

In a word the most dangerous sign is: silence. Silence is caused by denial. The band did play on after the Titanic hit the iceberg. Equities didn't crash after the bond market froze, even though the reaction should be immediate. If people are screaming about imminent disaster then chances are probably low. If they merely chatter about the iceberg and that ice is on the deck, then head straight to the life boats.

This nonsense is not over but default looks very very unlikely now. This means that not getting too excited was the right course of action. A real default would have been as least as traumatic as the credit crunch but it's not going to happen.

Meanwhile back at the portfolio this is where we are:

| | Quantity | Total Cost | Avg. Price | Price | Cur Value | Profit/ Loss | % | Daily Perf |
|---|---|---|---|---|---|---|---|---|
| Aquarius Plat. | 2000 | £1,026.90 | £0.51 | £0.50 | £990.00 | -£36.90 | -3.59% | £40.00 |
| Avocet Mining | 1377 | £1,027.50 | £0.75 | £0.15 | £209.99 | -£817.51 | -79.56% | £10.33 |
| Bank Ireland | 8529 | £1,032.50 | £0.12 | € 0.23 | £1,647.56 | £615.06 | 59.57% | £43.36 |
| Cobham | 398 | £1,000.00 | £2.51 | £2.84 | £1,129.13 | £129.13 | 12.91% | £43.78 |
| Creston | 950 | £1,048.62 | £1.10 | £1.01 | £954.75 | -£93.87 | -8.95% | £0.00 |
| Darty | 1276 | £1,030.00 | £0.81 | £0.71 | £902.77 | -£127.23 | -12.35% | £25.52 |
| French Cnctn. | 3200 | £1,017.00 | £0.32 | £0.31 | £976.00 | -£41.00 | -4.03% | £16.00 |
| Fyffes | 1625 | £1,029.37 | £0.63 | £0.64 | £1,040.00 | £10.63 | 1.03% | £8.13 |
| Firstgroup | 1297 | £1,692.07 | £1.30 | £1.22 | £1,586.23 | -£105.84 | -6.26% | £6.49 |
| Flybe Grp | 2000 | £1,035.03 | £0.52 | £0.79 | £1,570.00 | £534.97 | 51.69% | £10.00 |
| Land Secs. | 105 | £1,025.02 | £9.76 | £9.31 | £977.03 | -£48.00 | -4.68% | £17.85 |
| Promethean | 6000 | £1,017.45 | £0.17 | £0.17 | £990.00 | -£27.45 | -2.70% | -£15.00 |
| Songbird | 665 | £1,035.84 | £1.56 | £1.46 | £972.56 | -£63.28 | -6.11% | £21.61 |
| Total Produce | 1760 | £1,042.51 | £0.59 | £0.64 | £1,126.40 | £83.89 | 8.05% | £0.00 |
| Volex | 851 | £1,027.21 | £1.21 | £1.19 | £1,014.82 | -£12.39 | -1.21% | £44.68 |
| Walker Crips | 2600 | £1,037.54 | £0.40 | £0.41 | £1,066.00 | £28.46 | 2.74% | £0.00 |
| Total | | £17,124.56 | | | £17,153.23 | £28.67 | 0.17% | £272.73 |
| Cash | | 12881 | | | | | | |
| Current holdings | | 17153 | | | | | | |
| Market Value | | 30035 | | | | | | |

So we are flat once all costs are taken into account.

The next few days will determine if the US madness is resolved and if it is we can hope for a nice rally. Meanwhile we are busily doing nothing looking for nice cheap stocks.

# My Buying Is On Hold

## 16 October 2013

There is no way we are buying any stocks until the US default nonsense is over. In my head a default will cause a cascade of market disjuncture that can only be bad.

The market is saying, "don't worry." I would take notice but it is saying it with the market equivalent of a bull horn. Frankly I don't understand. It looks to me like the US government is going to sail past the notional 17 October without a deal and then along to what everyone agrees is disaster. But the markets say, "don't sweat it." I feel like hanging up my market guru hat.

Currencies are calm, commodities are calm. Markets aren't really moving much. Are we in the eye of the storm? I can't see we are. It's almost comical to watch me reading all the news and constantly checking all the markets. Why isn't the market responding? Even US bonds, which will be defaulting, are placid. Yet in the political forum it's chaos.

What does the market know I don't? The market says this issue is a "non issue." How come?

So this is where charts come in. They have the story so far. So you look at the charts and try to fix the story to the facts. This is my take: The upcoming ceiling has made the market fall heavily. That was in September to early October. But the solution to it was not broadly known by those in "the know" until about a week ago. This fix is some kind of Obama governmental edict. If the house and the senate can't sort it, Obama will overrule the process when default is very nearly real. If not we'd be 13,000 on the Dow already. So even as political gridlock is in place, default isn't going to happen.

Alternatively, the market is in denial. It is saying it can't happen. If it is wrong and it does the market will crater. However, it might be a slow collapse like the original credit crunch which began in late 2007 and came to a crescendo in the autumn of 2008, the best part of one year later, and the bottom the following March 2009.

But do all markets fold or is it only the US bond market? Right now it's unfathomable to me. So maybe it is for the market too and we are left scratching our head as the US lumbers towards the abyss. An abyss it can't fall intOOOOOoooooooooooooo............ (pooooooooof).

Meanwhile we are making money and back in the blue by a smidgen.

# Default Crisis Averted – We Were Right Not to Panic

### 17 October 2013

The US default situation certainly looks like a classic lesson for the value investor. We did nothing. Then nothing happened. It would have been easy to bail out last week. How scary does it get when the world's leading economy dashes headlong into a potential economic abyss? But we did nothing. We looked at the stock charts of the world and we saw a calm picture so we said, "well someone knows nothing is going to happen."

The market was right. To listen to the media, disaster was a 50/50 chance, not the one in a thousand the market was predicting.

So we didn't lose 5% of our portfolio's capital by selling only to buy it back. We didn't miss the rally when the market knew things were going to be OK which rallied well before the news. We are still basically in the dark as I write, but the market wasn't. To the aggregate of the market there were no surprises. On the scale of the impact of a default by the US, nothing moved.

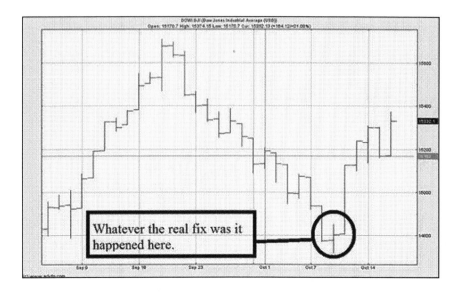

Personally I think Obama had/has an ace in the hole, which was known by the big players. If default was going to happen, he would pull the ace and there would be no default. There are many get out of jail free cards, the easiest being the Fed's ability to buy the debt coming due and to retire the $1.5 trillion of treasury debt it holds and hence bring down the net public debt position. But I don't know, I'm just guessing. Barry doesn't call me up anymore. However, somebody knew something.

This is the core use of charts. It lets you read the past. Sometimes that can be useful.

So we sat "pat" and nothing happened and we saved 5% of our capital. That is another tough aspect to proper investing: remaining calm.

Meanwhile Bank of Ireland is sitting pretty. I will poke that stock around shortly and establish whether we should keep on holding. Ireland is definitely on the up. As a kind of last man standing how high can Bank of Ireland go?

Meanwhile the Fed didn't "taper" last month as expected, but IMHO that was because of the "US default possibility." Now it might taper as this risk event is passed. As such, expect bumps ahead. Nothing new there really.

# Specimen Portfolio Update

## 22 October 2013

Here is an update of the specimen portfolio:

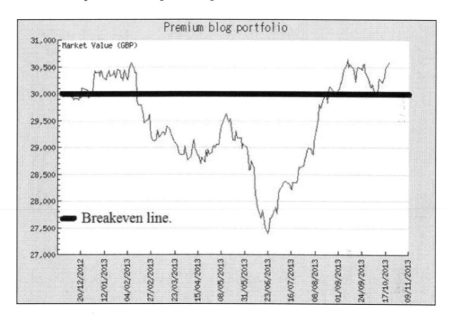

This is equivalent to 2.1% on £17,124 invested at the low bid price including costs of commission/stamp duty of about 3%. So you could tack on 5% or more to cover that and if your trading costs were lower or your unit size higher this cost percentage would shrink.

For example, if you had a £10 a transaction cost, you would save 1.5%. If you bought twice as much, £2,000, at the same cost you would save about 1%.

Costs are very important but I'm choosing £1,000 because most private investors will be buying in these sizes. Also if you need to buy 30 stocks, then the hurdle suddenly goes up from £30,000, to £60,000.

These hurdles are high, but they are piffling in comparison to those endured by people trading their capital, say once a month. You don't have to think about the commission, only the spread times twelve to see how much profit they have to make to even stay still. Of course they don't stay still, they lose their money. So the cost hurdle on this portfolio is high. You can get brokers that will make your costs significantly lower, but I don't want to do that in this portfolio. The idea is to keep it real, not ideal.

This is where the legacy portfolio is at:

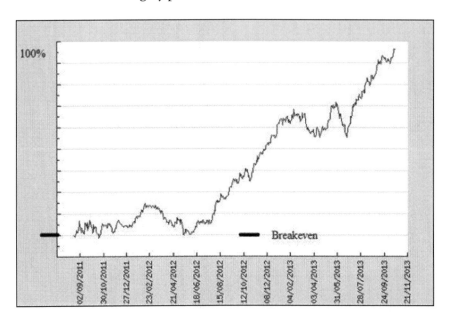

All the constituents of the specimen portfolio go into the legacy portfolio. At some point in the future they will be the same thing. You can see the similar trend, but the legacy portfolio is mature and has different levels of exposure to certain stocks because it has its wide diversification of over 30 shares which allows growing certain companies beyond one equal lump.

Here are the constituents:

| Company | Weighting | Buy | Current bid | P/L |
|---|---|---|---|---|
| Aga Rangemaster | 2.4 | £0.75 | £1.33 | 77.53% |
| Aquarius Plat. | 2.8 | £0.46 | £0.48 | 5.15% |
| Aviva | 2.8 | £3.27 | £4.41 | 34.55% |
| Avocet Mining | 2.2 | £0.82 | £0.15 | -81.63% |
| Avarae | 1.1 | £0.11 | £0.11 | 5.18% |
| Astrazeneca | 1.7 | £29.08 | £31.77 | 9.22% |
| Bank Ireland | 3.5 | £0.11 | 0.258 | 107.07% |
| Cenkos Sec | 1 | £0.76 | £0.96 | 26.63% |
| Creston | 1 | £1.09 | £1.01 | -7.80% |
| Darty | 1.3 | £0.79 | £0.79 | -0.26% |
| Drax | 1 | £5.20 | £6.57 | 26.35% |
| French Cnctn. | 4.1 | £0.26 | £0.31 | 16.54% |
| Fyffes | 1.7 | £0.63 | £0.64 | 2.17% |
| Firstgroup | 6.6 | £1.19 | £1.19 | -0.46% |
| Flybe Grp | 3 | £0.62 | £0.74 | 19.65% |
| Goldplat | 1 | £0.14 | £0.08 | -41.78% |
| Home Retail | 1 | £0.96 | £1.82 | 89.67% |
| Hornby | 0.9 | £0.65 | £0.78 | 20.12% |
| Lamprell | 0.7 | £1.01 | £1.54 | 51.86% |
| Land Secs. | 1.7 | £9.65 | £9.76 | 1.11% |
| Lighthouse Grp. | 1.8 | £0.06 | £0.03 | -49.66% |
| Lloyds | 6.7 | £0.32 | £0.77 | 141.46% |
| Pendragon | 0.8 | £0.13 | £0.36 | 183.46% |
| Promethean | 5.4 | £0.21 | £0.17 | -19.75% |
| Rds A | 1 | £22.82 | £20.81 | -8.84% |
| RM | 6.7 | £0.70 | £1.23 | 74.76% |
| Songbird | 1 | £1.53 | £1.52 | -0.91% |
| SSE | 1.7 | £13.72 | £14.53 | 5.90% |
| Trinity Mirror | 6.8 | £0.45 | £1.27 | 179.73% |
| Total Produce | 1 | £0.58 | £0.64 | 9.70% |
| Tesco | 1 | £3.29 | £3.72 | 13.16% |
| Volex | 1.2 | £1.19 | £1.26 | 5.78% |
| Walker Crips | 1 | £0.39 | £0.41 | 4.33% |

This is the legacy portfolio:

| Company | Weighting | Buy | Current bid | P/L |
|---|---|---|---|---|
| Aquarius Plat. | 1 | £ 0.5135 | £ 0.4825 | -6.03% |
| Avocet Mining | 1 | £ 0.7462 | £ 0.1500 | -79.90% |
| Bank Ireland | 1 | £ 0.1211 | € 0.2580 | 80.60% |
| Cobham | 1 | £ 2.5126 | £ 2.8400 | 13.03% |
| Creston | 1 | £ 1.1038 | £ 1.0050 | -8.95% |
| Darty | 1 | £ 0.8072 | £ 0.7925 | -1.82% |
| French Cnctn. | 1 | £ 0.3178 | £ 0.3050 | -4.03% |
| Fyffes | 1 | £ 0.6335 | £ 0.6400 | 1.03% |
| Firstgroup | 1.7 | £ 1.3046 | £ 1.1890 | -8.86% |
| Flybe Grp | 1 | £ 0.5175 | £ 0.7400 | 42.99% |
| Land Secs. | 1 | £ 9.7621 | £ 9.7600 | -0.02% |
| Promethean | 1 | £ 0.1696 | £ 0.1700 | 0.25% |
| Songbird | 1 | £ 1.5577 | £ 1.5200 | -2.42% |
| Total Produce | 1 | £ 0.5923 | £ 0.6400 | 8.05% |
| Volex | 1 | £ 1.2071 | £ 1.2600 | 4.39% |
| Walker Crips | 1 | £ 0.3991 | £ 0.4100 | 2.74% |

It is interesting to see the impact of buying £1,000 and significantly more of a stock in the two P/Ls. So buying a decent chunk of Walker Crips means 1.59% more profit. For big cap Land Securities it means 1.12%. However there is no good using wishful thinking in the market. The charges are real, even if not optimal. Sadly reality is never "best case," so I'm happy to be conservative.

Who knows: by Christmas we may have turned in a decent performance.

# Newsflash: Northamber

### 24 October 2013

We bought Northamber at 38p.

Net assets over 80p. Couldn't get more than 5,000 shares at 36p. Tried for about a week. Bit the bullet on the price. What a nonsense. More tomorrow.

# The Frustration of Buying Northamber

### 25 October 2013

It's maddening. I wrote recently I wanted to buy a stock but couldn't get a price that made sense. Well yesterday we bought it. The price has come back in theory but it hasn't helped, in practice I had to pay through the nose.

The company is Northamber. In a nutshell it has 80p+ in net assets. We bought it at 38p. Good deal, you'd think. However, the spread is/was insane. The spread has been 33-36p, let's call that 10%. That is an outrage. But it gets worse. Want more than bugger all, it's 38p. It's in the record, as two trades on Thursday, I bought 20,000 shares.

Whooooopy-doooo!

Now the price is 35-38p. Basically the market makers appear to have no shares. They may well be short. (But I doubt it.) As such the market makers are simply strangling the market for this company.

It's a good company, I will make a few coppers, but the process of buying stock is ridiculous, a market malfunction and a massive price gouge. It is also annoying that it is now in the specimen portfolio.

Firstly it might prove hard for some readers to get any if they want to follow on. Secondly it will immediately show up in the portfolio as a thumping loss as the bid offer spread is so huge. Lastly I hate getting ripped off by the market makers full stop. (£7,500 of stock should not take two weeks to buy and should not spike the market.)

However, it is in the portfolio for good reason too. I couldn't buy it for my legacy portfolio and not include it in the specimen portfolio, as over time they are meant to harmonise. It also fits one of my investment rules: if you can't buy it, it is likely a good buy. It is a solid company and a fat discount and there is likely to be a fat profit in it over time.

Nonetheless I'm galled!!!!

As of yesterday, before this buy, we were 3.27% up at an all-time high after piles and piles of costs. However, this buy will chip some of this profit off. Another reason to sigh, but this is the real game. It's long and frustrating, which is why few play it, but ultimately very fruitful.

Meanwhile Promethean spiked on an update, the first positive reaction to an update they've had since forever. I'm already loaded up on this in the legacy portfolio and I'm rubbing my hands with glee in expectations of great things ahead. I'm also trying not to top up on it as I already have enough. Greed is bad.

So I've just entered the Northamber trade and that chops a full 0.8% of our overall portfolio performance. Good job we have a portfolio is all I can say. Now I could cheat the numbers, because I could say, I could have bought £1,000 of this stock at 36p. But you can't, it is now 38p bid. Also I didn't buy £1,000 worth, I bought more, so I didn't get that price either. It would make the numbers look prettier for sure. Instead I'm showing worst case, a buy at 38p plus fat costs.

At 36p and a current price of 36.5p (the mid-price between bid and offer) I could suggest what a genius we are to be making money from the get go but actually we are booking a whopping 10% loss on it instead. So you see how reality can be radically different from slick presentation. We don't need baloney or "slippage" as some call it.

But why put ourselves through all this? Why not just walk away? Well, I'm happy to take some pain to buy 81p of assets for 38p, in a long established company with 60% of its market cap in cash, paying a 2%+ dividend and a management going back forever. The chart looks good.

Classically we should sell out when there is a 30%+ profit on the table, for this is a classic value investment share, but who knows what will pan out exactly. I say this so you can decide for yourself when to bail and not have to wait for me to tell you I'm out.

Apart from the whole process being galling, it is also a window onto the fascinating realities of the margins of the market. In summary, the market is broken for this company. As such the price is wrong, in this case far too low.

By taking the pain and risk, the market presents us a lucrative offer: assets on the cheap. So really I should be happy, but nonetheless I'm not, I'm still galled and disgruntled.

How is that for being ungrateful?

# Portfolio Update

### 29 October 2013

A quick update. We hit over 5% profit on the portfolio today (Monday morning) and came to rest at close at 4.4% up. That's £790.23 profit after entry costs and spread on £18,154 of stock. I can now climb out from underneath a rock and show my face. At these levels I'm an average hedge fund manager.

This is the cost of the spread on our stocks, as of today, to demonstrate how high costs really are:

| Company | Weighting | Buy | Current bid | P/L |
| --- | --- | --- | --- | --- |
| Aquarius Plat. | 1 | £ 0.5135 | £ 0.4825 | -6.03% |
| Avocet Mining | 1 | £ 0.7462 | £ 0.1500 | -79.90% |
| Bank Ireland | 1 | £ 0.1211 | € 0.2580 | 80.60% |
| Cobham | 1 | £ 2.5126 | £ 2.8400 | 13.03% |
| Creston | 1 | £ 1.1038 | £ 1.0050 | -8.95% |
| Darty | 1 | £ 0.8072 | £ 0.7925 | -1.82% |
| French Cnctn. | 1 | £ 0.3178 | £ 0.3050 | -4.03% |
| Fyffes | 1 | £ 0.6335 | £ 0.6400 | 1.03% |
| Firstgroup | 1.7 | £ 1.3046 | £ 1.1890 | -8.86% |
| Flybe Grp | 1 | £ 0.5175 | £ 0.7400 | 42.99% |
| Land Secs. | 1 | £ 9.7621 | £ 9.7600 | -0.02% |
| Promethean | 1 | £ 0.1696 | £ 0.1700 | 0.25% |
| Songbird | 1 | £ 1.5577 | £ 1.5200 | -2.42% |
| Total Produce | 1 | £ 0.5923 | £ 0.6400 | 8.05% |
| Volex | 1 | £ 1.2071 | £ 1.2600 | 4.39% |
| Walker Crips | 1 | £ 0.3991 | £ 0.4100 | 2.74% |

We have climbed this wall too and about 3% of commission and stamp duty. So in effect we are up 10% on the stocks themselves, but as far as the cash result, up about 4%. Don't forget the stamp duty selling. However, if you used a super cheap broker you could pop another 1% onto the current profits. If you bought in size (say £5,000 per share) you could probably save another 0.25-0.5%.

For now as far as profits are concerned we are a junior partner with the government and market makers and the broker. However, things will get better. The longer we hold the lower the costs to profit ratio will be.

We are looking to make 30% on average per average trade, perhaps more, so over time the fiendish costs of entry diminish as a percentage of returns. That's the plan.

But I'm repeating myself.

Here is the chart of performance as if we had a £30,000 portfolio pot:

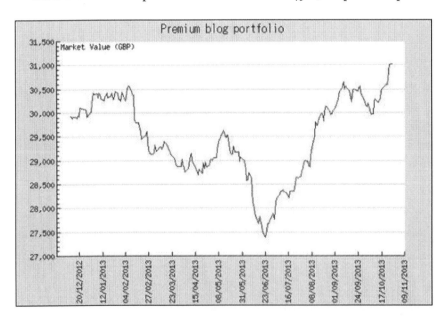

As luck would have it, the graph is showing a higher figure than I believe it should. (Have those crazy ADVFN engineers been at work? I'll get that looked at.)

However, you can clearly see the rollercoaster we've been on. Anyone joining us at the end of July who dived in would be well up (roughly 20%)

and think me a fine fellow. Who knows, if this continues I might make the full idiot to genius transformation. But that is in the lap of the gods.

This is the performance of the specimen portfolio:

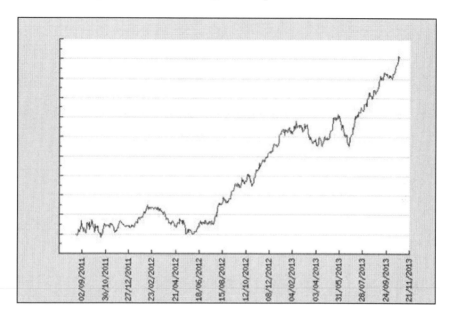

This rally really is eye-popping. Long may it continue. However, after we've taken the rough with the smooth a few times we will really see where we are. My target continues to be a profit of 25%, but anything over 15% is more than respectable and anything over 25% is good fortune.

However, the market will have to motor to get up anywhere near 15%, but if it can do 20% in four months almost anything can happen.

# Which Way is the Market Heading Now?

### 5 November 2013

I say this a lot. All you need to know in the market is whether it is going up or going down.

So which way for us? On the face of it the market should be near its top. The FTSE is at, and around, all-time highs. It's a safe bet to say, "It's going to fall." However I don't think it is.

In any event we don't really care because the long run deals with most corrections and makes them irrelevant. Unless we thought a crash was imminent, there is no need to worry about a slump. Slumps happen and happen often, but there is no immediate risk of a crash.

I think that this time is different, different that is from the last twelve years. (Those of you who know this meme should recognise how bullish it is for me to challenge it.) I think we are in a bull market for several years. This is another reason why we are not going to sweat the twists and turns of this bull market.

Of course, that's no reason to be complacent, but I do think the chances of a massive multiyear rally are not a fool's musings. The next few years will be historic for the European and US markets. (However I do reserve the right to change my mind.)

Meanwhile in the US, a situation in the markets is developing that to me is a classic investment opportunity. Firstly, I'm no US trading guru. The US market is different, more violent and definitely bi-polar. However, this situation gives me a chance to explain before the event a classic contrarian situation. I might be right or wrong, but foresight is about foresight, not hindsight.

The company is Blackberry – Research in Motion as it used to be called. The motion, however, has been down. You couldn't find a more reviled tech company. On the face of it, it is a dead company. You can go reading the media and you won't hear a good word for the company. Apple and

Android has killed it. Blackberry is now $6 a share, half what it was a few weeks back. Down from $225 in 2007, $75 in 2010.

I have just one thing that says it's a buy. 72 million subscribers. At three and a bit billion of market cap that is roughly $50 a subscriber. A cable company version of subscriber value is $2,000. You can run the numbers of many subscription businesses and a subscriber is worth hugely more than $50. $1,000 a subscriber is run of the mill. That would put Blackberry at $70 a share. So the subscriber base is a massive plus.

Then there are the massive write downs. These recent "kitchen sink" write offs give management lots of room for future profits.

But the home run is, New Management. Not only has the new management raised $750m, it is not the old management. I hope that makes sense. Even a chimp that did nothing but eat bananas in the corner suite would do better than the previous group. So any new group will be positive at least for a year or two. The new management group contains what looks like the right stuff too. That's a plus, plus.

Put all this together and Blackberry is a classic turnaround situation. Like Pace, like Trinity Mirror, like Flybe etc. It has all the field marks.

I could of course be wrong, it might work like this in the UK, but not the US, but if you are going to try and trade the US, this is the kind of gift horse contrarian situation that begs to be tested. So I will.

Meanwhile the portfolios are futtling around, so not much to report.

# Investing is Easy – but Difficult

## 7 November 2013

I can get guilty about my blog. Sometime I feel I should write more. However, that would risk me burbling empty musings. Even though the blog has stock tips in it, I'm really trying to help people learn how to invest properly so they can do it themselves.

Investing is not hard at a trivial level but the fact people don't do it attests that it is in fact very difficult.

Whether investing is hard or easy, in any event hyperactivity is lethal. Yet sitting pat on your positions for weeks and months can be nerve wracking. How do you tell if the market is about to go horribly wrong?

The thing most people would do to get a feeling for the state of the market is to look at the FTSE 100 chart. Does the index look good or scary?

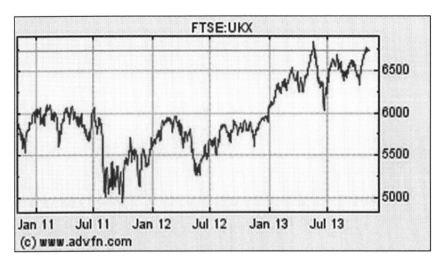

I would look at this chart and ask does the chart look like it is trending in a way that is stable. When you look at this chart you see periods of smoothness in the day to day changes and periods of craziness as per July 2011. This is telling you a story.

Craziness is volatility. Volatility is a measure of market uncertainty. The crazier the chart swings the less certainty the combined players in the market have of what is going on and what will happen next. If the market is smooth there is certainty. So smooth rises are a very reassuring sign that good market times are ahead.

However, the FTSE's day to day trading has all sorts of rubbish in it. It is not a pure stock index. It is only shares but those shares are not simply traded because of their companies. The index is used to hedge things like commodities, interest rates, forex rates and foreign markets like the US, Japan and Germany. So if oil goes mad it will mess with the FTSE 100. Why? Because investors might want to be long pound, so will buy the FTSE 100 as a proxy for pound versus dollar.

There are also FTSE 100 ETFs and more interesting and noisy: FTSE Futures and options.

People using the FTSE as a proxy fogs up the picture of the equity market's trend. These hedgers are like babes at a church service, they inject an element of random chaos and confusion. So in a perfect world we would want to watch an index with no noise injected into it. An index without a futures or options contract dragging it around... And here it is:

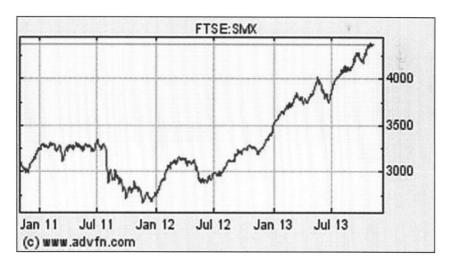

It's the FTSE small Cap index. Notice how smooth it is.

Here they are side by side:

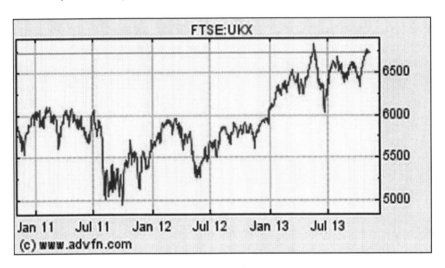

I use the small cap index to guide me on the general market trend as it does not get smudged about by many external factors. If you look at the FTSE 100 and ask yourself "where is the market going" you might be left "umming and ahing." The small cap chart says, "I'm going up in a straight line." That's a pretty good indicator to have. As such the small cap index is your favourite tipster, a key secret weapon to tell you whether the trend is your friend, or about to bite.

Currently it is looking pretty good.

# Flybe to the Moon

### 12 November 2013

Flybe is up again today and as I write we are up 122%. In the old days as a value investor I'd have sold yesterday. These days, however, I let these situations ride and rise. Here is why:

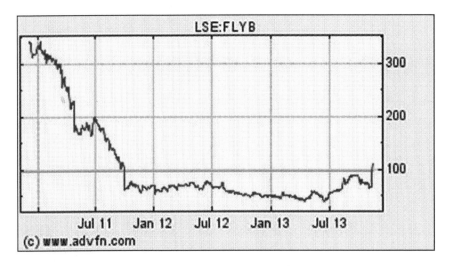

Flybe floated in 2010 at over 300p. There has been little or no dilution. Why wouldn't they recover fully? This is a bold statement, but even half way is 150p. Flybe would be nearer £10 a share if it was valued like Ryanair or Easyjet on a sales basis.

So time to stay greedy for now. As I started to write we were also 9.5% up overall but it's pulled back to 8.8%. That's almost respectable.

# Flybe – The Missing Post

### 13 November 2013

Because of the vagaries of the internet, yesterday a blog post got lost in the ether. It was meant for Tuesday morning, instead only the follow up went up. Below is the blog that went AWOL.

I'm in Japan, where Abenomics is boosting the economy there strongly, but the fight against deflation still rages. However, the morning of today is – because of the time difference – still yesterday in Europe, so timing work between the UK and Japan is a bit goofy for my newsletter.

I was kicking myself last night, having left the office, because my work couldn't go live. Then I realised, the key thing is, timing isn't important. We own the stock, we will be holding the stock. The important thing is why, not when. "You can't time the market," they say and that is generally the case, so it's important that you don't have to. The efficient market covered my arse, AGAIN.

So here is the delayed post:

Well, Flybe gave us a nice present today. Up 44%. Flybe is a classic as far as I'm concerned; it will be a big win for us.

This is where you might ask, "why not buy more?" The answer is, "I might be wrong."

Hardly anyone who has a car accident will say, "ah it was my fault." Likewise, many investors have never made an investment mistake in their life, even if profits escape them.

I make mistakes all the time. It is inevitable.

There is a whole theoretical framework for how to invest. These include gamblers ruin, which says, bet too hard and you will be wiped out even if you are mainly wrong; and, of course, portfolio theory. If you wanted to go digging you should look at the "Kelly formula," from which you can be optimal in your position size.

However, let's not knock ourselves out. If we like a share, we buy it. We don't fill our boots, we never put ourselves in a position of having to worry about being wrong.

If Flybe went bust, we would not be too badly affected, in the same way Avocet is a pain. Even though Avocet turned out badly we are still up 7.5%. This is not a shoddy return, especially when there is roughly another 4% of costs covered, equating to a 11.5% return. 7.5% is respectable. We will double our money every ten years at that rate. However, I'm not too happy with it. 15% is my target and who knows where we will be by year end.

Here is some fun with numbers:

While we started this portfolio at the beginning of the year, we haven't been investing the whole time. If you weight the portfolio by time we bought on average on 17 May 2013, roughly six months ago. As such we have a 15% net annualised profit. However, this is more an example of accounting tricks than reality.

Right now we are up £1,361 on the £18,154 we have in the market. So now I don't look stupid anymore, four months after looking a dunce. This is the core lesson of my blog. Consistent stock picking using a diversified portfolio is a recipe for investment success and long term wealth building.

It's still early days, but after a random rocky start, the portfolio is starting to get traction. Here is my performance chart:

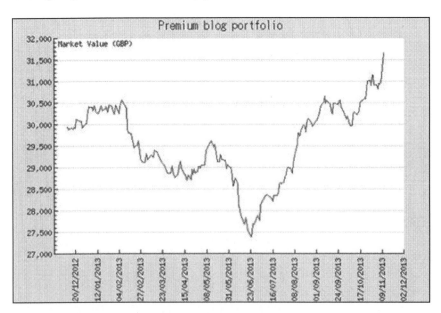

Meanwhile the legacy portfolio is up over 100% now.

# Flybe – It's Complicated

### 13 November 2013

Well, well, the Flybe situation "thickens." The recent share surge seems likely to be a successful attempt by the company's broker to unload the late owner's majority shareholding to the city. As I read it, off the cuff, the majority shareholder was the family trust of the late Jack Walker, owner of Blackburn Rovers etc and founder of Flybe.

This is how this kind of thing can go. New management wants to step things up. Old passive shareholders would rather like to not have all its eggs in one basket. New management zips around the city to whip up some institutional interest for a placing. Old shareholder informed something might be possible. Old shareholder names its price, "take me out in one go at 'the right price' or I'll niggle you to death and be a loose holder dribbling stock into the market." Brokers and management get a premium price because that way the institutions can get a fat slab of stock and be in for the ride that the new management promises.

If that is what has happened that's good news indeed... But you can never know... it's a cheap stock, so the price should rise over time.

It's better to keep it simple.

# Portfolio Suddenly Shows a Loss Thanks to Volex

### 14 November 2013

The market is getting lively. Just as I was enjoying a nice little profit on the open suddenly bang, there is a one per cent plus loss showing. Volex blew up! This is a cheap company going through ructions.

CEOs really shouldn't start off their statements with, "Volex is a fundamentally sound business..." It begs the question, "who said Volex wasn't a sound business?"

They have killed their dividend and have about a year's cash at the current rate of cash burn.

The report is full of corporate speak gobbledegook too. In a way this is good. I prefer a company to be cheap because of management confusion than anything else. And typos:

> "– Approximately one third of Group revenue and to be headquartered in Silicon Valley, California;"

Now these things happen, but a company with £500m in sales and advisers should be able to catch that. Likely no one wanted to look hard at this statement. So this company is officially a mess. As I have written, the company has jumped from a low of 81p to 89p and is down -21%.

Meanwhile Flybe has popped 5% and helped to fill in the divot made by Volex. Such are the joys of a portfolio. Back at Flybe, we find from the trade record that the institutions bought in at 70p. They include Schroders, Aberforth Smaller Companies, Polar Capital European Forager Fund and Quantum Partners. "Lucky" old them.

The legacy portfolio exploded today. Trinity Mirror's Interim Management statement went down a storm, spiking the stock 12%. I really hate holding out for more profit than I already have on this, 265%, but the lesson of the past is hang on to fat profits in recovery situations. Having bought Cape at 13.5p and sold it at 34p and then watched it go to 285p, the lesson is let a profit run and run. Later I bought Cape at 30p and sold it at 200, not bad, but it then went to 600p. As Captain Kurtz said, "Oh the horror."

So I'm hanging onto TNI because if it was DMGT (Daily Mail Group) it would be 450p. That would be nice. I do not expect my resolve to hold out anywhere near that far, but I'm focusing on the upside for now.

# Don't Buy Mining Shares. No, Really, Don't!

### 15 November 2013

I have to admit I want to throw £500 down the drain and buy Talvivaara for the sheer hell of it. The history of this company pushes the bounds of incredulity. (Excuse my use of irony.) It's trading at 3p as I write; it was 600p a couple of years ago.

I would urge all my readers to read their RNS since day 1. This is how you can invest in a company and turn your wealth into ashes. Can this story be anything but a confection from beginning to end?

I wrote a book about mining fraud called *The Twain Maxim* but in reality my fantasy is much more credible than the stories that litter the London market these last few years.

Talking of which, Avocet has just announced it has bought back its hedges. Just how these were made to be so loss-making is not a question worth bothering with as most gold miners have somehow managed to get their mining costs up to between $1,300-$2,000 an ounce.

Oh look TALV is now 3.3p, I'd have made 10%... let's sell out, at least in our mind's eye!

Meanwhile AVM is up 7.8%.

I will probably tattoo my arm with the following: Don't buy mining shares, you can't rely on their announcements, presentations or reported facts.

Trade them... you might as well go to Monaco and play roulette... Russian roulette.

# Status Update

### 19 November 2013

We are sat at roughly 6% profit. This is the current lay of the land:

| Holding | | Quantity | TotalCost | Avg.Price | Price | Cur Value | P/L | % |
|---|---|---|---|---|---|---|---|---|
| LSE:FLYB | Flybe Grp | 2000 | 1035.03 | 0.52 | 0.98 | 1960 | 924.97 | 89.37 |
| LSE:BKIR | Bank Ireland | 8529 | 1032.5 | 0.12 | 0.27 | 1920.01 | 887.51 | 85.96 |
| LSE:FCCN | French Cnctn. | 3200 | 1017 | 0.32 | 0.4 | 1280 | 263 | 25.86 |
| LSE:TOT | Total Produce | 1760 | 1042.51 | 0.59 | 0.71 | 1249.6 | 207.09 | 19.86 |
| LSE:PRW | Promethean | 6000 | 1017.45 | 0.17 | 0.2 | 1185 | 167.55 | 16.47 |
| LSE:FFY | Fyffes | 1625 | 1029.37 | 0.63 | 0.71 | 1145.63 | 116.26 | 11.29 |
| LSE:WCW | Walker Crips | 2600 | 1037.54 | 0.4 | 0.44 | 1144 | 106.46 | 10.26 |
| LSE:COB | Cobham | 398 | 1000 | 2.51 | 2.69 | 1070.22 | 70.22 | 0.07 |
| LSE:DRTY | Darty | 1276 | 1030 | 0.81 | 0.86 | 1094.17 | 64.17 | 0.06 |
| LSE:LAND | Land Secs. | 105 | 1025.02 | 9.76 | 9.61 | 1009.05 | -15.97 | -0.02 |
| LSE:SBD | Songbird | 665 | 1035.84 | 1.56 | 1.51 | 1000.83 | -35.01 | -0.03 |
| LSE:FGP | Firstgroup | 1297 | 1692.07 | 1.3 | 1.18 | 1529.16 | -162.91 | -0.10 |
| LSE:CRE | Creston | 950 | 1048.62 | 1.1 | 0.97 | 919.13 | -129.5 | -12.35 |
| LSE:NAR | Northamber | 2632 | 1030 | 0.39 | 0.34 | 894.88 | -135.12 | -13.12 |
| LSE:AQP | Aquarius Plat. | 2000 | 1026.9 | 0.51 | 0.42 | 840 | -186.9 | -18.20 |
| LSE:VLX | Volex | 851 | 1027.21 | 1.21 | 0.95 | 804.2 | -223.02 | -21.71 |
| LSE:AVM | Avocet Mining | 1377 | 1027.5 | 0.75 | 0.15 | 206.55 | -820.95 | -79.90 |
| | Total | | £18,154.56 | | | £19,252 | £1,097 | 6.05% |
| | Cash | | £ 11,851.44 | | | | | |
| | Market value of current holdings | | £ 19,252.42 | | | | | |
| | Market Value | | £ 31,103.86 | | | | | |

This is ranked in order of heroes and villains. They are actually all the same. Hopefully in various states of recovery, though I admit to thinking Avocet will never come good. However, you never know. Risk = reward, risk = uncertainty, uncertainty = reward. This sounds unlikely but it amounts to the market paying you to take a risk and it pays to the tune of your appetite for risk. Sadly that only works when there is no skulduggery and of course there is quite a lot of that about. Even so this should be compensated for too, but I must say I'm a little sceptical when we get too far into the bad lands of risk.

One thing about risk is, it must be risk. At the margin of the markets there is no risk, only certainty, certainty of loss. We try to stay clear of those but we will make mistakes.

Meanwhile I'm watching RSA and Petrofac. RSA is especially enticing but to be clear, I hate their long term chart. There is something wrong with it, it's too spiky and range bound. There is nothing quite like it in the whole market. This is a red flag for me.

RSA v Lgen:

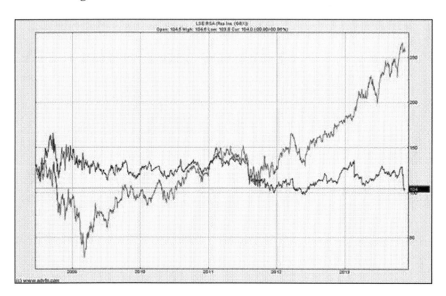

I'm interested in Petrofac as I have it down as a takeover candidate but whenever I dip my toe into it, I take a loss. This stock too doesn't feel right, so off in my punting account it has me nursing a loss.

I don't talk much about my punting account because it is there to crash and burn. Its success in the last year is down to the big rally we are in, titanic and dangerous leverage and a series of huge but lucky punts on the Nikkei and euro. I'm having such a punt on Nikkei long right now.

I've taken my original stake out now and as much again, so I can say I doubled my money in this account (even if it did take nearly ten years of fiddling around) so the remaining four stakes are there to continue the process of keeping in touch with the wild arsed trading community that loves to go all in. In the end they are ADVFN's "meat and potatoes" so it behoves me to ride that rollercoaster and let my winnings ride. It's a kind of masochism.

The market feels kind of expensive right now, but I'm just sitting and letting things develop. I might do some housekeeping shortly, but I'm taking it slow as sloth pays premiums.

Who knew?

# Bubbles are the Ultimate High Risk Trade

### 21 November 2013

Most people that get into investing in shares do so naïvely. They join the game thinking of trading to win, and buying ten baggers and other such dreams. Most blow their money fast and leave.

I often wonder if people are so reckless when they start out because they are used to automatically getting paid for work and are unfamiliar with losing. In most people's experience, if you lose you get reimbursed through insurance or compensation. Actually flat out losing your money is not how most of the world works for people in the modern world. Where the hell is mummy when you lose your shirt on a crazy stock? By the time most beginners realise more caution is needed, it's too late.

Meanwhile, for these unfettered high risk traders the ultimate attraction is the bubble stock. They don't think it's a bubble, of course, but the last thing they would do is look at the company's financial figures to check for a sane valuation. After all, everyone says it's going to the moon, it is on its way and nothing can go wrong. Sadly, bubbles are only bubbles after they burst.

So what does a bubble look like? It's all in the charts. Remember, charts tell you about the past and in the case of a bubble, a bubble in progress is a bubble spotted and hopefully a bust avoided.

The latest bubble out there was/is Tesla, though it has probably seen its bubble burst.

However, its current stock chart perfectly displays what a bubble looks like:

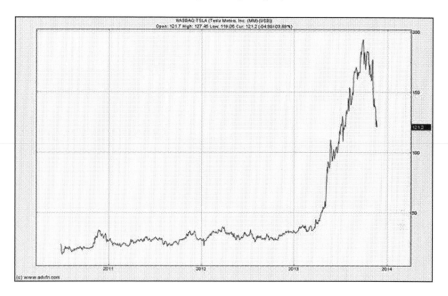

If you ever see a chart like this, you are looking at a bubble. Remember it well, because if you are unlucky enough to be holding when the bubble bursts you can seriously hurt your capital. Unless, of course, you are diversified, which our portfolio is increasingly.

In the market right now I'm feeling hesitant. The FTSE looks bearish. However, I believe Japan is about to go ballistic and this will blow through European and US markets and maybe set off another stage to this rally. We have had an excellent run in the last few weeks, so a hiatus or even a correction would be all part of the flow.

Meanwhile I'm on the lookout for a new stock. So far, nothing grabs me.

# The Market Feels Unsteady

**26 November 2013**

The market feels pretty shaky to me, but every time I think this, it rockets up. I did cut out my Ni225 trade earlier this morning though, as you can't afford many surprises if you use leverage. But we aren't here to gamble.

We are 6.2% up.

Hopefully my inertia will let some of you saving investors catch up with the current selection, but I must say I'd like to buy some shares but instead I must suffer ennui. So the markets are matching most people's investing reality. It has to go slowly.

Normally I'd be looking to buy shares like De La Rue that dumped 10-20% but these haven't been bouncing quickly, instead they simply languish for an indeterminate time. I use DLAR as an example because they bounced back today a good month after their fall. Dead cats no longer bounce, it seems, but instead wait for weeks before leaping up.

Meanwhile, for something worth writing about I'm left looking at Promethean. To me the chart looks full of imminent promise. I have, however, been wrong for a long time on this stock, so we will see. There is a reasonable chance the stock will move, but that's per my personal charting ideas.

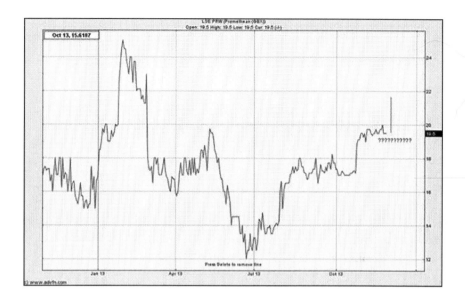

But we will see.

UK and US markets are toppy, but in a new era, with markets rigged by QE, you just have to hang tough.

# Not Much Action Right Now

### 2 December 2013

It's hard to write about stock picking when there is not much to pick. We could be trying to play nonsense stocks like Talvivaara but that way madness lies.

The correct way to go about that in my book is to open a spread betting account. I use IG Index a lot because their platform is solid. Drop in some money that you are prepared to lose. Then let off your gambling steam in there well away from your investments. Don't mix the two, because it will pollute your results and you will soon lose sight of your profits and losses which is disastrous for your motivation.

You will likely blow your gambling pot pretty quickly. If not, well done. However, your investing portfolio will bumble along growing and growing. At some point your investing portfolio will be large and your punting account still meagre.

Trading is hard, investing is easy. When you can make fat returns on your investing you might be ready to trade but I think you will see that starting with trading is doomed to failure.

Last night I went long pound v euro and I'm on the brink of jumping long on the Nikkei again if it breaks free, but I'm just flirting. Trading profits are temporary.

There are three types of games according to theory: zero sum, negative sum and positive sum.

**Zero sum game:** This means for every winner there is a loser. It is betting on a heads or tails coin flip game. There is nothing to be lost or gained in this game in the long run. Players are going nowhere. Why play this game?

**Negative sum game:** Every time players play the net result is less than they started with. Let's say it's like a World War. In the end everyone loses; the longer the game goes on the greater the losses. Only a genius can actually win, and probably not much, because the available pool to win from is being drained as the game goes on. This is how all gambling games work, and almost all markets. (This is why traders lose.) The only one to win is the mechanism draining the game, ie a broker or in a casino, the house. The rake or commission is the negative drain. You cannot win this game. Do not play.

**Positive sum game:** As the game is played so the potential winning pot rises. Economic competition is an example, or farming. As the game is played resources come to the game and add to the winning pot. Everyone can win at this game unless they are hopelessly outmatched by the competition. This is the stock market. Companies grow. You can play this game and win. However, the positive sum is important. If it's 7% a year, then you must spend less than 7% playing or you tip the game negative. This is why trading fails and investing wins. We play this game.

Trading = 7% – many commissions & trading costs = a significant loss

Investing over three years = 7%+7%+7% – one commission & trading costs = a decent profit

So trading and investing are different. However, investing can be very boring, but that is why it has to pay in cash not entertainment.

# Dead Quiet

### 10 December 2013

I'm not sure how I'm meant to write an exciting blog when the market is dull. It is dead out there. It has been my observation that the UK pretty much stops in the city and at the top echelons of business on 5 December. This has been the case as long back as I can recall.

It's a poor show in my opinion. It used to be that the slacker elite would return on 15 January but in the last ten years or so the pace of business seems to remain low till early February which leaves me believing that the real return date is not until the second month. It seems school holidays are holidays for all and the summer appears Exeat for all the top managers and their bosses.

So if you are serious about building a business you are left with only about half the year to do deals. This goes for the city deals too, of course. This is why I spend so much time in the US and Asia – you have to get about if you want to keep busy.

Sadly, the US is going the same way too. The old idea of ten days holiday a year is fast eroding. As America syncs up with socialist Europe, work life balances for the rich are getting as important as fat pensions for public employees and hand-outs for the lumpen.

Thus spake the grumpy speculator.

Let's hope the Indian and Chinese soon suffer the same malaise.

So here are the status of the two portfolios, the legacy and the specimen:

| Holding | Legacy | Size | Avg.Price | Price | % |
|---|---|---|---|---|---|
| LSE:TNI | Trinity Mirror | 7 | £0.45 | £1.86 | 309.68% |
| LSE:LLOY | Lloyds | 7 | £0.32 | £0.79 | 147.69% |
| LSE:BKIR | Bank Ireland | 3 | £0.11 | 0.259 | 105.21% |
| LSE:AGA | Aga Rangemaster | 2 | £0.75 | £1.52 | 104.00% |
| LSE:HOME | Home Retail | 1 | £0.96 | £1.90 | 97.81% |
| LSE:CNKS | Cenkos Sec | 1 | £0.76 | £1.37 | 80.72% |
| LSE:RM. | RM | 7 | £0.70 | £1.10 | 57.28% |
| LSE:FLYB | Flybe Grp | 3 | £0.62 | £0.96 | 55.22% |
| LSE:DRX | Drax | 1 | £5.20 | £7.83 | 50.69% |
| LSE:LAM | Lamprell | 1 | £1.01 | £1.46 | 44.19% |
| LSE:FCCN | French Cnctn. | 4 | £0.26 | £0.37 | 42.33% |
| LSE:AV. | Aviva | 3 | £3.27 | £4.34 | 32.47% |
| LSE:HRN | Hornby | 1 | £0.65 | £0.84 | 28.59% |
| LSE:DRTY | Darty | 1 | £0.79 | £0.99 | 23.97% |
| LSE:AZN | Astrazeneca | 2 | £29.08 | £34.60 | 18.97% |
| LSE:TOT | Total Produce | 1 | £0.58 | £0.67 | 15.27% |
| LSE:WCW | Walker Crips | 1 | £0.39 | £0.43 | 9.42% |
| LSE:FFY | Fyffes | 2 | £0.63 | £0.68 | 8.56% |
| LSE:SBD | Songbird | 1 | £1.53 | £1.61 | 4.96% |
| LSE:TSCO | Tesco | 1 | £3.29 | £3.34 | 1.67% |
| LSE:LAND | Land Secs. | 2 | £9.65 | £9.43 | -2.31% |
| LSE:FGP | Firstgroup | 7 | £1.19 | £1.17 | -2.39% |
| LSE:VLX | Volex | 1 | £1.19 | £1.15 | -3.66% |
| LSE:SSE | SSE | 2 | £13.72 | £13.15 | -4.15% |
| LSE:AVR | Avarae | 1 | £0.11 | £0.10 | -4.17% |
| LSE:RDSA | Rds A | 1 | £22.82 | £20.86 | -8.60% |
| LSE:PRW | Promethean | 5 | £0.21 | £0.19 | -10.31% |
| LSE:NAR | Northamber | 1 | £0.39 | £0.34 | -11.75% |
| LSE:AQP | Aquarius Plat. | 3 | £0.46 | £0.40 | -12.28% |
| LSE:CRE | Creston | 1 | £1.09 | £0.85 | -22.02% |
| LSE:LGT | Lighthouse Grp. | 2 | £0.06 | £0.04 | -45.79% |
| LSE:GDP | Goldplat | 1 | £0.14 | £0.07 | -52.69% |
| LSE:AVM | Avocet Mining | 2 | £0.82 | £0.14 | -83.16% |

| Holding | Specimen | Size | Avg.Price | Price | % |
|---|---|---|---|---|---|
| LSE:FLYB | Flybe Grp | 1 | £0.52 | £0.96 | 85.50% |
| LSE:BKIR | Bank Ireland | 1 | £0.12 | 0.259 | 78.96% |
| LSE:DRTY | Darty | 1 | £0.81 | £0.99 | 22.03% |
| LSE:FCCN | French Cnctn. | 1 | £0.32 | £0.37 | 17.21% |
| LSE:TOT | Total Produce | 1 | £0.59 | £0.67 | 13.53% |
| LSE:PRW | Promethean | 1 | £0.17 | £0.19 | 12.04% |
| LSE:WCW | Walker Crips | 1 | £0.40 | £0.43 | 7.75% |
| LSE:FFY | Fyffes | 1 | £0.63 | £0.68 | 7.35% |
| LSE:COB | Cobham | 1 | £2.51 | £2.63 | 4.63% |
| LSE:SBD | Songbird | 1 | £1.56 | £1.60 | 2.56% |
| LSE:LAND | Land Secs. | 1 | £9.76 | £9.43 | -3.40% |
| LSE:VLX | Volex | 1 | £1.21 | £1.15 | -4.93% |
| LSE:FGP | Firstgroup | 2 | £1.30 | £1.17 | -10.62% |
| LSE:NAR | Northamber | 1 | £0.39 | £0.34 | -13.12% |
| LSE:AQP | Aquarius Plat. | 1 | £0.51 | £0.40 | -21.61% |
| LSE:CRE | Creston | 1 | £1.10 | £0.85 | -22.99% |
| LSE:AVM | Avocet Mining | 1 | £0.75 | £0.14 | -81.57% |

The legacy portfolio is in good shape. Having been opened through 2011-2012 it's about 115% up including significant levels of profits taken:

And the specimen is still loitering around 5% profit. I'm somewhat disappointed even taking into account the fat costs, but really it won't be till this time next year that we can call a judgement and even then it might be another year or so before the true colours of a diversified portfolio begin to show through. Investing is a long game.

You can see how the legacy and the specimen charts are roughly the same. If you zoom into the relevant dates you can see them move in similar ways. The stronger performance of the legacy portfolio can be put down to its overweight positions in what the investment banks would call "conviction stocks." They are the ones held in multiple size, like Trinity Mirror. It has been the performances of those stocks that have catapulted the legacy portfolio.

However, you need a full portfolio of about 30 stocks before you can start fattening certain positions, as if you don't wait till then, a mistake picking a conviction stock can be horrendous to the investment pot.

As it is, these "conviction stock" positions are horribly overweight now, so I should really chop them back. But I've been focusing on running winners over the last few years and am actually aggressively trying not to sell conviction stocks that suddenly make the turn from "dog" to star. I hate running my profits, but in certain markets you have to.

In the old days I would religiously dump shares that made 30% and rotate into new opportunities, however with the dearth of companies I like and the tendency of shares to run and run I'm sticking to my guns instead.

The market is not about being right all the time, but being flexible enough to be able to adapt to being wrong and still persist to capture the profits of being on balance more right than in error.

You know you are bored when you start to wax philosophical. Meanwhile we sit and wait for the Santa Rally that probably won't appear this year thanks to the strong autumn rally.

Roll on 2014.

# Diversification is the Way to Go

### 12 December 2013

It's often overlooked but keeping track of a portfolio is a priority. Rather than flashy trading techniques, financial hygiene is important. You have to do consistent housekeeping on your investments. Money has a habit of evaporating if you don't give it attention.

Assets are like nice mohair jumpers – leave them lying around and before you know it a moth has eaten it full of holes, or worse someone shrinks it to a size only your wife can wear.

So today I was keen to buy First Group. It looks terrific from a technical and value point of view. A quick compare and contrast to Stagecoach is enough to get me excited, and with recent history taken into account it would make a great buy. But we already have a pile of it. So we have to hold off. We have enough.

Having too much of a single stock is bad. The more you concentrate your portfolio, the bigger the risk of a bone crunching loss. Big losses put people off investing. So in practice too much of a given stock risks putting the investor off investing for life. Many people suffer this fate and are thereafter doomed to keep their money on deposit at the bank for little return.

The extreme end of buying too much stock is risking so called "gambler ruin." Simply put, if you were to put all your money in one stock then flip it into another, then another, one day your latest selection will unexpectedly go bust and you will lose all your money. That's a hard fact, that at some point you will make a big mistake and lose the lot. It's just a matter of when.

With 30 stocks this can't happen. You could suffer a 50% crash, you could lose 30% of the companies in your portfolio in one slump, but even still, the years will see your investment portfolio swell. That's the core value of diversification.

That's why you should always aim for diversification even as your successes and failures pull your portfolio out of shape and unbalance it.

But don't be too fussed and just push gently towards keeping your portfolio balanced over the years. With investing time is on your side, there is never any rush to do much.

# Why Buy RSA?

### 13 December 2013

Small is not beautiful in investing. Today we bought into RSA. It's off 18%. Its Irish outfit is imploding and is bound to be a scandal. RSA's CEO for ten years has quit. The dividend is going to be cut by the looks of it.

I buy this stuff. Why? The trade is: Will this company go bust?? If not, it will recover. My bet is RSA will wobble a lot but in a year or two be back where it was before these problems came out. That's approximately 50p on 80p from here. There might even be a nice dividend stream along the way.

However, I probably should wait. For the legacy portfolio this will be the first buy, perhaps the initial one of several. For the specimen portfolio it will be the one and only.

You can't time the market, so on balance it shouldn't make any difference, but being stuck with buying only a single lump of such a position feels more nerve-racking in the specimen portfolio than for the bigger legacy portfolio which will happily plough in if the price falls more.

But anyway we are in. However, I have a fat reservation and it's this: The long term chart:

This is five years. That's a very unnatural looking chart. You might not see what I see, but after many many years of chart watching you develop an eye for what is expected and what is wonky.

This is Legal and General:

Aviva:

These are proper charts. They have proper ranges and proper volatility. RSA looks contrived.

It was the weirdness of the RSA long term chart that has put me off RSA as it suggested an invisible hand had been at work. Invisible hands are not our friends. But buying shares is about taking risks. So after this faux pas at RSA, we are betting on a successful – if painful – comeback.

This is why we have a portfolio. We are prepared to be wrong, able to take a loss and therefore about to position ourselves for the profits of buying when other are panicking (rightly or otherwise) to sell.

# May The Odds Ever Be In Your Favour

### 16 December 2013

I sold the RSA at open today. I very rarely do this. It looks like trading and I suppose it is but we went in to invest and have been given an opportunity to take a supernormal return.

The market is all about risk; risk versus reward. Risk and reward are all time based. If the time element is massively in your favour you should bank your profits. This is such a case.

You can stand by the cliff edge for a minute with almost no chance of falling to your death. Do it every day for ten years and you will likely fall off at some point. You will be extremely unlucky for a short time in the long term, so be careful to stay back from disaster.

The opposite is: if you are extremely lucky in the short term, bank it. This is the case here.

This is not value investing. However, here is the theory behind this move. There is always a horizon of profit that if you cross you should bank. It is like taking a bet with the odds in your favour. When it happens you should take the bet, bank the profit and keep taking new bets on the same basis.

Grossly speaking, the expected range a company moves is a function of the square root of the time. Here is a very crude exposition. Statistically, shares will move, as time passes, within the zone of the blue lines. This is subject to all sorts of other variables, like for example interference from reality.

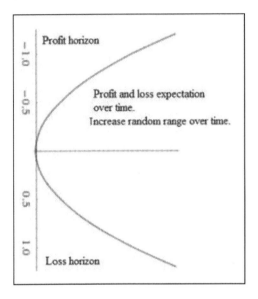

These range horizons give you a steer as to what can be expected. If your performance goes out of these boundaries something is up. A consequence is, if you are hoping for a profit of say 30% in three years from a share, but you get 12% on day one, you can think about banking your profit immediately, because you have got the lion's share for little exposure risk.

Indicative maths:

30% profit in three years
30% profit in 1,000 days
1,000 days roughly 30 squared
30%/30 = 1% a day

So we got roughly 12% and we bailed. As I write the price has dropped 5% from where we sold, so perhaps others in the city are thinking the same. However, the decision is not all maths.

As I said in my last piece I'm not totally comfortable with RSA, so an unexpected bounce back is another unsettling feature; I like my shares to behave themselves in line with how companies respond in such conditions. Only one in twenty companies make an intraday comeback like this.

Anyway, I'm afraid of wittering too much narrative. We buy good companies gone bad, so we bought. It bounced back fast and we grabbed a fat profit because we were happier with the money than the position. Too much rationalising can be counterproductive.

If RSA falls back in the future we will think about re-entry.

It made me chuckle because old style brokers don't charge a selling commission if it's a quick trade, as an encouragement to speculate your face off. How kind of them! So we saved an exit commission.

So we bought 1,226 RSA shares for £1,027.5 and sold them for £1,145.51 after all costs. This leaves us just shy of a 12% profit.

...back to investing dammit!

# I've Got the Portfolio Blues

### 17 December 2013

Damn and blast. I've got a problem with the portfolio. If I was a little slick I'd make the most of it to bump up the returns on the specimen portfolio, but that's against the whole ethos of what I'm trying to do here. To keep it real I'm trying to be more than fair in running the returns of the portfolio:

- I'm taking all the costs on the chin in the portfolio.
- I'm not using the cheapest broker option.
- I'm not valuing the portfolio at the "current price" but at the "bid price" which is the one you have to sell at.
- I'm trying to avoid hype wherever possible.

Now I have another problem: illiquid shares. I bought Arcontech yesterday. Or rather, I tried. I simply couldn't get enough for myself. I ended up with a messy £2,000 worth. What's more, it drove the price up 17%. I got mine at 0.136 (trade 6 on 16 December 2013) and immediately pushed the price up. Within minutes the offer was 0.16. You can't buy at the price I bought, not even close, nor can I as I would buy more but not at 0.16.

So I'm not putting it into the specimen portfolio because if my readers tried to follow they would be skinned alive by the market makers. So don't rush into this share. The offer is back to 0.15 now, a good example of why this stock is not going into the portfolio.

This is frustrating as I want the specimen portfolio to become the legacy portfolio over time by osmosis, and glitches like this will make this process imperfect. Arcontech will go into the legacy portfolio but not the specimen. At this level it's just a bit of noise in the legacy portfolio so it won't distort it by much.

Anyway, feel free to watch this stock. It has a long and tortured history and now has new management, rising cash (for now) and directors buying.

If you own enough, and that's many, of this kind of stock, the result should be good. The key is to buy into out of fashion tiddlers which actually have a business, not companies with plenty of dreams but no sales. It is unfashionable to think sales are important but then we buy unfashionable shares.

Meanwhile I'm not adding any new microcaps to the specimen portfolio as they are so illiquid I have trouble buying. If I think a stock is too illiquid I will mention it as I have with Arcontech, but I won't put it in the specimen portfolio. I tell you as we go.

Why did I buy this stock? Arcontech has a reasonable sales profile, it is in the financial exchange technology business and is basically valued at nil, £2m on £1.8 of sales. It used to be called KTS and I've kept an eye on it over the years.

It has directors buying. Directors' buys are an excellent sign, subject to special conditions. When I saw these buys, for example, I immediately checked the company for low/no cash, as directors can inject much needed cash this way into a company on the brink of imploding. However, the company has a solid enough cash balance, so I decided the directors fancied the prospects of 2014, which is why I bought some.

Arcontech is total risk because as I found out yesterday it has no liquidity. No liquidity is always a worry. So the fact I could get next to nothing in stock is ironically OK by me because I don't want to get locked into a share I can't sell, if and when it does go up. So a sprinkle of it in the portfolio is fine.

Illiquidity also underlines the case that this is definitely going to be a long term hold and who knows, I might get the chance to buy more when/if it falls back. It's a rule of microcaps to never chase the price, sadly the market makers will gouge you for all you have if you let them. As a tiny part of a big portfolio a stock like this it makes sense, but as a big punt it would be the road to ruin. This is why a portfolio is so key.

...and on we go...

# Why An Offline Broker Can Pay

### 18 December 2013

A quick update. I was raging about small illiquid stocks, namely Arcontech and how it's very tricky to play such companies. This has thrown up a further couple of small lessons. I couldn't get my original small order filled and the price went immediately from 13.8p to 16 after I bought only a tiny amount of shares.

So what to do in this situation? Firstly, the price went up because the market makers don't want to play. They don't have any shares to sell. In these circumstances they slam the offer price up, but not the bid price, creating a massive spread, which kills off interest. The price may well fall back a few days later when interest wains. This will enable them to get their stock back cheaply.

As such I left an order with the market maker, good for the week, to try and make up my position from tiny to at least small. Lo and behold, yesterday evening a market maker matched my bid and I got the stock. This remains tiny amounts.

So this is what you need to do if you wish to play the microcap minefield. Leave an order with the market maker and wait. If you aren't filled, so be it. Don't chase the price, ever. The share price of these microcaps is artificial and fragile and controlled by the market maker.

The second lesson is, if you are using an offline broker, it can often pay because you can do this kind of trade which is impossible online.

On £1,000 of shares this is an £87 saving, taking the offer to have been 0.15. At the 0.16 price the offer hit after the initial buy that improvement amounts to a £160 saving, ie 16%. That's huge. As such my non-cheap broker just recouped the cost of a lot of trades by being able to poke the market maker and leave my bid with them. An online broker could not help, with an online service you get a take it or leave the quote.

This is why I use a phone broker, because a good one saves me more money in price improvement like this, than I would save using online execution.

Meanwhile, Arcontech is still not in the specimen portfolio because anyone trying to buy will have the same nonsense to deal with so it is not practical for all but a couple of my readers to mirror this trade.

# How Will Tapering Affect Equities?

### 24 December 2013

The year is drawing to a close. US tapering has started and against many pundits' bearish predictions the market rallied.

Investors often have a problem understanding derivative values. Taper is one. Taper is not cancelling money printing, it is slowing the rate of growth. It's not the same as stopping, it's not slowing, it's a second order thing. Taper slows the growth. Money is increasing less fast, but it's still increasing.

Next year will be heavily affected by the perceived impact of decelerating acceleration of money, but the world will do just fine without it.

QE is really just replacing money lost when the private sector stopped creating money supply when the credit crunch imploded. Money is not only generated by government. For example, if you have £1,000 in a sock and you take it to the bank, that will generate anywhere between £8,000 and £20,000 of new money, because the bank will use it as a deposit to lend multiples of the cash you deposited.

You can do this by creating mortgages, car loans, inventing new financial instruments; this is the core paper chase of money supply.

So when the private sector version of the money printing press breaks, oceans of money and wealth get vaporised. Through QE governments have been putting it back. When the private sector spins back up, their money supply will reappear and with luck QE will be pulled back, but the economic balance remain. Fingers crossed.

The key question to me is, can we really be in a new equity era as I predicted this time last year? The charts look simply amazing! The Dow in particular has broken through the roof of its ultra-long trend. This means we could be in for amazing times. Now I'm not going to lever up and go for broke, but it's time to acknowledge that 2014 could be amazing.

For example: when I bought lots of Trinity Mirror on average around 40p, I planned to sell out at 90p. As I was bullish when it hit that I only sold some and left the core holding in place. I planned then to sell at 120p. That came and went as my general confidence held. I sold 10% this week at approximately 200p making back half the original stake. I'm still holding 90% because my confidence is high. But this is rare for me, I don't like to have so much of my profits and portfolio in one place, so consequently I'm relying on the big picture to keep me in such an aggressive position. The big picture looks great, but my innate caution is rather twitchy. Can this time really be different?

Well, the last few years have certainly been different, so why not?

Meanwhile on Christmas Eve the specimen portfolio is up 6.8% after costs, roughly a per cent better than the average hedge fund. This includes a 5% cost load of fat broker's commissions and various nasty bid/offer spreads. These won't affect us on these shares next year, so we should bag 11% if we have the same kind of performance in the next twelve months. Actually I'll be disappointed if we can't do better than that. However, the market doesn't care what I feel, it will do what it will do.

Meanwhile, Happy Christmas and a prosperous new year.

# Our First Sale

### 30 December 2013

We sold Bank of Ireland today. This has made us a 76% profit. It has been higher.

We have bought Lloyds. We want to have a bank and in the long term Lloyds will hit 150p, possibly sooner than later. Banks are horribly opaque, so I resort to hand waving to explain my reasoning.

Banks have been very cheap because they are pariahs and as above, opaque. However there will be banking. So the question of picking a bank is stability and relative valuation.

I resort to sales. Here are the key examples:

|           | Sales | Mkt    | Sales/Mkt |
|-----------|-------|--------|-----------|
| HSBC      | 34891 | 123665 | 3.544324  |
| Stan      | 11235 | 32904  | 2.928705  |
| BKIR      | 2898  | 8000   | 2.760524  |
| Lloyds    | 23535 | 55838  | 2.372552  |
| Santander | 30821 | 57172  | 1.854969  |
| Barc      | 25291 | 43608  | 1.72425   |
| RBS       | 17941 | 20937  | 1.166992  |

My idea is that all these companies are banks. They do banking stuff. The only differences are: do they have financial skeletons about to rise from the tomb, are they being nailed by regulators/governments, do they have robust/clever management? Everything else will be blurry. Profit margins, assets etc are all so opaque you may as well say on a medium term moving average, they will be fungible.

So "Sales to Mkt cap" is a clearish indicator of valuation/upside. The market could be right about the valuation, but if you believe banks will be recovering over the next five years, you need to ride the cheapest/soundest.

Right now in my book that's Lloyds. Barclays is still mired in scandal and seems to have big government gunning for its scalp. RBS is horribly mired in politics and Santander is simply "incredible" to me.

So that leaves Lloyds in the purple patch. I'm itching to buy RBS to be honest but you simply can't trust politicians not to utterly destroy value so I'm hesitant.

Quick chart check...

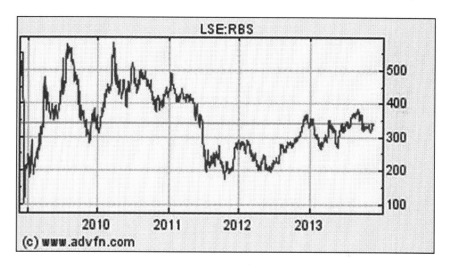

Not a bad trend on RBS, but rather indeterminate.

Lloyds:

Lloyds gives a clear un-noisy trend. Right now it is resting. If it breaks up, it could be 130p in 2015 (Alakazam!!!)... Sorry, just can't resist the hocus-pocus of charts.

Bank of Ireland:

Credit crunch and near destruction of this company suppresses current action.

Let's zoom in:

Similar to Lloyds.

What spoils the picture for me for Bank of Ireland is the rescue of BKIR by US financial investors. I simply don't trust them. They are sat on a fat profit, now at a good valuation. They will sell and when they do they will pin down the upside for the stock for an extended period even as Ireland recovers.

Meanwhile, Lloyds has a 30-40% upside if it can regain parity with HSBC and STAN and all the upside of a UK recovery. Of course the UK government has a wedge, but that is absorbable. Lloyds also seems to be the least hated of the rescued banks.

The legacy portfolio also sold its BKIR and already has Lloyds which it holds so it will help the portfolio harmonisation process as well.

We will buy £1,000 worth and bank the balance for a new purchase when it comes.

# Shares That Pay Dividends

### 7 January 2014

I like dividends. For one thing, you don't have to worry about them like the daily changes in prices. They come, they sometimes rise or fall, but you pretty soon forget about them unless you have the cheques themselves dropping through the letter box.

If you trade crazy stocks, dividends can feel like free money if and when they appear. Most crazy punting stocks don't pay dividends which is no surprise, but a trader can end up with them sometimes by happy accident. For a trader, dividends are a rare thing. Not for an investor, however.

I've just calculated the specimen portfolio's dividends for last year and they come to £88.34. It's hardly a bonanza, but it's a curry for two. So as I write we are approximately £2,000 up on approximately £18,000 that we put into the market over roughly a year. That's not bad, but not amazing either. About 10% would be considered fabulous in certain quarters but not to me.

However, I am no longer wearing the dunce cap, even though the Nobel prize for stock picking is still not on the horizon.

Having said that, it has been a very interesting exercise for me to start a portfolio from scratch at a small size to suffer all the issues a small investor must face with costs and spreads. There is also the issue of the rollercoaster provided by the market when you are building up a portfolio. Investing is not a smooth process to begin with and that makes persisting tough work, especially if there is a bear market along the way.

So here we are at the start of a new year. The US market is booming and near bubbling. This likely means there is a slump over the horizon somewhere, so I'm prepared for a knockback come the late spring.

Yet who knows where we will be then, we could be riding high or not. You are simply left guessing. The only thing to do is to look for cheap shares and buy them, then wait. We will carry on doing so.

Today we bought Shell, £1,000 worth as usual. Shell is as boring as a stock gets. Shell is cheap, it has been forever. Why? I have no real idea. All the oil companies are, from Exxon to Total, big oil is low P/E, in Shell's case under 9, and it pays a fat dividend, in this case 4.9%. Shell is not going to make us rich overnight but it's a cheap stock, which is what we buy. If we snap 20-30% we will likely sell. That might take a year or three. It is also a nice bit of blue chip stodge, giving the portfolio a bit of backbone in bad times and a 5% dividend year in and year out.

# We're In The Money

### 8 January 2014

They say money goes to money and this is indeed the case. Having sold Bank of Ireland and a small block of TNI my legacy portfolio has a chunk of cash in it and I have added to my Walker Crips position.

I can do this as the legacy portfolio is fully diversified. My position in it is also a bit on the small side. As the portfolio is roughly up 120% in two years I need to use profits to grow positions to keep them balanced.

It is remarkable that the two portfolios can be so similar and yet the performance be so different, but the key is the stellar performance of Trinity Mirror, Lloyds and RM, over half the performance in three stocks. This also makes this portfolio fragile, because should these stocks dump like Mothercare did today, then the punishment would be severe.

We can't weight our portfolio in the specimen portfolio because we aren't diversified enough yet. After another twelve shares we can think about taking bigger positions in some shares. (We also probably don't have the cash reserves to go loading in a hurry and I don't want my readers to get hopelessly left behind by a fast acquisition of shares. I want readers to have a chance of following the action. Watching is one thing, doing another altogether.)

So after moaning about expensive broking here is a good example of how an expensive broker can work out cheap. The Walker Crips offer price is 46, but my broker wrangled with a market maker and got me my stock at 44.75. Great. Let us call that a 2.5% improvement. That is the approximate cost of 3 commissions. Of course it means the broker has stock he wants to shift, but this is not a trade, we will be holding no doubt for ages.

This reminds me why I like phone brokers. When they are good they are very good. They can't really do this on big caps, but on minnows they can really score big on the buying and selling price. Online shops simply don't offer that. It also works well when the market blows up because the broker can always call a human and try to do a deal. You can also call from the train and not worry about getting cut off by tunnels, or dropping your PC off a boat into the harbour. Sometimes you get what you pay for.

Overall the market has been raining me money... this is when I get nervous. When the market loves you it's time to worry that the party is over.

Fingers crossed that it isn't.

# Why We Hold First Group

### 9 January 2014

So we have a lot of First group which we bought before their wild/weird rights issue. Why did we buy this? It's a simple calculation.

Let us imagine that all bus and train businesses are broadly the same. As such there should be a similar valuation. A bus ticket or train ticket is fungible, so sales should be valued roughly the same. So let's look at the competition in this sector:

|  | Sales | Mkt Cap | Sales to mkt |
|---|---|---|---|
| Nat Express | 1831 | 1498 | 1.222296395 |
| Stagecoach | 2804 | 2111 | 1.328280436 |
| Go Ahead | 2571 | 796 | 3.229899497 |
| First Group | 6900 | 1648 | 4.186893204 |

So for £1 of First Group you get £4.2 of sales. To be in line with National Express or Stagecoach, First Group would need to triple. Of course Nat Express and Stagecoach could crumble, but you see the simple logic.

What could make a company so lowly valued? Bad management and/or a need for money. The rights issue fixed that and a new Chairman could be the shakeup required to the management.

This doesn't mean First Group is going to £5. It just means there is plenty of upside if the company doesn't improve things worse.

Here is the chart:

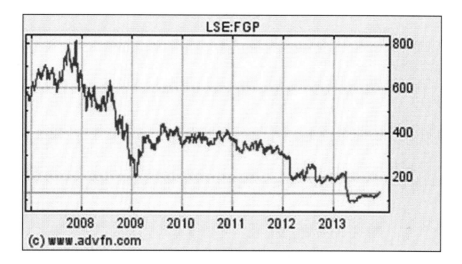

This is Stagecoach's chart:

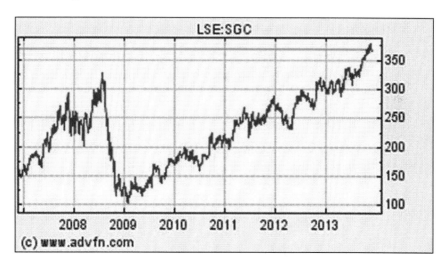

Note how Stagecoach went from £3 to £1 and FGP £6 to £2 in the same period.

Now you can drill a lot deeper to try and get confirmation that this is not a mad idea. There are balance sheets to analyse and statements to read, but it's best to start with a glaring observation like the sales valuation above to start the process of research. This might throw up lots of ugly reasons not to buy. However, with a good selection of glaring anomalies in the market there is no need to get clever.

Keeping it simple is the best way to go because temporary but extraordinary reasons for shares to be cheap ultimately go away.

# Portfolio Up Today

## 15 January 2014

I tend to be very bearish in January. This year is no exception. However, the market is chugging along. So while I'm feeling bearish the portfolio is up over £100 today.

It is of course most people's dream to live off their portfolio and that takes a lot of capital. If you are an average hedge fund manager you are bringing in 5%, so for those wishing to pull in £100,000 before tax, you need £2m. To have £2m in cash is a nice place to be and most people can only dream of it.

If you were aiming at 15%, which I consider my base line, that number is about £650,000. However, 15% is a high bar, even if you beat that year in year out. But it is doable.

This is much more attainable and anyone between 20 and 40 has a fairly good chance of building that kind of cash pot up by 65, if they build a portfolio diligently. However, saving is tough as there is always a pony to be bought or a car to be savoured or a kitchen to be fitted.

It will be interesting to see where we are at the end of three years. I will be buying as if there is £30,000 in the pot and may add to the cash a little in year three.

We have actually needed £19,348 to build the portfolio so far and if we had done it this way we would have a few hundreds in the account spare.

We are up £2,209 including dividends. We have eighteen shares with another twelve or so to come.

Another 10% would of course not be too shoddy but I won't be happy unless we get close to my 25% target. However, this might prove tricky as the market does feel well priced and 25% is theoretically an extremely high hurdle.

This is where the portfolio lies:

| Ticker | Name | Return |
|---|---|---|
| LSE:FLYB | Flybe Grp | 114.49% |
| LSE:DRTY | Darty | 46.80% |
| LSE:TOT | Total Produce | 21.55% |
| LSE:COB | Cobham | 16.89% |
| LSE:PRW | Promethean | 16.47% |
| LSE:FFY | Fyffes | 10.50% |
| LSE:FCCN | French Cnctn. | 9.34% |
| LSE:WCW | Walker Crips | 9.01% |
| LSE:LLOY | Lloyds | 7.08% |
| LSE:FGP | Firstgroup | 6.93% |
| LSE:SBD | Songbird | 6.57% |
| LSE:LAND | Land Secs. | 2.23% |
| LSE:RDSA | Rds A | -1.41% |
| LSE:VLX | Volex | -10.11% |
| LSE:CRE | Creston | -11.22% |
| LSE:NAR | Northamber | -13.12% |
| LSE:AQP | Aquarius Plat. | -25.99% |
| LSE:AVM | Avocet Mining | -88.60% |

Forgive the column order as with thirteen winners versus six losers I feel I should put my best foot forwards.

I have put an order in for a new addition to the portfolio but I have left an order with the market maker some 2.5% below the offer. If they are reasonable then I will update you, if not then a "pox on them" – we won't buy. There are enough stocks in the market to await the right price for the right share.

# Investing Is Like Gardening

## 23 January 2014

Well, now we are starting to look clever. We are up £3,134.76 on the £19,348 we would need in the brokerage account to do all the trades to date. That's 16%, in 261 days of the money being at risk, ie on average time invested. Annualise that and it's 24% per annum.

But you could say, well I stuck £30,000 in an account about a year ago, so what is my return? That would be roughly 10%, also not bad, but most of the money was un-invested for that period and "safe" sat in cash in a segregated account at the broker.

But I could add, "well, we've got about 4% costs paid for to add on to the return, including the broker and the spread, so actually we're making 28% or 14% depending how you want to look at the capital you sent to the broker."

Then you might say the costs have to be paid and then I would point out, we've effectively paid up front and if we hold for three years those costs will be defrayed by the effects of time.

And then you might say...

Well, we could go on forever.

We can say categorically, right now, we are £3,134 better off on eighteen stocks we bought a thousand pounds each of, in 2013. So in any event my dunce hat is off and the mortar board is on instead. That is nice. I have definitely justified your subscription. (NB: good advice. Never confuse your brilliance with the effects of a bull market.)

So here is the chart of our performance taken from the ADVFN portfolio:

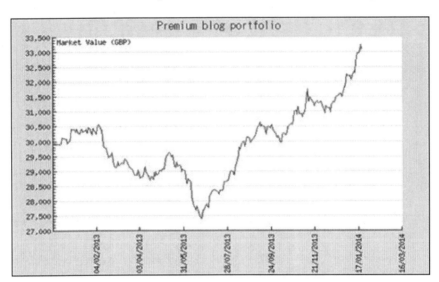

Promethean is currently doing some heavy lifting, up 80% for us most of which has been over the last few days.

Flybe is up 128% and Darty is up 56%. In my opinion these stocks have a long way to run if the bull continues.

The question for me is, what to buy, and the answer currently is, nothing. Never mind.

I wanted to buy Essendon a week or so ago. I mentioned I refused to be gouged by the market to buy a stock but didn't say which, well that was it. They wanted, if I recall, 46p on a 5p spread. That's obscene. Now the bid offer is 59-64p. (Sigh.)

So was I smart or stupid not to buy? I don't know, but I "feel" you should never play games when the market has all the cards and you have to grovel. Grovel to buy can quickly turn into grovel to sell. I refuse to play against someone who is dealing from a loaded deck. However, letting this stock go does rankle.

So does selling a share and then seeing the stock run away upwards, like Bank of Ireland.

Yet the thing to realise is that investing is not an exam where you aim to get all the answers right, it is an activity like gardening where you hope to end up with a nice garden with fine plants, lawn and vegetable patch. You have to dig and chop and sow, enjoy the process and see how it turns out. No plant is sacred, no result perfect, there is no hope of complete control of the elements.

When we started we did well for a bit, then we went down 20% like a balloon with a hole in it and now we are up 15%, all in about a year. The first six months were like getting beaten up, the costs hurt, the spreads hurt, the market beat on us. Why play the game at all?

Then the market turned. With absolutely no change in strategy our result improved 35%. (That's 35% from the 80% trough, which is actually a 44% improvement.)

You might say the market didn't change much either.

This is a key lesson about investing. You must keep plodding along and over time you will do well if you are being sensible and diligent.

We have a thesis: buy cheap companies in a diversified portfolio, using P/E, sales to market cap, directors buys and charts to select candidates. We simply stuck to it.

Over time having a successful method becomes the satisfying part of investing. You know all those people thrashing around chasing the next big thing are wasting their time and money and coming unstuck and you do well by simply plugging away carefully at your method and it will make you a nice pot of wealth over the long term.

It is nice to see the portfolio begin to sprout as it should and see the fruits of patience start to form. At 10% a year you begin to get rich slow. At 25% annualised, it's not so slow. But the territory is hilly; tomorrow we might be a dunce again, but in ten years...

# The Market is in a Correction

### 30 January 2014

Well, the bull market had to get checked and here we are in the correction. Who knows if it's over or just starting.

There are lots of interesting issues about these kinds of things. One is that everyone wants to identify and blame a correction on a trigger. That trigger is best if it is a person. However, markets don't need a villain or even a solid reason to fall except that they have got too high. A market slump is like an avalanche, all you need is plenty of snow and a steep slope. The rest is inevitable.

This avalanche was likely caused by two things.

A credit crunch in China combines with their year end tradition of settling bills around the last day of the year. The Chinese will have been pulling cash out from under their global mattresses and this has hit equities and currencies hard.

The second is the Fed was going to taper. These days central banks make it very clear what they are going to announce a week or so ahead of the official news, so that no banks are caught out, they can make money out of the insider information and thereby spread the shock so on the day nothing much happens. This is called advanced guidance. If you got this inside info and used it, you'd be slammed in jail, but thems the breaks in the new reality of interest manipulation.

Interest rates are a grand manipulation and all markets follow them, so it makes sense to smooth their effects by letting the major players know your intent early. So the way to win the game for us is to run along with the market because you know it's not random anymore and big moves days before big news is merely the early release of the info. As such you can ride the wave.

However, we are investing and like a deep sea fish, we shouldn't care about the storm above. Only occasionally do we need to swim fast and swim away from what is going on above. This is unlikely to be such a time.

The legacy portfolio is taking some punishment as Trinity Mirror is taking a beating – it's down over 20% and its outsized place in the portfolio is making a nasty hole. Shouldn't complain as the results thus far have been way over the top.

In the specimen portfolio we are still £2,800 up on roughly £19,000 used. Not bad for about a year. I'm not going to bother with all the different calculations I could make, but I call this 15%. That's 5% taken and 10% running.

Top of the pops is Flyby up 101%, then Promethean World 83%, then Darty 61%. I didn't expect so much of Darty this fast, but you simply never know how your picks are going to pan out, you simply hope for a good average result.

Here is the chart as the ADVFN portfolio shows it as if you put £30,000 in from day 1:

For all the bumps of the last few days, this chart makes the picture look serene. Which is the whole point of a portfolio.

I'm imagining that if we get a slump then we will buy three or four stocks in close succession, but we will have to wait and see.

If China doesn't implode, which is the likely outcome, things will get back to normal. As far as tapering goes, the US is still pumping $60 billion dollars of QE into the world economy every month. That remains a giant tailwind. However, you can't take anything for granted.

Interestingly, the US just issued its first floating rate treasuries, a sign of things to come and an expectation of rising interest rates and perhaps inflation.

Meanwhile the best response to all this is to go back to sleep. Investing should be boring.

# The Diversification Rule

### 31 January 2014

On Wednesday the legacy portfolio was pummelled by a big drop in Trinity Mirror. This portfolio has much too much of that stock in it in money terms because TNI started out at the top end of my portfolio allocation and then went ballistic. As such it is perhaps 20% of the portfolio's value. This means the portfolio is not as diversified as it could and should be.

Now I'm left having to decide between my opinion of the share and my belief in the theory of diversification. It is not a happy place for an investor to find themselves.

I should at least sell half of the position. I have sold about 12% as I wrote earlier but that is not enough.

Today Trinity Mirror rallied and put all the losses back.

The pain and pleasure of this whipsaw is not good for investing but I'm left holding because I believe there is a large upside. My fear and greed are at loggerheads. What I must do therefore is constantly watch and keep making the hold or fold call. It is unsatisfactory but since the moment of becoming undiversified in this share, the profits have been very solid and rewarded my rule bending. Breaking rules is dangerous, but having none at all is lethal.

Next week will be a good indicator of whether this new bear market we've been suffering is all about China and the Fed taper or something else. If it was the Fed and Chinese New Year the markets will rally as these events pass. It is looking to the upside as I write.

Now you will hear me say from time to time, trading won't make you money but investing will. You may occasionally hear me say you can't make money trading too. But that's not strictly true.

Look at this chart. It's yesterday's FTSE:

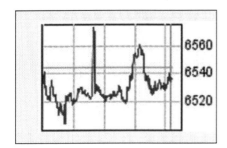

Can you see anything to trade there? If not, don't worry... even if you can, you wouldn't like the process.

Now here is the chart of HSBC today:

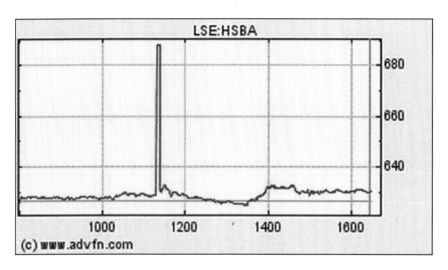

See the trade now? This is what I used to trade. I would bet against the sudden rockets and dramatic collapses caused by malfunctions. Here I would short HSBC at about 670. You have to be very quick but it can be done if you are set up for it.

This fat finger trade caused the spike in the FTSE you see above. Someone made a hash of their trading computer algo and >>BANG<< lost a million or two in a few seconds. If I still traded this kind of thing I would have made about £2,000 in three minutes of blind terror. You could make a larger amount if you have the nerve and capital. Try to go short

£1million of HSBC and you'd make £50,000. But remember, you have moments to respond and no time to check to see if HSBC just got a bid in from someone...

The market pays you to make it more efficient and when things go horribly wrong it pays you well to take the other side of the error and make things right again.

But to do this you have to sit and wait, and wait, and wait ,and wait... Then when lightning strikes, in an instant make a big gamble that someone made a big error. The result is often a fat trading profit... An occasional big loss and fairly big stomach ulcers.

It does feel heroic, but ultimately there is much more money to be made compounding a portfolio than scalping £2,000 here and there. As time passes the investment portfolio grows and it gets easier but the trading profits stay the same and the boredom and struggle is always the same day in and out.

Who needs the stress? Trading is not a lifestyle, it's a pathology.

# Don't Panic!

### 7 February 2014

What to do when there is a crash? Sell, of course...

No. That is the wrong answer. That's really annoying. You really want to sell when the market goes bearish. It feel like the right thing to do. But it isn't. You only sell out if the think it's nearly the end of the world. For example, China is about to explode in a revolution or a zombie plague breaks out in Los Angeles. Otherwise, grin and bear it.

Here is a chart of my 2008 portfolio which I sold in 2010. (The chart is a little cranky but you'll see the result.)

I sold out at just over 100% profit, which was stellar. But I could have gone on holiday instead and put on another 150%.

It looked sensible for about a year. However, in the end the market showed it was just as well to sit tight.

You could say I was safe for a large part of the dip. So that when I re-entered about a year later I'd avoided all the potential harm and for that matter paper loss but selling and buying is an intangible cost all its own.

The point is, ugly markets like the current one should be seen only as potential opportunities to buy stocks cheap if they really do tank. Unless the zombie hoards are destroying London or NASA has spotted a meteor heading our way, do not liquidate your portfolio. Continue to buy cheap shares and sell them when they are not cheap. Try to block out all else.

You want to hear that French Connection shot up 20% today and know why. The answer is: it's a cheap stock and it should go up. This feel unsatisfactory, where is the narrative?

There was a funny cartoon I read yesterday. One character says: "We've got a release of more random economic data."

The other characters says: "Let's work with it to make a narrative that explains today's market."

This is how I view the market.

Instead of narrative we buy cheap and sell not cheap. The only two questions we have is what is cheap and when is it not cheap. On a day to day basis there is little to do and not many stories to tell.

# The Art of Doing Nothing

### 12 February 2014

We continue to have a nice run. Even though I'm bearish and the market is jittery the portfolio is going up nicely. This is why sitting on your hands is such a good investment attribute.

We made our first buy on 11 December 2012 and as of today our portfolio has been going for 295 risk weighted days. We have needed £19,348 to make all the buys necessary to mirror it.

We have a £3,977.57 profit. That's 21%. So we are now in the zone I expect to be in and the journey there has been unexpected.

Whether we will be up or down from here on the 365 day mark is another matter. We could have a crash or a manic boom and probability say its 50/50 we will be no better off.

In any event I've earned your sub. However, I'm not too sure about the entertainment value recently. Making more tends to be boring.

Meanwhile, back in the market, I'm looking closely at Barclays. They will be a buy sometime soon. They are on the radar! I'm also toying with a gold play. I should lock myself in a cupboard instead but in my stupid punting account I've been picking up a splash of gold.

This has been quite profitable in the last couple of days but it could swing around suddenly and bite me. I think there is some good inflationary news around the bend and the last few days has been aided by the insiders hearing it first. We will see.

In crazy punting land I went heavily long Nikkei which then folded further blowing my stop. It then fell 600 points and I refrained from jumping in; now it is 800 points higher. I've decided Nikkei is now too dangerous and the outcome of bank of Japan vs Abe is too hard to know. Such is the short life of a speculator. Happily, I keep punting down to a sideshow to keep my hand in with the antics of most of ADVFN's users.

Meanwhile, I can just sit back and do nothing on my investments and make hay without a whisper of adrenaline. (This is not strictly true, but you follow my drift.)

This is the chart of our portfolios progress:

(Note this is plotted as if you put £30,000 in an account from day 1. If you had, not that I suggested you did, you would be 13% up with over £10,000 sloshing around in cash in the account.)

So what now?

Not much. Keep looking for opportunities. Sit back and relax.

Meanwhile, I think I will start positing some of my techniques, just to keep you entertained. You've probably learnt all you need to by now and if you didn't you could buy my book *101 Ways to Pick Stock Market Winners* for nuppence for your Kindle on Amazon and learn the rest.

I think I need to go on a course for pressure salesmanship in the meantime. At the moment I am temporarily an investment genius... tomorrow, who knows?

# Why I am Dabbling in Gold

### 14 February 2014

Of course you are absolutely bored with me saying, "Wow we are making good money aren't we?" I would be too. Profits from risk are boring; it is losses that drive the bulk of excitement. We want to make money but pretty soon the desire to gamble can overcome this goal.

You might not agree but it is my observation that gamblers gamble to lose, it's the emotional loop caused by losing that drives them on. It is easy for people who are prepared to take risks to be waylaid by the urge to gamble. It's a slippery slope easily slippery sloped down.

Consistent winning, on the other hand, is kind of dull. As soon as a game is a winning one, it becomes work.

If you told a degenerate gambler you would pay him £300 to travel 200 miles, walk a long way, then stand in a cold windy field all day, he'd laugh at you and never agree to do it. Tell him to go to Pontefract races and give him a bus ticket and he would be on his way.

So anyway, rather than talk stock, let's talk techniques. The below is the chart that made me buy a little gold. This is the chart today:

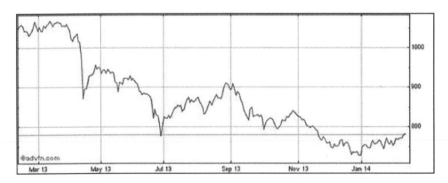

This is where it was yesterday when I saw it:

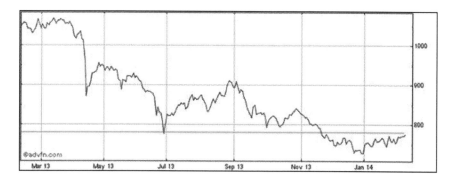

To me it looks like it has made a solid base for the last six weeks. The volatility has died. It's sneaking its way up.

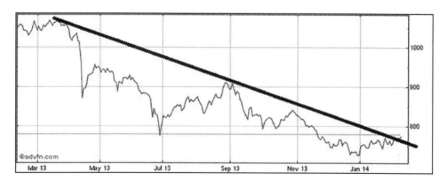

It looks like it's out of the trend. Certainly out of this one:

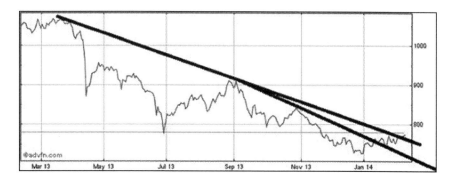

I always look out for a trend reversal where the volatility dies and the path is slowly but surely upwards. The chart needs to say: the trend looks like it's over, something else is up. Now that doesn't mean it has changed but it swings the chances your way.

I do think gold is too low. So I am looking for a signal to reverse. I can take positions and get stopped out as wrong. I don't have to be right. I just need to be more right than wrong.

A chart is all about hindsight. I like to say, it predicts the past. A useful past is one where the uncertainty has died away. Then you hope, all things being equal, the next moves define a new direction.

Now I'm definitely not saying buy gold because this blog is not a trading blog. I'm simply trying to show you a technique to learn for the future and your own investing, because this works for cheap companies just as well as crazy commodities.

# Stop Press: Petropavlovsk

### 14 February 2014

Bought POG, Petropavlovsk, from my sick bed. Can't resist. Update follows on Monday.

# Buying Gold

### 17 February 2014

I have the swine flu in Tokyo so sorry for this ramble. We bought POG, the unpronounceable and difficult to spell Petropavlovsky. It's a real gold mine. It's down 90% in three years. Its auditor assure us it digs $1bn in gold a year. Gold is flying and the charts look good for the company and the metal.

All the deep value is in mining, but then so are all the profound crooks. I've sworn off these stocks but I have to take a pinch.

This is the power of the portfolio. With twenty stocks the worse it can do is hurt us 5%. So if it does implode it will just be this year's Avocet mistake.

...back to sleep for me... no Lemsip for old men.

# The Portfolios are Strong

### 18 February 2014

Yesterday was a massive day for the legacy portfolio, adding nearly 2.5%. The specimen portfolio was strong as well, as you'd expect. We are now making £4,320 on just over £20,000 (£20,196 according to the ADVFN portfolio). I hope readers are understanding that I can be bearish and hold and be wrong and make money.

The golden rules of investing are: buy cheap shares and sell them when they aren't cheap. Nothing else. The tricky bit is judging cheap.

Timing the market is impossible. Well, at least, so very difficult you should not attempt it. However, if you do try to time the market you will win some and lose some. Likely on a 50/50 basis but you will blow your money on costs. I like to reiterate this because some take losses as a kind of tragic but heroic thing. However, they are losing money trading because they are just paying their capital away in costs.

Our costs of getting in and out are about 4% on average, so every time we jiggle our positions it costs us dear. You will bleed yourself white in brokerage costs trying to time the market. It will also put you off the stock market entirely, because it's no fun to be whipsawed by randomness.

So this is the ride so far. Recall how horrible it felt to be a fool at the bottom of this chart and how cool it is right now.

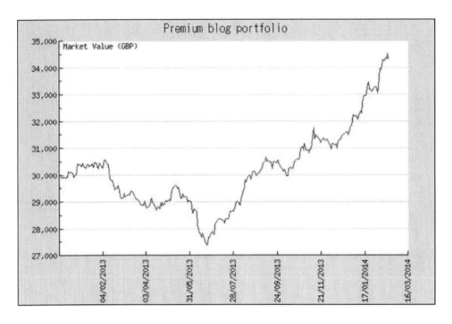

The key thing to remember is our luck or technique hasn't changed, the market just caught up with our thinking. We just got in too early in effect. But that's OK. You can't time it.

This is the legacy portfolio:

It's almost too good to be true. However, you can revisit this portfolio's performance since this blog was started, see the constituents and the various updates and marvel at the result. Long may this performance continue. That's 175% profit over roughly two years. Call it a 60% yearly compounding return.

I believe that this is unsustainable. I still think 25% is the number for yearly profits and that's a huge hurdle and these results have been created by exceptional times.

Perversely I also think there is a lot more to come, so I have to shrug and thank my good fortune. Realise, however, if this bull goes on for a few more years it's going to get rough. Volatility is going to explode.

Meanwhile we are watching:

- RSA for a further fall
- Tate
- Rolls Royce

These stocks are all fragile and if they take a fat tumble I'll be tempted to grab some. Barclays is also worth watching. If it too fell heavily, to say 170p, I'd jump on it. Meanwhile it's wait and see.

# Small Cap Spreads are a Disgrace

### 20 February 2014

I find myself selling stock out of the legacy portfolio. This time it is Cenkos which bagged a nice 115% profit. I'm starting to build up a pile of cash there now which is irritating.

Because the size was large (actually tiny really in the galactic scheme of things) I had to take an extra 1p haircut to sell. This is the sobering realities of small caps, that you are at the mercy of the market makers.

The regulators should do something about small cap spreads. Arcontech, which I refused to buy for the specimen portfolio, is a perfect example: it's up 50% from where it was bought but with a 10% spread and with a tiny market cap, it won't be a viable share for anyone who follows this blog to put into their portfolio as a tiny number of buys will spike the price up and a few sales crush it back down again; meanwhile the market makers will be skinning my readers for 10%.

As for Essenden, now bid/offer 65/72, there are plenty of more fish in the sea. (OK yes, it is really annoying but you have to stick as much as you can to your rules. As often as not these shares will pull back, in this case it didn't.) If you look closely you will see the price shot up 12% on about £8,000 of trading. So imagine trying to sell a few tens of thousand pounds of stock into the 10% spread. I hazard to say that the price is at best fragile.

Although the portfolios are pounding on the profits, I continue to feel bearish. Of course, the May slump is just around the corner but I don't think it is that. The market is not cheap any more. It is not expensive either, but I'm good at cheap and not cheap makes me nervous.

If the market keeps going, as I think it will, I'm going to have to look at more sketchy reasons to buy shares rather than make simple calls against market fashion. I'm OK at that but I'd prefer to buy dog shares and wait, than have to start putting on my speculator hat.

However, if we enter a boom bubble phase we are just going to have to buy the least expensive shares and let the market do the rest. It is not so difficult, it is just not my preferred game.

Meanwhile, I'm starting a curated list of tomorrow's dogs, so I can keep an eye on them all. For all the talk of buy and hold, and leaving stocks alone and coming back in a year to see how you've got on, there is I'm sure a positive profit to be had watching shares closely. You shouldn't pounce too often but unless you keep watch you can easily miss both buying and selling opportunities.

So on the "in the dog house" list is:

- BG Group
- De La Rue
- Games workshop
- G4S
- Ladbrokes
- Morrison
- Mothercare
- Rolls Royce
- RSA
- Sainsbury
- Serco
- Tate

I wouldn't buy any now as I expect them to potentially fall heavily, or at least some of them. If they do, then I'll watch them closely to see if any get into very cheap-land.

As I am currently bearish, I'm not going to take any risks. We can always buy in the May slump if and when it comes.

# Promethean and Flybe

## 21 February 2014

So yesterday Promethean announced it had sold kit to 10,000 US classrooms. This has spiked the price nicely. More to come I believe.

Promethean is an internet, educational technology company; dammit, it should be valued at ten times sales... Sadly that would make it £7 a share, not 38p. Ah to be on NASDAQ now the bubble is here.

The other big news was that Flybe has raised £150m to get on with its business. This is the new ex-EasyJet management at work. £55m of this is to come from a two for three rights issue aimed at existing shareholders. Crudely, the existing shareholders will be left with half the business in return for stumping up 66% more cash. I have mixed feeling about this.

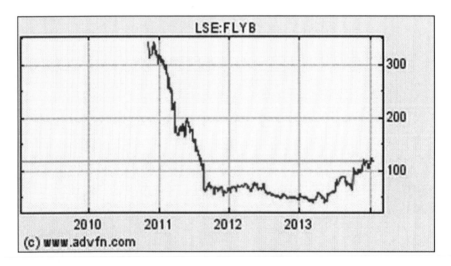

Taking the slow boat to China the new management should be able to get Flybe back to its IPO value. That's a triple from here. It's risky, but 1 unit of capital has a good chance of getting 500-600% return or a further rise of roughly 180p. What's not to love in that?

Now with the new money raised the same result cuts that in two. 150p. But wait, let's add the cash onto that, roughly 65p and maybe we can hope for 200p. So we've gone from a massive upside of a further 280p upside on 1 unit of risk, to an 80p upside on 1.66 units of risk. I can feel a little cheated at that.

This is, of course, why the city gobbled up £150m of Flybe when it currently only has £85m in outstanding shares. It smells a bargain.

The management will say, "look let's crack on, look at EasyJet, it has a £7 billion market cap and the loathed Ryanair £10 billion. This can be us in five years, so hold on to your hats." Clearly the share is £150m less risky now, but it's still a bit galling.

It must be said if Flybe was valued like EasyJet, even after this dilution it would be worth close to £5, but it's nasty to see the upside cut in half, just because the management wants to go hell for leather and the city wants to eat our lunches.

But we will pick up the rights and we will plough on. In the end I believe we will be crying all the way to the bank.

# Flybe Rights Issue Gives Us a Good Profit

### 25 February 2014

The city appears to like the Flybe rights issue. This is good. While we might have liked the long term upside that has been top sliced by this money raise, we are still sat on a nice profit, with a further option to buy well below the current price.

Currently the price is at a premium of 20p so we have a paper profit of £266 on the rights, another 26% profit to add to our 151%.

I'm going to take up the rights even though it means putting up another £1,465. We will end up owning 4 units of Flybe in relation to what we buy as a base unit for a member of the portfolio. We will grin and bear that for now, though we might top slice at some point.

In effect the city has voted in confidence of the new management by signing up for such a big rights issue and they will likely keep buying up the stock as that is what funds tend to do. This is one of their little tricks to make returns. They pick what they think is a winner and buy and buy and buy the share, hence pushing the price up. This makes their fund look good, as their picks are rising, even though they might be the ones causing the rise. So people see the fund has good returns and invest in that fund.

So the fund has more money to invest, so the fund buys more of their selections and up the price goes again. It's a virtuous circle until >>poom<<, suddenly it turns into a vicious one.

But these are early days for Flybe so the rise could run and run for a long time, regardless of fundamentals. What is not to love? As such we are going to suck up the rights and hang on for the ride.

Meanwhile, I have another stock in my sights. I like it, but it's a woolly one. Watch this space.

Right now we are 23% up... And like Lord Byron after his swim, I have got the ague.

# Buying a Hedge Fund

### 25 February 2014

It's hard to find old style value because the market is high. So the choice is to look further afield or to do nothing.

Now and again I will buy a company down on its luck and the decision may just be technical. This one is. Here is the three years chart of Man Group:

It's a hedge fund with 50 billion under management. It's in the dog house because its famous fund hasn't been doing so well. Mainly one suspects because trend following hasn't been such a clever strategy recently. I could be sarcastic about hedge funds but Man is famous and was illustrious.

Here is the seven year chart:

Now I really like the flat performance at the chart end. It says, "it's harder to fall any further."

Over the last few years it's happily sat at £5 and again at £2.50, though right now it's 84p.

Well we know what has gone wrong. The market. We also know change is upon us. Man has blamed QE for its poor performance and with taper, the coming months will give it a chance to prove this idea right. We will see, but in any event it won't take much to deliver us a 50%+ profit and if the price breaks much below its recent channel the share will be giving us a warning something else is wrong besides simple "market conditions."

So one more piece of diversification to the portfolio.

# Man Group Brings Profits

### 28 February 2014

So we were lucky with Man Group. Sorry – I should say, I was brilliant with my selection of Man Group. We are up 17% on this pick in a couple of days. The yearend figures were obviously better than expected.

OK, so we were lucky. But to paraphrase the golfing legend Gary Player, "The more I invest the luckier I get."

Today we bought Serco. They have hired a new CEO, Rupert Soames, who was the highly regarded CEO of Aggreko. It bends a rule of mine which is "do not invest in political footballs," but I've been watching Serco, which is cheap, and this news and the sub 10 P/E has pushed me off the fence. This new broom should give the company a 30%-50% hike in the next year or so, so we are in for this hoped-for rise. It is not the sort of spectacular upside we have baked in with some of our picks, but nonetheless it is irresistible.

We buy what's cheap and sell what isn't.

For the followers of my legacy portfolio, I've been selling out of Trinity Mirror. It's not that I feel it won't go higher, it's just that after a 400% rise it is bending my portfolio too much. It started out as a horribly overweight 10%, so thanks to that fact the profit since then over the whole portfolio has been up 150%; but the position was still flirting with being between 20-25% of the overall portfolio. This gave me the heebeegeebees. So I decided to top slice it. I've halved the position and may halve it again. I already feel better.

Diversification is extremely important and I'm not naturally comfortable to run my profit like I did with TNI, but sometimes you have to hang tough.

# Reading the Charts

## 4 March 2014

It's enough to make an investor paranoid. So this is the FTSE chart:

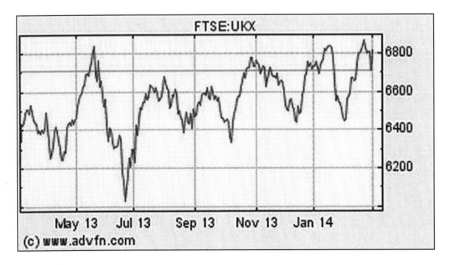

As a chartist believing in the mumbo jumbo of charts you can clearly see that we are due a dip back to 6,500, if the current cycle of up and down is to continue.

So how exactly did Putin know this and the Ukrainian revolution sync up with the FTSE??? You are left either scratching your head or believing in the "new world order." Or of course coincidence... "But as a policeman I don't believe in coincidences..." It's at least very odd.

Anyway, yesterday the portfolio was kicked down the stairs £500 by the trouble in the Crimea and today it's back up £300. It is probably not over by a long mark but it's a nice example of how fragile and fickle the market can be. It's better to be numb and just roll with it.

In the legacy portfolio I've been hacking away at my massive overweight Trinity Mirror position. It's now just 25% of what it was. Which means it is still a bit overweight at 5% or so. However, it feels much better. I'm expecting it to go a fair bit higher but now the risk of a portfolio cracking fall of TNI is gone. The money is off the table.

It leaves me with a big pile of cash, however. Some of it is going to be mopped up by Flybe's rights but I kind of feel the need to mop up this cash, even though I still feel bearish. So I've added to my Total Produce position. Which was initially a 1 unit position but with the big profits in this portfolio since Total Produce was bought, it's now underweight. I will slowly go round my portfolio constituents and see if any need punching up. This will suck up some cash.

There are quite a few candidates begging to be sold but I'm letting them ride for now, because they are as good as any other stocks I can find right now to have my money in. Value is hard to find.

So yesterday it was war but today it's peace. This is why it doesn't do to care too much about the news. If you are reading the news, it has already moved the price.

Only something massively bad, so big it can't be taken in all at once, should make you think about selling. Ukraine is unlikely to be it.

# Going Bananas: Fyffes Takeover

### 10 March 2014

Hey-diddle-di a takeover!!! There is nothing as nice as having a takeover in your portfolio. Rights issues tend to turn out well but takeovers are a slam dunk win. Over time we should get a lot.

So the unspellable Fyffes is merging with Conchitas, sorry Chiquita, and ending up with 50% of the resulting company. Now here is the rub, the merger is at 101p for Fyffes. Fyffes closed at 75p on Friday.

Now it gets better. Fyffes is getting 50% of the business (OK 49.xxx% but nice round numbers are better for investing) and it has 33% of the combined sales of the combined company. Bananas are bananas you'd think, so in effect Fyffes is getting a bigger share of the result by 2/1. So let's say the new company has a value of 300, Fyffes is getting 150 for its 100. This should mean that the company gets to be 400, another 33% upside.

Then on top of that, the bigger resultant company might catch institution interest and that might add another 50%. All this on top of a 38% pop today. (We have a 53% profit on the company as I write.) It doesn't get fatter than that. So we are not selling.

In fact I bought for the legacy portfolio. I doubled up. We cannot do this in the specimen portfolio as we are not yet diversified and what is more I doubled up when the price this morning was 93.5p on the way down to 90p as happy punters sold this morning. You wouldn't have been able to catch that move. It's now 98.25p so that's a few per cent missed for us in the specimen portfolio, but we are not traders and we aren't diversified, so we shouldn't think like that. Sorry.

However, let me explain what happened so you can do the same one day. Fyffes is a small cap and institutions aren't crawling all over it. It has a fat spread. When the news came out, private investors took their profits and there was no one there to buy, so the price fell off. Around 9am when the markets started to be awake pros and perhaps institutions bought the stock up until now it's only a couple of pence off the correct merger price.

But investors should be blind to this nonsense; we are sat on a 53% profit with more to come. Happy days.

Interestingly, we are now 313 days into the portfolio on a risk weighted basis and it is not till 1 June 2014 that we will have had our roughly £20,000 in the market for a year.

Right now we have a £5,394 profit on a total of £21,226 invested/in play – that's 25.4% profit. This is where I hoped to be when I started this newsletter but I can assure you I didn't expect to be down 20%+ this last summer and be here now... but in the end you can't predict the swings of the market, you can only hold onto a technique you believe brings you results. And here they are.

# Is That a Banana in Your Portfolio, or Are You Just Pleased to See Me?

### 10 March 2014

The not totally efficient market looks like this:

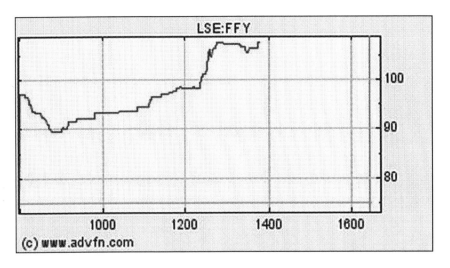

So you can say for a relatively illiquid small cap share it takes four hours for the market to get the price right. This is where the trader makes his money. While the market and institutions are waking up they have a chance to make some money. In the case of this lucky trader with Japanese jetlag that's about 18% on a nice chunk of change. I should sell on the basis of a fat quick profit but this share has a 50% chance of a 100% upside over the next three years, so I have to hold.

Inefficient markets at work can be caused by things like the confusion caused by a stock listed in the UK in euros, as is Fyffes. What is worse, try trading this when no one knows the ticker and no one can get the Fs in the right order to find the share... seconds of lag turns into minutes.

Get the currencies upside down and you can be in a pickle. If you already have your spreadsheet in place for a FTSE 100 company with this issue then you won't have any problem, but for a semi-obscure small cap you are going to be double checking a lot before you punt an amount of cash on the mispricing. As it is there are only 1,500,000 shares traded today so there aren't many people who want to take that much risk in this fat mispricing.

But anyway, "kerching" for all of us.

# Morrisons Takes a Fall So I've Bought It

### 13 March 2014

Today Morrisons announced their year end and the price immediately dropped 10%. We bought a clip. Or rather I bought a clip for the legacy portfolio and we therefore mirror it in the specimen portfolio. This is probably a bit early for us but we are mirroring to attempt at least, over time, to harmonise the specimen portfolio with the legacy one.

However, I will likely buy more Morrison for the legacy portfolio as it might have a long way to fall (or maybe not.)

Under the hood, I very happy because all the other supermarkets tanked too. This is a fantastic signal. It proves to me that the city is going zombie on supermarkets and there is a good chance supermarket share prices are going to get stomped into the ground over the next year or so, offering a fabulous opportunity to get in big at a ludicrously cheap price.

If a wonderfully cheap bottom is reached I will load up and make a killing. I will acquire as the sector falls, feeling for that bottom. This Morrisons buy is a first dab at that.

As beginner portfolio buyers we don't have the luxury of someone with a big portfolio who can keep buying, but even so, Morrisons is currently cheap, with a fat divvy and low P/E, so it fits our current criteria.

We buy cheap and sell not-cheap, so on that basis it's not a terrible time to buy. However, there may be far better times to buy in the future – and who knows, perhaps we will. I'm just happy because I think a whole sector is out of fashion which is the engine of stupidity that feeds me.

# The May Dip Is Coming

### 19 March 2014

I haven't felt bullish all year but for the first section of it the market kept making me money. That's the kind of wrong I like to be. If you can bank fancy profits being wrong, it's the sort of wrong you can bottle and sell.

I don't feel any more positive now and May is coming. We are going to get thumped, I feel, but not seeing when the hammer will fall means you just have to be prepared to suck it up when it finally comes out of the blue.

I'm now about 20% in cash, which is not really that big a cash pile, but I'm normally 100% in equities, so it does leave a nice chunk of so called "dry powder" for any slump that might show up. If the market dives I will invest that money.

Not only is there not much value out there, there are a lot of companies that are expensive. This can be a strong signal for a large correction to be on its way, except if the market is going to go into a boom; it might simply keep going up against all logic.

That's the funny thing, I think the market has a big chance of going bullishly ape and frankly I'm not used to dealing with that. I don't do boom investing. Booms and bubbles are about a kind of systemic pressure that drives prices mad. They are caused by financial alignments that cause eclipses of financial logic. Well, actually they make perfect sense but you have to start sketching equations and drawing curves to illustrate them and in the end they represent the part of a curve when the calculus goes what the mathematicians would call non-linear. In plain English, the market gets too dangerous to play. That's not here yet, but it's a reasonable possibility.

The most likely outcome, however, is correction and that's fine, we will buy the dip. If this is to be, it's close: no later than June. But a boom will be very interesting/tricky to get right.

I did fine in the dotcom boom, but so did everyone, it takes no skill to go long in a bubble and make money. It's the getting out at the right place that takes luck and skill.

For example, an acquaintance did well in the dotcom boom, because he got run over in a car park by a van. His friends helped him close his positions while he was in ICU, just before the market imploded, so that dark cloud ended up having a seven figure silver lining.

I did OK in the dotcom slump too but that might have been luck, so frankly I'm not sure how I'm going to handle a massive bull market if we go into a new boom and bubble. Hanging on for giant profits is not really my style even though I've been working on that skill since 2008. Perhaps we have already boomed, now will just be a bubble. It's very imponderable.

However, I'm not wedded to this theory. Invest in what you see. The world has no need to agree with me. It's the cold superego that makes market profits not the egocentric id that thinks the universe rotates around them.

The fact is, people are getting greedy and therefore I'm getting scared. But I'm going to sit pat and just make sure I'm keen on what shares I'm holding.

Meanwhile this is where we are:

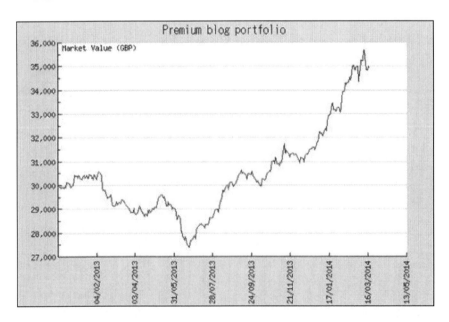

I'm expecting the portfolio to, at best, go sideways from here for a bit. (This is the chart presupposing we started with £30,000 of cash in the account, which of course none of us have.)

But that means little. You can't predict the short term, I constantly remind myself of that simple fact. In the short term the market is random; only in the long term does your edge turn into profits.

So in conclusion, agonising is just a waste of time... But it's so difficult not to.

# Betting on Ladbrokes

### 20 March 2014

I simply had to do it. We've been watching Ladbrokes and waiting for a dip to get in. Well, today it happened when George Osbourne slapped the gambling stocks with some more taxes.

We seem to have got near the low of the day at 1.369 but sadly this probably isn't the bottom. That's because the maths say the chance of hitting a market bottom is one in ten. Another reason not to try. But for a few hours we look smart.

Ladbrokes is a unfashionable dog. And we like to buy those. OK, so we don't like the general market right now but we are trying to ignore that. Bargains are not to be had on good days.

Here is some technical reasoning. Ladbrokes is at the cheap end of the market but it is in an established down channel:

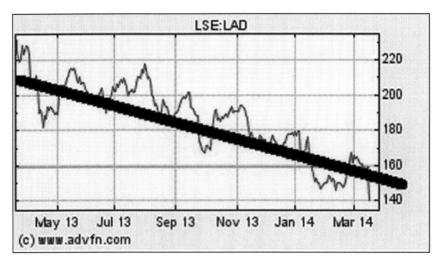

We are not going to fight it by buying anything but the bottom of that trend, ie today after a 11-14% drop.

The long term low is near:

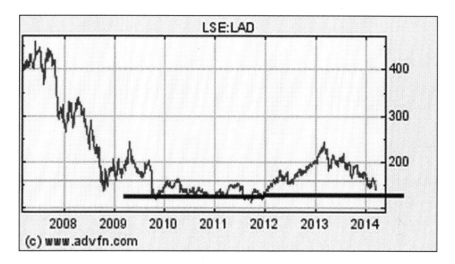

It's a sector thing, not just Ladbrokes.

See, the pattern is the same for William Hill, only the valuation is different. So it is time to think about getting in.

Again, we don't have the luxury of buying lower down, if it gets cheaper, but that's one of the disadvantages of being in the early stages of building a portfolio. However, it does come out in the wash.

There is apparently a 6%+ dividend in the pipeline if the company maintains it, which would be nice... but big dividends are always TBA (to be announced) and can get savagely chopped.

# Essenden, Still Right to be Wrong

### 21 March 2014

Remember we wanted to buy Essenden because it was cheap, but didn't because we couldn't get the right price for even a small position as the spread was massive? If memory serves me right, it was around 40p. A few weeks later it is now 95p.

This is galling but it is still right that we didn't buy because the liquidity is not there. When I buy a stock I have to remember that many people are reading my blog for tips and will buy the share. That means in general there must be enough shares of that stock in the market to at least give my readers a chance to follow. If there isn't, it is going to be bad for those that pile in.

I will try to avoid shares that give no hope to readers of a fair investment. This is why we didn't buy Essenden: because the spread was unfair and even small buying risked bending the price. A certain amount of liquidity is required.

Right now we don't have anything too illiquid in the portfolio, except maybe Northamber, which is a little bit low on liquidity.

However interesting, I will try and avoid microcaps which do not trade in enough size to be able to support a reasonable amount of buying or selling without going mad. There is no point being in a share if you can't get out without being gouged. Microcaps can be a game of "find the lady" and that doesn't work out well for the player.

# Tidying Up the Legacy Portfolio

**26 March 2014**

I'm lightening up a little in the legacy portfolio. Trinity Mirror is almost gone... down to 10% of the original holding. So I am back to a much better level of diversification in that portfolio, which is now awash with TNI profits in cash. I will use it if we get a May/June slump.

I have lightened up on RM just a little. Again, the position was out of hand with profits and near my initial target. It could go a lot further so I just top-sliced it a bit, selling down 20% of it.

The stupid punting account isn't doing so well. It seems that I am no longer in favour with the gambling Gods. It hasn't been hit that hard but whatever the trading market psychology is, I don't have it right now. I might just close all of that and forget it and leave all that free money for gambling to just sit there collecting dust.

So having written that, I closed my gold, stop-lossed the rest and now I can leave it be and forget this exists. The thing with this account is that after an excellent string of luck last year there is a significant amount of money there and using it can be a distraction from the main event. It is interesting how a small amount of speculation can be totally distracting from the sensible investing of even 100 times more money. This is yet another reason to avoid messing around with speculation.

Meanwhile, this is where we are with the portfolio. Nothing dramatic has happened:

However, I'm still nervous as a rabbit.

We don't have any of Premier Foods but this is an interesting situation right now. Premier Foods' price has slumped since the announcement of an underwritten rights issue of £353 million. The price has been smashed down towards the 50p rights price as no doubt the underwriters/overburdened holders dump the new stock for a profit.

That seems to make the stock cheap and therefore tempting:

However, the balance sheet sucks. This is the pre-deal balance sheet:

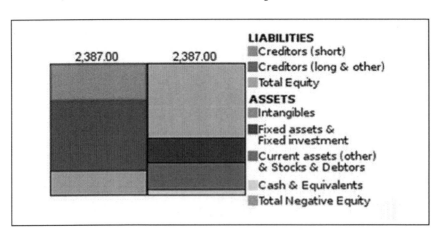

|  | 31 Dec 2012 (GBP) |
|---|---|
| **ASSETS** | |
| fixed assets | 374.2 m |
| intangibles | 1390.9 m |
| fixed investments | 1 m |
| current assets - other | 81 m |
| stocks | 116.2 m |
| debtors | 370.5 m |
| cash & securities | 53.2 m |
| **TOTAL** | **2387 m** |
| **LIABILITIES** | |
| creditors - short | 691.6 m |
| creditors - long | 1290.5 m |
| creditors - other | - m |
| subordinated loans | - m |
| insurance funds | - m |
| **TOTAL** | **1982.1 m** |
| **EQUITY** | |
| ord cap, reserves | 404.8 m |
| prefs, minorities | 0.1 m |
| **TOTAL** | **404.9 m** |

Note £404m of net assets includes £1,300m of intangible assets, so net tangible assets = -£896m. So £353m in cash brings that down to a -£566m... let's call that half a billion pounds.

Now the company's sales are £1.7 billion so the £500m hole is about four months sales, which doesn't sound too bad. However, the company only makes around £50 in a good year and when it loses money it loses hundreds of million. Since 2004 it has lost a total of roughly £600m. First Group, in comparison, made pre-tax of over a billion pounds in the same period.

So that's why we aren't swooping. If the share price goes way low, which it likely won't, we may go for it, but it's nowhere near there now.

The multilevel rights average out at 80p, as the company's share price should be, after a resultant recalculation of the pre-announcement valuation (it was around 160p at the time) of 89p, if you care to fiddle about with a spreadsheet.

The share has now fallen to 68p. This is 18p above the cheapest tranche of the rights which is 50p. Which is somewhere between 12p and 20p too cheap if you are to believe the underwriters. But we don't like it! I just can't see how Premier Foods can dig itself out of its balance sheet hole without another such raise down the line. The balance sheet remains broken and we try not to buy shares in truly broken companies.

Meanwhile, the company borrowed £500m at 6%, which for a company that has made no more than £58m in any one year since 2004 while losing £400m and £259m in 2008 and 2011, is quite a trick. It will keep the wolf from the door for certain, but not forever.

My guess is somewhere down the line the company will dilute again. I can't see how it could avoid it. It might sell assets to pay down the debt, but that's no good for us. It would need to sell business at two times sales to "get out of dodge," but with a market cap of one-sixth of sales before the rights issue, that doesn't look like a likely result.

Venture capital creates disasters, for example HMV, by gutting the host company of capital and then relisting the husk back to the public and the same kinds of institution they bought the company from in the first place, at an inflated valuation. As such beware "private equity" IPOs. If they could strip any more assets out of the company before IPO they would have. It leaves the relisted company on the very edge of solvency and very nearly doomed to failure. It should be a crime, but it isn't. Who pays? Pensioners through their deprecated pensions and anyone mistaken enough to buy shares.

In any event, now is not the time to buy shares in such an ugly situation. So we haven't.

# A Good Day For The Portfolio

### 31 March 2014

There is a limit to stoic investment and that is definitely passed when the stock you didn't buy because of evil market makers' silly bid and offer goes up 150%. For us, this is the sorry case of Essenden, which we passed at around 40p and is now over £1.

However, this would have been the story a lot in 1999 during the dotcom boom and crash. Sometimes the rules of the game change and you look silly. They change back, though, so as long as your technique makes you money you should stick to it and let random short term aberrations run their course.

I am of course gnashing my teeth as I type.

Back to the portfolio: Friday was a very good day. We made around 2%. Apparently it is such days that account for most of the profits of a portfolio. This is why getting out and jumping back in is so dangerous because you have a tendency to jump in after great days and be out when they happen.

The authors of this profit were French Connection and Songbird.

Songbird is Canary Wharf; the company has a market cap of £1.6 billion, so I simply look at Canary Wharf and the price tag and say, "hey, we're going into a boom and a bubble, what is Canary Wharf worth?" City people don't like this kind of no-brainer thinking because any fool can do it but on Friday the company announced it was doing really well and letting was hot. It jumped 14%.

Meanwhile, more intriguingly, French Connection jumped 9%, probably on an Investors Chronicle tip. They could go straight to £1 from here, which is a classically stupid prediction to make. Whether they do or not we are already up 104% and now I mention it up 42% on Songbird.

We now have a little over £22,000 in the market and some of my readers might not have been able to invest that much and be worried about being left behind. The answer is that over time they will catch up. I make no good or bad choices, they are all the same, the result is a function of averages and over time you will get the same averages. It will just take you time to catch up. The only difference in outcome will be a function of volatility. The fewer shares you have the wobblier your results will be.

If you only bought Avocet you'd be down 89%, or if you had only bought Flybe you would be up 153%, but it's all part of the same spectrum that has our returns in and around 25% per annum.

We've ridden that wave of volatility to get here and I couldn't have designed a better example of how you can invest in a simple way and go to a 20% loss then to a 25% profit all in a year of slowly building up a portfolio. Pretty soon the specimen portfolio will be complete in terms of initial constituents and we will start to pump up the size of our positions. That is, of course, if we don't get a crash, which will slow us down somewhat if it happens. However, it won't stop us even if it does happen. We already have in profit the equivalent of most of the damage of a normal crash.

# The Songbird Connection

### 31 March 2014

So today we are up nearly 3% again, driven by Songbird and French Connection.

The lesson is underlined that even when you feel bearish, do not sell. You have to keep holding because buying cheap stocks is a completely different thing from trying to time the market.

One, buying cheap shares, you can do and the other you cannot. You can't time the market. Only break this rule when you actually see the comet enter the atmosphere to kill all life on Earth. Do not do it because you think it is coming.

I'm still negative on the market but I have made nice money in the last few days. My mood tells me nothing about the market. My gut doesn't read charts. I will be right half the time and wrong half the time.

This is where my gold miner's axiom comes into play: if you think it's gold, it isn't; if you know it's gold, it is.

I will paraphrase it. If you think it's going to crash, it isn't; if you know it's going to crash, it is.

"Knowing" is so definite you can tell the difference between being certain and simply worrying.

# Portfolio Spring Clean Continues

### 2 April 2014

I've done a little housekeeping, adding dividends into the portfolio and getting the Flybe rights correctly accounted for. This is what we find: We have invested £22,779.59 and we are 41p shy of £6,000 profit. This means we are 26.4% up.

1 May is the first year anniversary of capital at risk but now we have bought more shares that horizon goes back, so I'm going to stop using it or I'll go mad.

We are £6,000 up, having put roughly £23,000 in, starting roughly around winter 2012. That is the sanest way to look at it. Now we have a proper portfolio, although not wide enough yet, which has some months behind it, we don't have to unpick our performance so much.

That's pretty good by any standard especially when all the small investor privations of high broker commissions and fat bid/offer spreads are taken into account.

Meanwhile, Flybe is steaming ahead. It is good for £2, but we aren't wedded to anything.

# Not Buying Gold

### 7 April 2014

The only thing I really want to buy at the moment is gold shares but I know that would be bad. As a contrarian value investor I'm like a Pavlovian dog. I see certain numbers and I want the stock. However, gold shares are nearly impossible to buy because their track record on delivering on promises is so low.

How can you invest in a company that makes a product that went up 400% in a decade yet still didn't manage to turn in great profits? I suppose I will have to look deeper, but every time I consider a gold mine and begin to read their old news flow I'm horrified. However, the Pavlovian investor looks at the numbers and starts to bark "buy."

Everybody I'm meeting in the city is telling me how they predicted the recovery. That makes me nervous. But while I'm bearish right now, I'm massively bullish about the next few years.

Our performance says I should be more relaxed but it'll soon be May and then if the market dumps I will stake claims to my seer-like prescience. A long bear can have his cake and eat it.

This is the current state of progress. (As if £30,000 went in the account from day 1.)

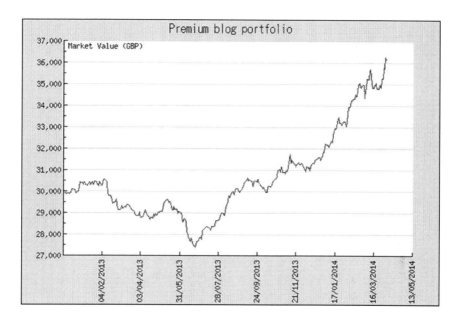

Don't forget to tell all your friends to subscribe.

# Fasten Your Seatbelts...

## 14 April 2014

I didn't write anything for the blog last week, because I've been to Boston at an internet conference and then on holiday.

In my leisure time I am a treasure hunter and a lovely rolled field awaits, so this will be short.

I'm convinced we are in for a nasty correction, in fact we may already be in it. The question is: sell or hold? The answer is: HOLD and store up cash to buy at the bottom.

I don't see a 2008 although we may get a 2011-style dip. I sold out in 2011 and felt quite clever missing a nasty correction. However, I didn't add much on my returns by doing so. I still have that portfolio running on ADVFN. Here it is:

(Note it is so big and started so long ago the chart process stops before it reaches its end point, hence the end spike.)

So this looks quite clever and I was reopening at the bottom that October for the legacy portfolio I show here. However, for all that effort I probably saved 5-10% and the risk of missing the next boat was much more important than that.

FYI – this portfolio is now 3.5 times the size of its original investment, or put another way has made 2.5 its value in profit. That's huge by anyone's standards. However, it is just about 25% a year, my target.

My point is, even though the portfolio had a fallow period for over a year, it still performed excellently without lifting a finger after April 2011. This is what buy and hold is all about.

However, having studied this a bit, what happens is the portfolio concentrates into a few big winners, so over time the portfolio becomes undiversified and therefore fragile.

This is the benefit of occasional pruning that buying and selling has. It keeps the portfolio robust and diversified. But that portfolio concentration takes many years, so it's of almost academic interest.

Anyway, please fasten your seatbelts, we are about to put our resolve to the test.

BTW, the ADVFN UK Investor Show was a huge success last week. Try to come next year and I'll happily shake your hands.

# Portfolio Profits

## 14 April 2014

This makes an easy blog. Let's crow a bit before the market tumbles and we all look foolish again. I remember wearing the dunce cap last summer so I'm making the most of us doing well.

Here is the FTSE:

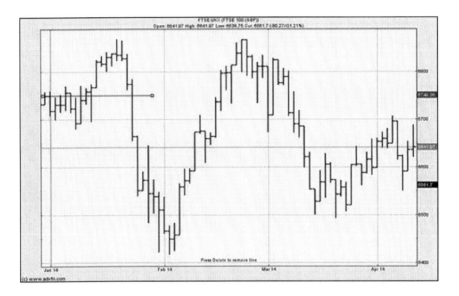

It opened at 6,748 in January 2014, it is now 6,642, that's down -1.57%.

Here we are, up roughly £4,000 on £24,000, 16.6%, or if you started with $30,000 in cash at the start, 12.5% up since the new year.

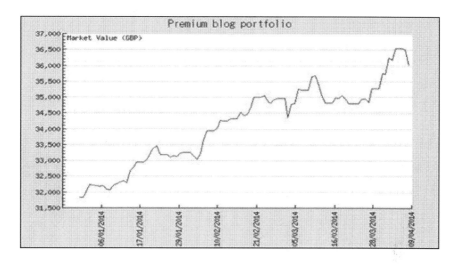

We can feel good about that and hold the thought as the coming weeks yank us around.

According to the doomsters at Zerohedge this performance outstrips the best US Hedgefunds: http://www.zerohedge.com/news/2014-04-11/best-and-worst-performing-hedge-funds-2014-full-list (bar 4 by the lowest estimation of our performance.)

In any event we are doing OK. When the correction comes – and it always does – the trick is to fall less than the market and rally more on the bounce.

So far so good, but I can't help feeling we are going to get a pretty stiff correction. However, you can't time the market, so my gut should be ignored.

Meanwhile Walker Crips had good results and shot up 25%. This could go a long way if we are entering a boom. Solid directors buying very encouraging.

# Aquarius Platinum Rights Issue Shenanigans

### 23 April 2014

So we have more rights issue fun and games. This time it's at Aquarius Platinum.

This is the deal: own one, buy two at 14p. The price before the deal opened on Tuesday was 40p. So this is the math:

(40+14+14)/3
68p/3

22.66p is the value of the resultant share. So today the share price of AQP opened at 23p and closed at 23.5p. That looks like a horrible loss when you open ADVFN, however you have rights to 2 shares at 14p. These are listed as AQPN, the N denotes the rights. These are valued at 9.35p although throughout most of the day they were 9.6p.

So your shares are now worth: 23.5 +9.35+9.35 = 42.2p. So we are actually nearly 5.5% better off. Whoopie!

However, we have to cough up an extra: 4,000 x 14p = £560.

But it doesn't stop there; we have a couple of weeks (until 9 May) to decide whether to chip the cash in or sell the rights. If the price of AQP went up the rights would get more valuable but if they went down the rights would start to fall in value accordingly. Now tomorrow small investors might wake up and go: "darn I don't have £560 spare," or big investors might say "a pox on your house," and sell the rights, which could well hammer them into the ground.

However, in theory after the dust has settled AQP should be worth 22.66p so if the rights and share price tanked the thing to consider would be to buy them up. (If you have a stomach for that.)

What we are going to do is take up the rights. We aren't going to do anything fancy. From my point of view miners are tawdry, louche and sordid, sorry I meant high risk. And we need a little bit of that in the portfolio because if we can spot the "low risk" in the pack the future will bring fine results.

If you are tempted too much by mining stocks, read the book Brett Kebble: The Inside Story (look it up on Amazon). That should help calm your fervour. Amazing story. The ex-CEO of Eidos got mixed up with this mining fellow and, eh... disappeared for good. You couldn't make it up, nor would you want to, nor do you need to.

Anyway, we will take up the rights.

We are now in a bear as far as I'm concerned, for four to six months. Hopefully our beaten down portfolio of comeback kids will miss a lot of the pain... but we will see.

A bear will give us opportunities to buy. This is more important than you might think.

# The Bear Necessities

### 24 April 2014

We are in a bear market. It will likely last a few months.

How can we tell the difference?

It is odd, but the most striking day to day features of each intuitively feel opposite to the reality. The market has jumped hard on occasion in the last week or two and that feels BULLISH. However, it's bearish. Sharp jumps and slow slides are bearish and slow rises and sharp drops are bullish. It doesn't sound right, does it?

Here are the examples:

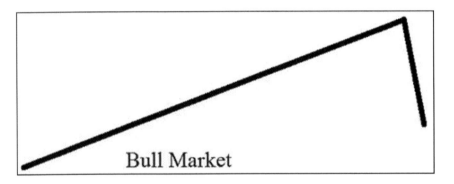

If you keep repeating this pattern you see how the market rises.

This is a bear:

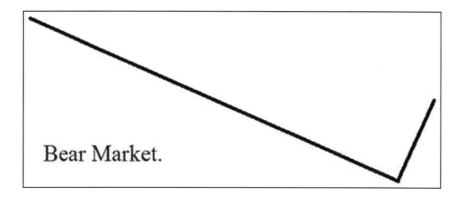

The move against the trend is steeper and more extreme than the trend. The sharpest move is the gyration away from the trend.

Here is the FTSE:

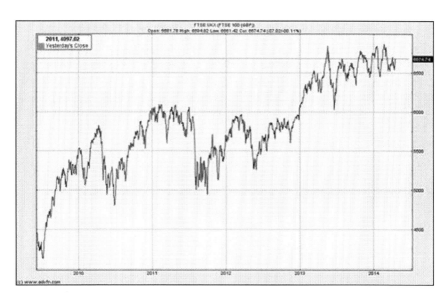

Through this long BULL, you see the falls are sharper that the rises.

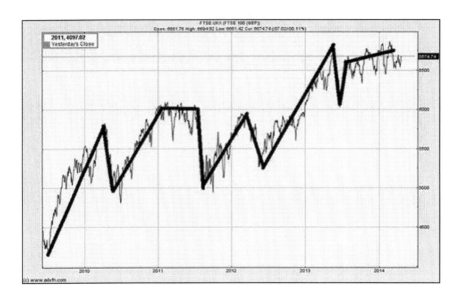

If the falls and recoveries are the same you are in neither a Bull or a Bear. You can elaborate to your heart's content but that's the core of it.

Right now we've been falling steadily and getting sharp recoveries.

Here is an example:

This tells me GSK is in a bear even though it's not really going anywhere. Now the Pharma takeover circus has begun, it's interesting to note the company's underlying trend is bearish, even though the price action doesn't show that. It doesn't mean tomorrow it won't change, but the first order of play in investing is to know if you are in a bull or a bear. The rest is detail.

Meanwhile the portfolio is basically churning:

You may have noticed Quindell and Iofina crashed. I hope you didn't have any. Asos, which I shorted in my stupid gambling account after Christmas, (it went up, I closed, it slumped) has also dived recently.

(I only have one stupid punt on at the moment: long pound v euro. The market doesn't want to cuddle up to me this year, so I'm sulking and nestling my pile of ill-gotten profits until sunnier times.)

Why do people buy these stocks? I look at the market cap and look at the sales and that's enough for me. These companies do not have a cure for cancer or the latest sexy tech widget on the shelf.

Yet say you do a bit more digging. How do these companies make investment sense apart from within the narrow bounds of the financial equivalent of magical thinking? Their market caps do not match their enterprises; in a bad way. They are the very opposite of the stocks we buy. However, it takes way more faith to buy a crazy small cap that rockets than an established business that steps in a pile of horse manure.

I know people laugh at a joke when there is a laugh track to prompt them. Do people trade in the same way? I don't understand it, to be honest.

Some poor speculator was yesterday damning shorters for destroying his pension invested in Quindell. I'm just astonished anyone would put themselves in that position even in Shell, let alone some no name, new venture.

Yet hosts of traders seem to be totally comfortable to put £10,000 or more, of which they have few, into a crazily high risk stock often making unlikely to occur promises, with no track record etc etc... on which they stand to lose £5,000 instantly.

If you ever feel like doing that, DON'T.

# Welcome, New Subscribers

### 28 April 2014

ADVFN ran a promo for my newsletter and as a consequence we have quite a few new members. Welcome.

Interestingly, some of the email we got back after the mailout were along the lines of "25%???? Haha, is that all?"

Over the years I have heard that time and again. 20-25% is just not enough to satisfy speculators. The trouble is, I have yet to meet one who has any money or isn't in the process of pouring what they do have into the pockets of their broker.

I founded ADVFN in 1999. So let us say fifteen years ago. At around 25% you multiply £30,000 to around a million. At a higher rate you'd be incredibly rich. At 100% you would have tens of millions in profits. I think it is safe to say ADVFN does not have a single user who has managed to achieve anything like that.

Of course, because of the mathematical probabilities of trading, some make a fortune AND lose it. I have seen that happen a few times... but make a fortune and keep it, I'm still waiting to applaud that.

Of course, we can take a step back and see a bigger picture. Who is the richest man in the world? Why, it's the world's most famous investor. The richest speculator is? Do you see any successful old traders? Search for "traders" on Google and summarise the articles in your head... you won't see a lot of happy outcomes. Do the same with investor.

However, my readers probably already know this which is why they read my newsletter. They don't want to be the next Wolf of Wall Street. They aren't seeking quick riches or the "thrill" of speculation; they just want to get to grips with building their capital through successful investing.

25% a year is not just a good result, it is an excellent result. It is so high that it makes me a bit nervous mentioning it, even though I've got that return consistently over the years. The past is a very uncertain guide to the future, so every successful year is a unique achievement. Approximately

25% annual returns compounded is the same result that has made Buffett the richest man in the world.

However, becoming billionaires is not what we are trying to do. We are trying to buy cheap shares that in due course will go up and make us a nice profit. The wealth building will come as the product of that.

In the first year of my newsletter we have achieved that, even with a background of high costs. I'm happy with the resulting profits but the method and the viewpoint is more important. I'm keen to focus on the fishing rod, not the fish.

In the last year we've covered how to build a portfolio and done so step by step in a way that anyone can emulate. That process will take another year to complete and then we will be focusing on to how to maintain one. This will actually be less dull than it sounds.

Many might think the share tips that the portfolio contains are the highest value item of my newsletter/blog/whatever you care to call it, but again I feel it's the method that is key. Stocks come and go but successful investing is a constant process.

Going forward, the tide of the market is going to ebb and flow. Some days we are going to make money, some days we are going to lose. We are going to have good luck and bad, great picks and dumb picks but the outcome should be similar over the long term.

When you read the newsletter from my first post onwards, you will see we looked pretty stupid by the middle of last summer and pretty clever by the New Year and you should see for yourself I did not change my investment stance even once. There is no hindsight on show. See for yourself the process, get the insights, see how it's done.

So I'd like to welcome again my new readers and thank all my subscribers for reading. 2014 is going to be fascinating.

# AstraZeneca Share Price Up 15%

### 28 April 2014

I'm in California and should be asleep, but checking the UK opening before I put my head down I note AstraZeneca, a member of the legacy portfolio, is up 15%. Clearly it is felt that the takeover of the company by Pfizer is on. Well, I can understand why.

"You can't compare apples and oranges," so they say, but as a Dilbert cartoon points out, you can as they are both fruit, they are both from trees... etc.

I like that because it's a method that has made me quite a lot of money over the years. I'm told it's nonsense, you can't compare two extremely similar companies like for like. I just laugh as I count my profits.

The first instance was Vodafone v Orange. Remember when Orange was listed? That's a long time ago. A pound of Orange sales was about 20% of a pound of Vodafone sales. Needless to say Orange went up and got taken over, still on the cheap, but I bagged a fat profit.

So let us take a look at AstraZeneca. Who shall we compare it to? GSK? Why not. "Apples and pears," no doubt the analysts would say. I'd reply, if you saw both companies from a spaceship you'd think them the same. Professional detail mongers hate generalisations of course or else the value disparities would be there.

Compare the two companies in two browsers or whatever method you like to use to put both companies' fundamentals side by side.

Balance sheets are roughly the same, sales roughly the same, even profits over a 2-3 year period are similar, although they are a bit choppy. AZN is worth £58 billion, GSK £81 billion; even though AZN has been rising fast in the last two years and GSK has been going sideways, there is still a big disparity. It was roughly 2:1 as far as I was concerned, that is to say GSK was valued at twice AZN pound for pound.

Have a look at BP and Shell. There is a similar disparity there, with BP significantly more "expensive" in my book than Shell. It's not as fat as AZN/GSK was but it still sticks out.

So keep your eyes out for this kind of thing. To me it's glaring. Apparently to Pfizer it's glaring too.

Off to bed I go.

# Serco Slump Shows the Importance of Diversification

### 30 April 2014

Dagnabit, I forget to put Serco in the portfolio tracking on ADVFN.

The result shows why diversification is important. Even though Serco has dived it doesn't make much of a mess now we are starting to be diversified.

Serco just plummeted because they are going to have a rights issue by the looks of it. The new boss who is not in place just yet has obviously had time to look under the hood and probably had to swallow hard. We are plum in the thick of rights issue-land at the moment but that's fine, rights are opportunities.

However, the plummet since we bought Serco is still quite a lot. About 25%. If we had three stocks this would crease our performance. As we have 22, it is only a flesh wound. You can divide 25/22.

Diversification even with and perhaps because of the generally random nature of the market makes our life so much more comfortable. Bad luck or errors get flattened out as sometimes they work in your favour, other times against.

Meanwhile Petropavlovsk is lining up for a rights issue too. (Note to self: don't buy any more mining stocks. I don't care if they are on all my filters, they are not proper companies.)

So after all these annoyances, including Serco, we are here:

Not much drama to be seen, at least yet – but there is the "Sell in May" slump potentially just around the corner.

That's why I go on and on about diversification. Without it, you are going to have a hard time.

# The Dogs List of Shares to Watch

### 1 May 2014

I've added Carclo to my dogs list. This is going to be a great buy sometime in the future. It's not in the dustbin yet but the market seems to want to throw it there. I can practically smell the blood lust.

This might take a year or even two but I need to put it on the list so I don't forget.

This situation is hard to guess but in time it will flatline or something else will trigger an entry. Maybe it will never get that low, but the dog list is there to keep the opportunities on the radar.

They are:

| | |
|---|---|
| LSE:CAR | Carclo |
| LSE:DLAR | DE LA Rue |
| LSE:GAW | Games Workshop |
| LSE:GFS | G4S |
| LSE:LAD | Ladbrokes |
| LSE:MRW | Morrison (WM) |
| LSE:MTC | Mothercare |
| LSE:RGD | Real Good Food |
| LSE:RR. | Rolls-Royce Hlg |
| LSE:RSA | Rsa Ins. |
| LSE:SBRY | Sainsbury(J) |
| LSE:SRP | Serco Grp. |
| LSE:TATE | Tate & Lyle |
| LSE:BG. | BG Grp. |

Some of these one day will be in the portfolio, some won't make it.

# Winning with French Connection

### 6 May 2014

It is often said it is the winners that make you the big returns and for us this is French Connection. We now have a 185% profit on it – that is to say we have nearly tripled our money.

In the last few days our profits have come from FCUK, countering general losses in what remains a bear market.

We are in May and I'm expecting some hard weeks, but of course a good group of stocks will break the fall. With a solid portfolio you go down less and up more than the rest of the market in general. We shall see.

This is the French Connection chart. I love this kind of pattern:

It simply tells a story of popular to unpopular to popular.

Where's the ceiling? Who knows but I think it could be a fair way higher.

We are still approximately 25% up.

# Taking a Crazy Punt on Barclays

### 8 May 2014

In the cause of disclosure I bought some Barclays in my crazy punting account. Here is why:

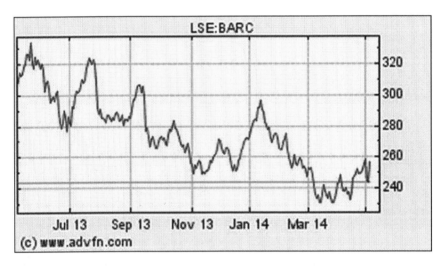

When I look at this chart, I see something changed in early March. Since then the chart is moving differently.

Charts tell you about the past, not the future. Always remember that. The rest is speculation.

I noticed this because Barclays jumped today and when I saw that chart I went "Hummmm..." That "hum" went like this:

1. Something has changed.
2. It's going up.
3. Oh look an RNS saying we've changed strategy.
4. I can put a tight stop on this WAP "wild arsed punt" and let this rally run.

I'm writing this because I know none of my readers will be able to resist looking at charts so it's good to share some T/A now and again. This is an example of practical common sense T/A, with no mumbo jumbo in sight.

Theory says that chart reading is rubbish but in my experience if you sling out the Bollinger bands, moving averages, RSIs and the like, charts can be useful if you use them to explain the narrative of the past then think about how that might pan out in the future. If a chart doesn't scream at you though, forget it.

Meanwhile, as I write, French Connection just shot up...

Also Supergroup, which we don't own, got smashed 20% and bounced 10%. I used to trade this crazy stuff. You make money but you lose your constitution... it's simply bad for your health.

Imagine you have £100,000 of this on leverage:

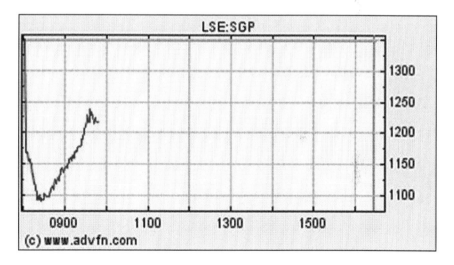

and say you bought in at 1150 on the way down. Gives me indigestion just thinking about it.

I also note its long term chart:

This is why we buy cheap stocks not stocks with a 27 P/E. These glory stocks are getting hammered. (That's off 25%.) We aren't.

# The Market is Flat

## 13 May 2014

"Meh" is the new young folks word. That is just how I feel about the market. It's not going anywhere for us. The market is just sloshing about.

It must be said I'm always down on the market in the new year and it must be underlined the market is often really soft in the new year too.

Here we are:

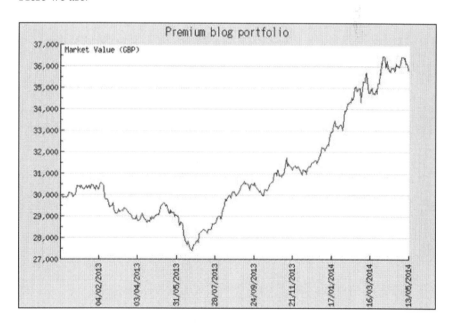

It just feels like I'm waiting for a nasty correction but it might not come. Right now nothing is going on and that makes it hard to write much.

Petrofac took a hit, which was interesting. This is a stock I always get wrong. (It happens.) It was interesting to see it take a punch to the temple.

RSA consolidated to boost its share price quotient, if not its value. Apparently it's meant to make institutions like a company more. Ridiculous if true. I always put it down to institutional computers not liking too many zeroes to print out, but in the era of Excel you'd think that kind of problem long gone.

Anyway, this kind of window dressing still happens, so it's either a waste of time and money or a crack in the efficient market hypothesis.

# Going Bananas

### 14 May 2014

I bought some more Fyffes for the legacy portfolio today. Being able to grow positions is another benefit of being diversified. You can build up lumps of a single share as you see fit without the fear of messing up your portfolio if you have made an error.

Fyffes has a great merger deal going on with Chiquita and it may fall through because of fears of a banana monopoly. That would be temporarily bad for this cheap company, hence weakness in its share price.

Google can monopolise the whole internet with impunity, but heaven forbid a Vulcan death grip on global bananas. There is a risk some clueless bureaucrat will step in and save the globe from evil banana oligarchs.

But according to the magazine Eurofruit (I kid you not) "ChiquitaFyffes will have a more seasoned management team." It will also have the world's least spell-able corporate name.

I like the prospect of the combined company. This is why I have bought more: It feels like a cheaper offer to buy a share I like... this is very "Warren Buffett-ty!"

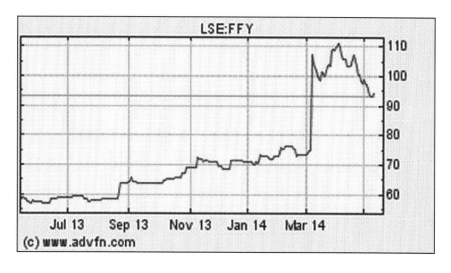

The right price is 105-110 and I want to hold the share for the future of banana supremacy, so while the price is soft I'm going to buy more. Apologies for the fruit puns, but it is nice to buy some shares after what feels like a long pause.

Another reason for buying more is that with the dramatic increase of the portfolio I need to boost the position size. With the legacy portfolio with over 20% in cash knocking around, awaiting the phantom May correction, a chance to put a little to work punching up some positions is welcome.

Meanwhile not a lot happening.

# Here Comes the Slump

### 16 May 2014

We got absolutely smashed yesterday, Thursday 15 May. Of our £6,000 in profit £1,000 went pooof! I think this is the start of the May slump but we will know in the next few days for sure.

All the market dogs went up (supermarkets) and the darlings slumped. This is a sign of hedge closing. This in turn is a sign of the closing of long term positions.

French Connection dropped 15% and Flybe swooned, but there were big fallers all over the market.

The press said it was growth fears... Blah blah. (Note that a couple of months back growth fears meant more QE which meant a rally).

Anyway, here we are with the slump underway. FTSE 250 is off another 200 points today (Friday) and all the while the FTSE 100 isn't moving. (At least at around 11.00am while I'm writing this.) This feels like a "risk off" where the big players move from high risk/high return ideas, into boring safety play.

It could just be the Fed is about to taper again and all their "uncles" have got the nod. Overall we don't care about a slump, it's short term, impossible to time right and will wash out by autumn and we will have some new cheap picks in the portfolio.

So brace yourself though, here come the dip. (Maybe!)

# AstraZeneca Takeover Off

## 19 May 2014

You say you want to invest but you really want to trade.

So today Pfizer's takeover of AstraZeneca is off, at least for now. As I speak it is 15% down. I've bought some as I type for the bounce. This is one for the mad punting account. These sudden moves are one of the few trading opportunities you will find and it is all about the initial over-reaction.

AstraZenica is a massive company and a move of 15% should create a counter move of 4-5%. So we buy near the awful opening and sell sometime around midday before the Americans arrive. The pattern generally goes something like this:

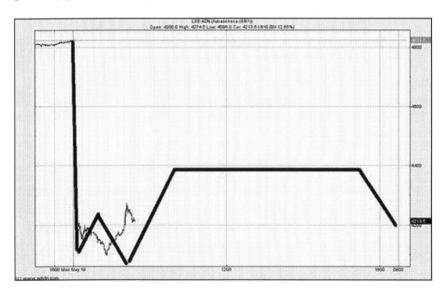

It's the mid-morning bounce we like the look of.

Now the scale doesn't have to be this big, it's the shape. It could be:

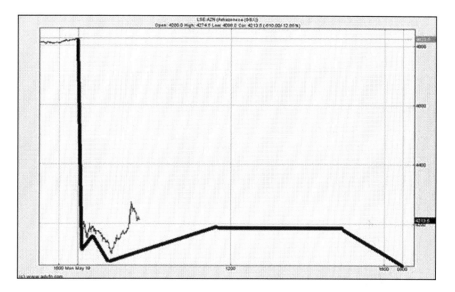

However, this is the pattern and it's patterns that traders trade.

You do need Level 2 and you do need a tick by tick chart if you are going to play these games. However, remember you're an investor and as such all you should care about is the intrinsic value of AstraZenica – and that's about £60 a share.

# The AstraZeneca Punt: Results Are In

### 22 May 2014

So how did we do on the WAP (wild arsed punt) on AstraZeneca on Monday?

Pretty good.

Recall my outline of how it would pan out and/or how this kind of thing generally pans out?

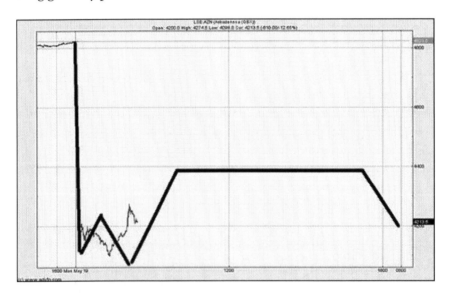

Well this is what happened:

I set my profit take at 4,398 and left it alone, but kept an eye on it. Saw a fat profit at 10am so pulled the rip cord. Why?

1. Because doing this kind of trading is just a pain. The risks are huge.
2. I didn't know it would hit exactly my prediction. I'm not the hero of my trading novels who has both steel and crystal balls. It looks impressive but was it objectively a WAG (wild arsed guess)? You can never be certain.
3. A lot of money in 90 minutes is the same result as twice as much in 360 minutes. (Risk is the square root of the time. Square root of 90 minutes is 9.5 units of risk, square root of 360 minutes is (let's face it, uncannily) 19 units of risk.
4. Investors fly in private jets, traders go to jail.
5. Real trading opportunities are a handful a year, investing is all year long.
6. If you can make 25% a year investing you are ready to try trading... but if you can you don't need to bother.
7. Etc...

But anyway, you saw it live. Remember this was a massive FTSE company getting socked by major news... not some dodgy outfit with a batpoo mine in Antartica...

Meanwhile I'm still hating the market, even though it's sneaking our way.

Really liking RDSA right now but we have it already.

# Summer Lull is No Fun

### 28 May 2014

I should really love the summer lull. It should mean, I watch the markets closely in the dark cold days of the years and then bug off to the playgrounds of the rich and famous in the summer to enjoy my work life balance.

But I don't actually have one of those. I love my work and I love the markets. So summer is frustrating.

So where is the summer correction?

Last year I posited that there should be the regulation big correction but if we are in a new equity era we wouldn't get much of one. The latter occurred. So is this just a continuation? It makes sense but I can't shake the cold fact that the market is high and there is little deep value about. However, that fits a long bull on equities followed by a bubble. You can't expect value to be about when there is a boom and bubble underway.

Argh!!!

Patience is a virtue etc...

So for me this is the key chart to watch in moments of doubt and wavering:

It's the small cap index. Unlike the FTSE it's not full of macro nonsense. You simply can't use this index to hedge.

This is the FTSE 100:

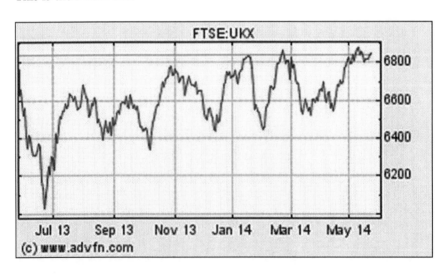

Look at that noise in the FTSE 100. The reason is, it's the playground of macro trading. FTSE 100 is a liquid index used for hedging currencies, commodities and you name it. It has futures and options and EFT. It's bound by the hip to the world through global trading behemoths. So it's full of noise and hard to read.

The SMX isn't. It goes up in a bull and down in a bear. It's a great indicator.

This is the long term:

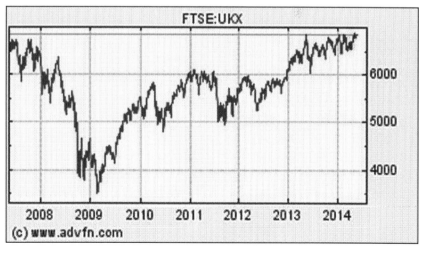

You can see the clarity even over the long term. SMX says, "hold on a mo we're on pause," but the FTSE, at least to me, seems to suggest business as usual. Perhaps even a breakout. (Really, that seems very unlikely even if the chart shows the possibility.)

To me it's clear we are on pause and for the "rock star" shares like Asos it looks like "game over" for their vertical rises.

There are only four months of a lovely summer of easy living to go before markets get back to work... dammit!

# One Way to Pick Stocks

### 30 May 2014

So you might wonder how I go about picking stocks. It's a mix of browsing and using filters. Here is an example of one browsing method.

I looked at top movers on top lists today. I always do because it brings names to the fore and gives a starting point for investigation.

Today Caffyns is up a few per cent. Its figures are good. It's a car retailer. I like car sellers because they sell a lot of turnover yet are worth about 10% of what they sell against a benchmark of 1:1 in general. Why? Because car dealers don't make much money as their margins are wafer thin. It is odd but understandable.

Caffyns is small, too small for me and it's a family firm which is a red flag to me.

I know Pendragon, PDG is way bigger. I also know that PDG has made me oodles of money in the past, so I have a good feel for the stock having owned it for long periods.

I go look at PDG. £3.8 billion in sales for £430m in market cap, that's 9:1. I like that. It has also got a 10.5 P/E which is cheapish, but not really cheap. The UK is booming/going to boom, so cars are going to sell. House prices go up and people go out and buy cars. It's the good ole bad ole days.

However, Pendragon is not painfully cheap. We are also in the pre-slump summer, as I still wait vainly for the correction, so that's two turnoffs.

I look at the chart:

Pendragon is not going up, it's been drifting off since November.

Of course you might say why do you care? There is always tomorrow for it to go up. This is why I care:

What I see is this: Pendragon trends. When its tendency is up, down or sideways it keeps on that path for long periods.

Unlike for example RSA :

Unlike RSA, you know where you are with Pendragon. Pendragon goes in one direction for long periods.

Note how smooth its long term chart is. There is what I class as certainty. RSA on the other hand spikes all over the black. The market displays uncertainty.

So the market appears pretty certain that PDG is kind of boring and not about to go anywhere but faintly down. It's a yawn, but it's not cheap, so why buy?

When Pendragon changes direction that will be the time to reconsider, or when it hits a level where the P/E looks irresistible, at least below 10.

So it's a watch and wait.

# Conclusion

I was considering annotating this book at various stages, but I realise that hindsight has no value at all. You can regret past decisions as much as you like but the markets show that regrets are pointless. They are pointless because even a few more right decisions versus mistakes when applied to the financial markets would make everyone immensely rich. Even a splash of hindsight would make us all billionaires.

Thus mistakes in general cannot be avoided, only suffered with good humour, dammit!

Many shares go up like a rocket and down like a rock. If we could be tipped off by a time traveller to just a handful of these companies we would be trading zillionaires.

Sadly it is not to be. We must blindly fumble about the markets, groping for the future while we stumble over the cobbles of imperfect information.

As we have hopefully learnt in this book, the journey might be uneven but the only difficulty to making money in the market is determination, grit and a positive mental attitude.

- You need a method.
- You need to be patient.
- You need to be able to let yourself be fallible.

That aside, the rest is just "practice by doing." It is easy for me to say it is easy, because it is easy for me in practice. Meanwhile it appears that many people lose a lot of money playing the game of trading the stock market.

However, as I have said – repeatedly – Trading is not Investing. Few investors, who invest even in a rudimentary and sensible fashion, lose money.

Conversely: few traders, who trade in a rudimentary and sensible fashion, make money.

Why?

Because the rewards from shares are limited.

That limit is somewhere around 25% a year. It might be a bit more, it might be less, but somewhere there is a threshold that is a hard limit to the profits you can reliably make from shares.

You can go looking for a case where this is wrong but you will look high and low and what you will find to contradict this hypothesis will be sparse and likely unreliable.

What this means is, if you buy and sell a lot, ie trade, all your profit potential will get eaten up in costs. This is why traders lose money. It is that simple.

I maintain investing is like farming. You do not need much of a plot to gain an interesting result from your work. It is pretty easy to farm for a living.

Whereas trading is like hunting. You really have to hunt a lot to feed a family and there are limits to how much you can catch. To make a decent living hunting, you have to have a lot of fragile, at risk capital – think fishing boats. In the end, the easiest outcome to make a interesting return from hunting ends up serving people who want to hunt – think leisure fishing, game keeping etc. – or in the markets, being a broker to traders.

The bottom line is, the richest man in the world today is an investor. Meanwhile there are a lot of traders in prison.

Stress testing that assertion is highly recommended.

However everyone wants to trade, few want to invest. You want to trade. You do, don't you? Well, you can, with one proviso.

Let us agree trading is harder than investing. So when you can make 20% a year or more investing, for say three years, then you will have skilled yourself up enough to give trading a try. Remember, the other side of the trade is likely Goldman Sachs or some other trading Cthulhu, so skill is essential. So put £2,000 in a spread betting account, kiss it goodbye and give trading a go.

If you can make 20%+ investing you should just about hold your own trading. If you don't, you can still become wealthy compounding a portfolio at 20% in a Sipp or ISA. Doubling your money every three to four years really does make you rich.

If you put the same lump sum into a brokerage account, every year, at 20% compound a year, you will create a pot 200 times larger after twenty years. Put in £1,000 a year and end up with £200,000 in twenty years.

£10,000 goes to £2m+. After ten years it will be 30 times more, ie £30,000. This is the game you should play, not the trading one.

At 25% the numbers start looking silly. It's the kind of silly we all can use. So invest and Be Rich.

It is one of the few avenues open to almost anyone to become wealthy through diligence, patience and hard work.

I hope you enjoy the journey.

# About the Author

Clem Chambers is CEO of ADVFN, Europe and South America's leading financial website.

A broadcast and print media regular, Clem Chambers is a familiar face and frequent co-presenter on **CNBC** and **CNBC Europe.** He is a seasoned guest and market commentator on **BBC News, Fox News, CNBC Arabia Newsnight, Al Jazeera, CNN, SKY News, TF1,** Canada's **Business News Network** and numerous US radio stations.

He is renowned for calling the markets and predicted the end of the bull market back in January 2007 and the following crash. He has appeared on ITV's **News at Ten** and **Evening News** discussing failures in the banking system and featured prominently in the **Money Programme's** *Credit Crash Britain: HBOS — Breaking the Bank* and on the BBC's *City Uncovered: When Markets Go Mad.*

Clem has written investment columns for **Wired Magazine,** which described him as a 'Market Maven', **The Daily Mail, The Daily**

Telegraph and **The Daily Express** and currently writes for **Forbes, Business Mirror, Index Trader, Traders** and **YourTradingEdge**.

He was The Alchemist – stock tipster – in **The Business** for over three years and has been published in titles including: **CityAM, Investors Chronicle, Traders Magazine, Stocks and Commodities**, the **Channel 4** website, **SFO** and **Accountancy Age** and has been quoted in many more publications including all of the main UK national newspapers. He also wrote a monthly spread betting column in gambling magazine **Inside Edge**.

Clem has written several books for ADVFN Books, including **101 Ways To Pick Stock Market Winners, A Beginner's Guide to Value Investing, The Death of Wealth** and **Letters to my Broker**.

In the last few years he has become a successful financial thriller writer, authoring **The Twain Maxim, The Armageddon Trade, Kusanagi** and **The First Horseman**. His new fiction book, **Dial Up for Murder**, is a techno-thriller set during the dawn of the internet.

Clem also writes for the ADVFN newspaper and has two premium newsletters: Diary of a Contrarian Investor and Building an Income Portfolio.

# Also by Clem Chambers from ADVFN Books

## THE GAME IN WALL STREET

### by Hoyle and Clem Chambers

As the new century dawned, Wall Street was a game and the stock market was fixed. Ordinary investors were fleeced by big institutions that manipulated the markets to their own advantage and they had no comeback.

*The Game in Wall Street* shows the ways that the titans of rampant capitalism operated to make money from any source they could control. Their accumulated funds gave the titans enormous power over the market and allowed them to ensure they won the game.

Traders joining the game without knowing the rules are on a road to ruin. It's like gambling without knowing the rules and with no idea of the odds.

*The Game in Wall Street* sets out in detail exactly how this market manipulation works and shows how to ride the price movements and make a profit.

And guess what? The rules of the game haven't changed since the book was first published in 1898. You can apply the same strategies in your own investing and avoid losing your shirt by gambling against the professionals.

Illustrated with the very first stock charts ever published, the book contains a new preface and a conclusion by stock market guru Clem Chambers which put the text in the context of how Wall Street operates today.

Available in paperback and for the Kindle.

# THE DEATH OF WEALTH

## by Clem Chambers

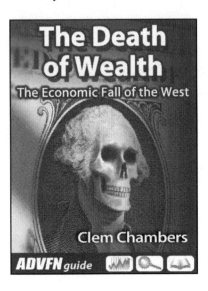

Question: what is the next economic game changer?
Answer: The Death of Wealth.

Market guru Clem Chambers dissects the global economy and the state of the financial markets and lays out the evidence for the death of wealth.

*The Death of Wealth* flags up the milestones on the route towards impending financial disaster. From the first tentative signs of recovery in the UK and US stock markets at the start of 2012, to the temporary drawing back from the edge of the Fiscal Cliff at the end, the book chronicles the trials and tribulations of the markets throughout the year.

Collecting together articles and essays throughout the last twelve months along with extensive new analysis for 2013, *The Death of Wealth* allows us to look at these tumultuous events collectively and draw a strong conclusion about what the future holds.

2012 started with the US economy showing signs of recovery, and European financial markets recovering some of the ground lost during the euro crisis. It ended with Obama's re-election and the deal that delayed the plunge off the fiscal cliff by a few months.

In between, the eurozone crisis continued, but none of the affected countries actually left the eurozone; quantitative easing tried to turn things around with the consequences of these 'unorthodox' actions yet unknown; and the equity markets after the mid-year correction became strongly bullish.

*The Death of Wealth* takes you through the events of 2012 month by month, with charts showing the movements of the FTSE 100, the NASDAQ COMPX and the SSE COMPX throughout the year.

With an introduction by renowned market commentator and stock tipster Tom Winnifrith and a summary by trading technical analyst Zak Mir, this collection chronicles the rocky road trip the financial systems of the world have been on and predicts the ultimate destination: the death of wealth as we know it.

Available in paperback and for the Kindle.

# LETTERS TO MY BROKER

## P.S. What do you think of the Market?

### by Clem Chambers

*"Why is it the minute I sell my stocks, no matter which they are, right away they go up?"*

Meet Joe, a rich but hapless investor who makes every mistake possible. Just when you think he's learnt something, he finds a new way to lose money.

Populated by rogues, hucksters and fools *Letters to my Broker* is the classic comedy of errors revived for a new generation that teaches you the rules to trading the stock market haven't changed in the 94 years since its original publication.

*"I want some advice. Not that I'll follow it."*

Aided by the acerbic commentary of No. 1 bestselling author and ADVFN CEO Clem Chambers, *Letters to my Broker* tells you where Joe's going wrong, what you should do to keep your shirt and how to avoid his hilarious errors.

Stock market tips so old they're new: Read *Letters to my Broker* and trade like it's 1919.

Available in paperback and for the Kindle.

# ADVFN GUIDE: THE BEGINNER'S GUIDE TO VALUE INVESTIN G

by Clem Chambers

The stock market is not only for rich people, or those intent on gambling. 'Value Investing' is how Warren Buffet became the richest man in the world. A method of investing in the stock market without taking crazy risks, 'Value Investing' will help you build your fortune, no matter the economic climate. Perfect for novice investors, the book clearly outlines how to choose the best stocks and how – thanks to the Internet. It is the perfect way to ensure you 'get rich slow' with minimal stress.

Available in paperback and for the Kindle.

# ADVFN GUIDE: 101 WAYS TO PICK STOCK MARKET WINNERS

by Clem Chambers

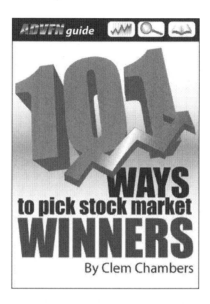

101 tips to help day traders, investors and stock pickers to focus on what characterises a potentially successful stock. Personally researched by Clem Chambers, one of the world's leading authorities on market performance. Incisive, brutally honest and occasionally very funny, *101 Ways to Pick Stock Market Winners* is an invaluable manual for anyone wanting to make money out of the markets.

Available for the Kindle.

For more information, go to the ADVFN Books website at www.advfnbooks.com.

Printed in Poland
by Amazon Fulfillment
Poland Sp. z o.o., Wrocław